FORMULA 1
DECADES

FORMULA 1

DECADES

AN ILLUSTRATED HISTORY OF

GRAND PRIX

1950 CHAMPIONS -1996

HAMLYN   JOHN TIPLER

First published in Great Britain in 1996
by Hamlyn, an imprint of Reed Consumer Books Limited
Michelin House, 81 Fulham Road, London SW3 6RB
and Auckland, Melbourne, Singapore and Toronto

Produced and designed by Brown Packaging Limited
255-257 Liverpool Road, London N1 1LX

ISBN 0 600 58976 5

A catalogue record for this book is available from the British Library

Printed in China

Contents

Introduction

For as long as cars have been around, people have raced them. The first motor race – the Paris-Bordeaux-Paris event – was held in June 1895. However, the competitors in that race just over a century ago have little in common with the modern daredevils who speed round today's Grand Prix circuits. Drivers such as Michael Schumacher risk everything on a series of

split-second decisions that have to be made at the same furious speed at which their cars are moving. This is the story of the men who have made the Formula 1 World Championship the glamorous, fascinating sport that it is today. Every World Champion since the inception

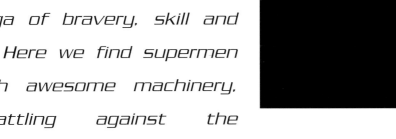

of the Championship in 1950 is featured here in a saga of bravery, skill and perseverance. Here we find supermen struggling with awesome machinery,

battling against the elements and each other. The tale is told against a backdrop of dangerous circuits, demanding sponsors and complex regulations.

The Fifties
Gentlemen Drivers

The drivers of the 1950s drove for the love of it. The sportsmanship of the playing field prevailed and the mood was calmer than it is today. There was more close racing, with lots of frantic wheel-to-wheel dicing, yet there was none of the deliberate barging now prevalent in F1. If it was clanging metal you wanted, the stock-car stadium was the place.

The cars themselves were difficult to control. The drivers sat on, rather than in, the chassis, so technique was all arms and elbows, the driver close-up to the wheel and fighting it with his biceps. There were no fuel or weight restrictions. Tyre technology was still in its infancy and the driver was putting some 400bhp through very narrow treads.

Circuits were normally adaptations of public road systems while Grand Prix race distances in the 1950s were of a minimum 300km (186.41 miles) distance or three hours in length, rising in 1954 to a 500km minimum or three hours' duration. In 1958, the requirement fell back to 300km distance or two hours' duration.

The World Championship calendar listed less than half the number of races which count for the title today. But those Grands Prix were interspersed with many non-Championship races, often titled 'Grand Prix', and not lacking much in terms of atmosphere compared to a proper GP. There were also fixtures for F1 cars or free-formula – 'Formule Libre' – races at regular Bank Holiday meetings in which the F1 cars and the stars could participate.

In addition, the Grand Prix aces drove a wide variety of models, from F1 and F2 cars to sports-racing cars and saloons. They even took part in rallies! Go to an historic event today and watch the 1950s Grand Prix cars in action, and you'll be astonished at just how quick they are. The 1950s was indeed a spectacular decade.

Nino Farina

(1906–1966) World Champion 1950

Dr Giuseppe 'Nino' Farina was one of the three drivers hired by Alfa Romeo for its assault on the World Championship in 1950. The other two were Juan Manuel Fangio, embarking on only his second season in Europe, and Luigi Fagioli.

Farina may have gone down in history as the first Formula 1 World Champion, but he had been in motor sport a long time before that. As such, he belongs to the previous era. Having started driving aged nine, using a two-cylinder Temperino, he first competed in 1925 while still a law student at the University of Turin where he was awarded a doctorate in Political Sciences. His first event was the Aosta-Gran San Bernado hill climb, in which he was not only beaten by his father but also crashed his old Alfa and broke his shoulder. A sporting all-rounder and cavalryman in the army, he persevered at an amateur level in the early 1930s in Maseratis and Alfas, and was sufficiently competent to attract the friendship and patronage of the great Tazio Nuvolari, the premier racing driver of the 1920s and 1930s.

He joined the Alfa Romeo squad run by Enzo Ferrari in 1936, and finished second in the Mille Miglia after driving through the night without lights. He raced for the official Alfa team, driving the new 158 Alfetta to victory at Antwerp, the Coppa Ciano and at Berne in 1939, and, in 1940, at Tripoli – avenging the defeat by Mercedes the previous year.

After the war he started off well by winning the 1946 Grand Prix of Nations at Geneva. But internal politics caused him to leave Alfa Romeo, and he returned to the scene in 1948 driving a privately entered Maserati. By 1950, his star was, if not on the wane, not exactly in the ascendant.

A sophisticated background

He was born in Turin on 30 October 1906, and was nephew of the famous coachbuilding carrozzeria of Farina – Giovanni and 'Pinin', later Pininfarina. Nino exemplified the 'gentleman driver', aloof, suave and sophisticated. He also practiced a more stylish driving style than was customary at the time, which entailed leaning back further away from the steering wheel. His wife Else owned a fashion house, and was rarely seen at races. Farina is said to have been 'difficult and disagreeable'. Certainly he was at times forceful, ruthless even, yet capable of abandoning a race in the middle of a scrap. At Monza in 1949 he gave up his pursuit of two Ferraris, simply because he thought his Maserati unable to catch them. Enzo Ferrari once likened him to a 'thoroughbred race horse, liable to break through the starting tape in its eagerness; yet capable of the most astonishing follies one or two laps from the end. As a result he was a regular inmate of hospital wards.'

Nino Farina's weapon was the Alfa Romeo Alfetta 158, brought out of mothballs after the war. Alfa Romeo had several potential race winners at its disposal, all pre-war designs of course, including a pair of mid-engined flat-12 Tipo 512 voiturettes and seven Tipo 158 Alfettas, which had been hidden during the war. Apart from the first event they competed in, at Paris in 1946, with Farina and Jean-Pierre Wimille losing through clutch failure, the Alfettas won all but one of every event in which they were entered. (One they didn't win was the 1951 *Daily Express* Trophy at Silverstone, given to Reg Parnell in the Ferrari Thin Wall Special when rain forced the race to be abandoned; the Alfettas had won the heats, however.)

Two-stage supercharging in 1946 brought power up to 254bhp. Alfa Romeo did not appear during 1949, fearful of an opposition which failed to materialise.

The Alfetta's early rival was the 4CLT/48 'San Remo' Maserati, a supercharged four-cylinder voiturette which in evolved form used a tubular chassis and coil spring suspension. With Alfa absent, the Maserati won the British Grand Prix in 1948 and 1949.

The French Talbot-Lago had flowered in 1949, with Louis Rosier and Louis Chiron driving to victory in Belgium and France.

A winning start

At the de-commissioned wartime airfield of Silverstone on 13 May 1950, in the presence of King George VI, the Queen and Princess Margaret, 21 drivers lined up at the start for the British Grand Prix. The three Alfa 158s had started at the front of the grid, and that's where they finished, with Farina leading Fagioli and Reg Parnell – the token British driver – with Talbot Lagos fourth and fifth, two laps down. They'd covered 70 laps of a three-mile circuit, Farina's average speed being 90.9mph.

While Fangio scored at Monaco, Farina took the honours at the Swiss Bremgarten, Berne, another street circuit, with Fagioli second and Rosier's Talbot a lap behind. At the Belgian round on the 8.76-mile Spa circuit, Fangio was the winner from Fagioli, while Farina followed Rosier home in fourth place, setting the fastest lap at 115.1mph on the way. This says a lot about the man, since Spa has always been a daunting high-speed affair. At Rheims-Geux for another high-speed blind down the long straight roads of rural France, it was Fangio's turn to win, from Fagioli again.

The points scoring system in 1950 was based on a driver's best four results from seven races – including the Indianapolis 500 – with eight points for a win, six for second, four for third, three for fourth, and two points for fifth. It stood like that until 1961, when the winning tally was raised to nine points. A single point was also scored for setting the fastest lap in a race. Thus the first World Championship went down to the wire at Monza, with Fangio on a total of 26 points from three finishes, Fagioli on 24 points from four second-place finishes, and Farina on 22 points from three finishes.

There was an air of nationalistic fervour at Monza – there always has been, just as the tifosi are fanatical about the fortunes of Ferrari today – and just possibly Farina may have received preferential treatment in the Alfa camp over Fangio. At a non-championship race at Bari prior to the Italian Grand Prix, Fangio had mysteriously run out of petrol during his dice for the lead with Farina; Farina's tank contained sufficient fuel to take him to the chequered flag.

The front row at Monza was made up of pole-winner Fangio, Alberto Ascari's Ferrari, and two other Alfas driven by Farina and Consalvo Sanesi. As the flag dropped, the Alfas out-gunned Ascari's Ferrari, but he quickly fought back to second behind Farina at the end of the first lap. On lap seven, Fangio set fastest lap, and on lap 14. Ascari passed Farina, only to be retaken. With Sanesi's Alfa retired, Fangio lay a comfortable third. As is so often the case, the shrewd driver bides his time, waiting perhaps for the two leading protagonists to take each other out. But Farina was safe for the

Nino Farina on his way to victory in the first ever World Championship race, at Silverstone in 1950.

moment. On lap 22 Ascari's back axle broke and, on lap 24, Fangio's gearbox failed. He took over Taruffi's Alfa – a perfectly legitimate move then and the product of an age of sportsmanship and chivalry – and Ascari was sent out again in Serafini's Ferrari, two minutes in arrears. However, Fangio's Alfa burned a valve on lap 35 and, despite making a second fuel stop, Farina beat Ascari by 1minute 18.6secs. It had been Farina's year. He had gained the Championship with 30 points to Fangio's 27 and Fagioli's 24, and Alfa were champion constructors. But although Farina was a front runner in many races during the following years, he was usually behind the young lions, Ascari and Fangio. This is not to denigrate Farina. Just to get on to the front row of the grid was no mean achievement.

After the world title

The following year belonged to Fangio. The results show the Argentinian scored two Grand Prix wins at Rheims and Barcelona, with two second places, at Silverstone and the Nürburgring. His chief rival was consistently Ascari, while Farina, who won at Spa, was third at Monza and fifth at Rheims. At the fast French circuit he was plagued with magneto problems, due to the heat and the 9000rpm the Alfas were pulling. His colleague Consalvo Sanesi, also having magneto problems, heroically pushed his 159 about a mile against an uphill gradient to cross the line in tenth place, and he was given a greater reception than the one accorded to Fangio, the race winner.

On 2 June, Farina took a works Alfa 159 – instead of his own Maserati 4CLT – to Dundrod for the Ulster Tourist Trophy race. This event, highly prestigious in its day, was attended by the Queen and Princess Margaret, with prize money donated by the *News of the World*. It was a case of overkill, really, as very few provincial racing cars stood a chance against a GP winner; amongst ERAs, Altas, elderly Talbots,

Farina shows off his relaxed driving style in the Alfetta 159 at Silverstone in 1951.

Delages and Maseratis, his only real opposition came from Reg Parnell in the Thin Wall Ferrari, who led while the thirsty Alfa refuelled. Farina would himself drive the Thin Wall to second place in the Woodcote Cup race at Goodwood the following year. Interestingly, we find Peter Collins winning the supporting F3 race in a 500cc JBS, and Mike Hawthorn taking the honours in a Riley in the saloon car event.

Farina took the Alfa to Goodwood in the September. The car was transported over the Alps from Italy in a vast Dodge truck, accompanied by three mechanics, and trounced much the same opposition in two races, including the notable Daily Graphic Goodwood Trophy. In a third event, he managed to catch Stirling Moss' H.W.M. on the last corner to win by a short head.

Meanwhile in the World series, a fastest lap at Monza showed he could still shine with the best of them. In fact *Motor Sport* described this as his finest race. Although his own car gave up on lap 5, he was given Bonetto's 159, and was back on terms with Ascari and Gonzalez in the new Ferraris. Farina was hauling in Gonzalez at the rate of five seconds a lap. Both teams were scheduled to make two stops for fuel and tyres, and this strategy may have proved Farina's undoing. It was a long stop, compared with the Ferrari's, but Farina set off at an unabated pace. It soon became clear that the Alfa's fuel tank was ruptured, however, as fuel was pouring out of the tail. Without that, he might well have claimed second place.

If 1951 was Fangio's Championship, it was also the year of a titanic battle for supremacy between Alfa and Ferrari. In 1951, the Ferrari squad included Alberto Ascari, 'Gigi' Villoresi, Piero Taruffi and Froilan Gonzalez, with 24-plug head cars. The Alfa 159s were beaten at Silverstone, with Gonzalez the winner, while Ascari was the victor in Germany and Italy.

The Spanish Grand Prix, held in front of an estimated 250,000 fans on the Pedralbes circuit at Barcelona in late October, showed Farina in his true colours. Fourth fastest in practice, it was he who tailed Ascari at the end of the first lap. But Fangio was soon ahead of him and, on the fourth lap, he led Ascari. One by one the Ferraris' tyres shredded their treads – according to Lampredi, the result of an ill fitting stand on the pit wall – and Fangio kept going with no fresh rubber and just a refuelling

stop. Despite new tyres all round, the Ferraris, and Ascari's blue-cowled car in particular, were in continuous trouble. The anticipated inter-marque battle was not half as intense as it might have been.

Farina, running second, was to be seen making mysterious gestures to his pit as he sped by. His second refuelling stop saw Gonzalez's Ferrari supersede him in second place, and that was how they finished.

But when Ferrari's Aurelio Lampredi-designed 4.5-litre unsupercharged Tipo 330 and 340 cars began to vanquish the Alfas quite early on in 1951, the game was up and the latter withdrew from Grand Prix racing at the end of the season. The main problem was that, in order to keep up, the supercharged Alfas, now designated Tipo 159s, ran on 98 per cent methanol fuel, which burned at the prodigious rate of 1.5-gallons a mile. This speed was not achieved without a price, as the additional weight of 66 gallons of fuel upset the car's originally excellent handling. In its final incarnation, the Alfetta Tipo 159 produced 425bhp at 9300rpm.

A fallow year

Perhaps Farina had been in some way de-motivated in 1951; resting on his laurels maybe, or simply bettered by Fangio and Ascari. Even Gonzalez scored more points. They had the silly season of rumours even then, about who's going to drive for who, which engines are going to be available, and so on. After the German GP, it was rumoured that Farina was unhappy and wanted out of the Alfa team.

In 1952, Farina was recruited to drive for the Ferrari team. Although he scored no wins, he did raise his game, clinching three second places at Rouen-les-Essarts, the Nürburgring, Zandvoort, and a fourth at Monza. The title was Ascari's, on 36 points, with Farina on 24 points to Taruffi's 22. Farina was none too happy about playing second fiddle to Ascari, and he had no hesitation in making his feelings known after the French event. In fact there was a general air of unrest among the Ferrari drivers throughout the whole season. *Motor Sport* reported Farina desperately trying to out-do Ascari at Marseilles, 'going through the sweeping s-bends past the pits more by the grace of God than skill.' Farina spun himself out of contention in a late-braking bid when Ascari stopped for a tyre change.

In 1953, Farina was still at Ferrari, following in the wake of the dynamic Ascari. Also on the strength was the young Englishman Mike Hawthorn. Villoresi brought up the rear of the old brigade, while

Fangio had gone over to Maserati to drive the new 250F model. Tragedy struck at the Argentinian Grand Prix – a new event on the calendar for 1953 – when Farina went off and mowed down 15 spectators. Accidents were a regular occurrence, and the public was often poorly protected; it seemed to be accepted as a matter of course.

Farina took second place to Ascari in the Dutch GP at Zandvoort, and fifth in a close-run French grand épreuve at Rheims-Geux. At Silverstone he was third, two laps down behind Ascari and Fangio.

There was an altercation between Farina and Ascari after the Swiss GP at Bremgarten, the penultimate round in the Championship. Seventeen years earlier, there had been an argument between Rosemeyer and Caracciola at the same circuit, with the Auto Union driver accusing the Mercedes maestro of using blocking tactics; Hill and Schumacher behaved in much the same way in 1995.

Teamwork wins the day

But in 1953, if Ascari won at Berne, he would be Champion, as neither Fangio or Farina could overhaul him. It was a sinewy circuit, unchanged since Rosemeyer's day, and the Eymatt corner claimed a host of fatalities where the track plunged downhill and thence out of the sunlight up into gloomy forest section. At the start, Farina's Ferrari misfired, and he was overtaken by the next four cars. By lap 11, Farina had recovered and was running second to Ascari. When Ascari's Ferrari hit carburettor problems, Farina was through into the lead, followed by Mike Hawthorn in another Ferrari. This was good for the team prize, and the Ferrari pit signalled to Ascari to hold station. It's a Ferrari house rule that if two of the prancing horses are out in front, they don't challenge one another – it's the car that wins, not the driver.

However, at Berne, Ascari, now firing on all four cylinders, had the bit between his teeth. He passed Hawthorn on lap 52 and Farina on 54, setting fastest lap in the process. Farina felt humiliated and cheated that Ascari had overtaken him, and went for Ascari in the paddock after the race. Ascari's response was that the sun was in his eyes and he hadn't seen the signal – quite possibly true – and that in any case, he had won the Championship for the second successive year. Farina didn't speak to him after that, although they shared a Ferrari in the Nürburgring 1000km sports car race a week later – and won. The row between Ferrari team-mates Gilles Villeneuve and Didier Pironi after the latter overtook at Imola in 1982 was on identical lines.

The last Grand Prix of 1953 was at Monza, and this event too was not without controversy. Despite Ferrari's statement that this was to be their last official race, there were new cars for Ascari, Farina, Villoresi and Hawthorn, while Maserati had new six-cylinder A6 models for Fangio and his compatriot Onofré Marimon, plus old models for Bonetto, Mantovani, Platé and de Graffenreid. For the race Fangio swapped with Bonetto. The race quickly settled into a duel between the two Maseratis of Fangio and Marimon, and the Ferraris of Farina and Ascari. The lead changed hands many times, until the last corner of the last lap, when Ascari and Marimon went off, Farina took to the grass, and the wily Fangio nipped by to win from Farina by two seconds. It appeared that Marimon had pushed Ascari off; but the nose of Farina's Ferrari was crumpled by someone's rear wheel, presumably Marimon's. No-one knew for sure what had actually happened, as it had all happened so fast. The official version was that Ascari had spun on some oil. One thing is certain. Team tactics meant that slower drivers often assisted quicker team mates by deliberately blocking their opponents, and maybe there was a certain amount of that going on in Italy.

Farina ended the season third in the Championship table with 26 points, behind Ascari on 34.5 points, and Fangio on 28 points.

Farina featured in the results only once in 1954 – taking second place for Ferrari at Buenos Aires, nearly two minutes behind Fangio's Maserati. Having been badly burned in a crash during practice for the annual Monza 1000km sports car endurance race that year, he was sidelined for a while. Buoyed up with painkilling morphine injections, he did extremely well to repeat the result in the Argentinian event the following year. Confusingly, Farina also drove the third placed Ferrari of Maglioli. They could do that in those days.

Farina was fourth at the 1955 Monaco Grand Prix, and third at Spa behind Fangio and Moss. But his injuries from the Monza fire indicated that it was time to quit, and that was the last time he featured on the results sheets. He practised a Lancia D50 for the Italian Grand Prix, but decided enough was enough when it shed a tyre tread at 170mph – leaving him shaken but unhurt.

He maintained contacts with the sport, however, and continued to run his Alfa Romeo and Jaguar franchise. But Farina's luck ran out eventually. Driving his Lotus-Cortina through the Savoy Alps near Aiguebelle, on the way to the French Grand Prix at Rheims in 1966, he skidded into a telegraph pole and was killed. He was 60.

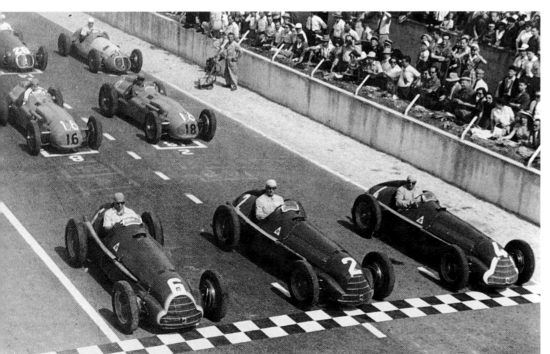

Three Alfa 158s – of Fangio, Farina and Fagioli – on the front row of the grid at Rheims-Geux for the 1950 French Grand Prix.

Alberto Ascari

(1918–1955) World Champion 1952, 1953

Alberto was the son of the 1920s star Antonio Ascari. At the time, the 1950s, father and son racing heritages were rare. Not until the Andrettis, the Brabhams, the Hills and now the Villeneuves, did we find sons following fathers' tyre tracks.

After his father won the 1924 Italian GP, having led from start to finish and heading an Alfa Romeo 1-2-3-4 victory, the six-year old Alberto posed with him and the P2 Alfa for the paparazzi. Enzo Ferrari, the team driver, was on hand, along with his cousin Giovanni Minozzi, also involved with Alfa's racing effort. It was, therefore, inevitable that Alberto would be raised in a competitive environment.

Born in Milan on 13 July 1918, he grew up riding trials and racing motor cycles, and won several races in the late 1930s. Enzo Ferrari entrusted him with one of his new Tipo 815 straight-eight 1.5-litre sports racers for the curtailed 1940 Mille Miglia, and Alberto was set to run with Minozzi as his co-driver. The young Ascari treated the car with scant respect and was soon out with a dropped valve. Half-shares in Taruffi's 1938 1.5-litre Maserati saw him finish ninth in the 1940 Tripoli GP, and retire in the Targa Florio.

Alberto was of a physical type rare outside club racing today, in that he was, well, plump – although not as big a man as Froilan González, nicknamed the 'Pampas Bull'. Ascari's nickname in Italy was Cicco, meaning 'butch', or 'meaty'. He was also placid and genial, aware of his own limitations and those of his car. Thus he tended to avoid mistakes or breaking the car, and finished races looking relatively unruffled.

In 1947 his career got going again with second and fifth places at Cairo and Albi in an 1100cc monoposto Cisitalia. Driving the Scuderia Ambrosiana Maserati as number two to Villoresi, Ascari was active most weekends, improving his technique. He placed fourth at Nice in 1947 and won at Modena.

Ascari's winning Ferrari 500 leads team-mate Farina at the start of the 1952 French Grand Prix.

The leading man

Typically, Ascari preferred to be out in front, rather than using a pacesetter and harrying rivals from behind. He drove the brand-new 4CLT/48 Maserati to its first victory at San Remo in 1948 – earning the car the eponymous title 'San Remo' Maserati. He won the Pescara sports car GP, followed by fifth places at Monaco and Berne, fourth at Monza in the wake of the Alfa 158s, and second at Silverstone in the RAC GP. On the strength of these results he was given a drive in the Alfa team in the French Grand Prix, in which he finished third.

For 1949, Ascari and Villoresi forsook Maserati for Ferrari, and Alberto ended the season as Italian champion, having scored victories at Berne, Bari, Silverstone, Rheims and Buenos Aires. Still on the threshold of the championship, he improved his standing in 1950 with wins at Penya Rhin, Buenos Aires, the Nürburgring, Rheims, Rome-Vallelunga, Luxembourg, Garda, Mons, Modena, and Buenos Aires.

It was Ascari who presented the strongest threat to Alfa Romeo's swan-song 159 Alfettas in 1951, and he won the German Grand Prix at the Nürburgring and the Italian GP at Monza as well as the non-championship San Remo GP driving the 4.5-litre Ferrari. Success in F2 events included wins at Monza, Naples and Modena, and, partnered by Villoresi, he won the international Sestriére Rally in a Lancia Aurelia.

Alfa Romeo had withdrawn at the end of 1951 because no state funding was available to develop a new challenger to the Ferraris; some rather desultory attempts were made with the Disco Volante in sports car racing, but thereafter Alfa was not seen in Formula 1 until 1979. (Through the 1960s it concentrated on touring car racing with the hugely successful Giulia GTA and in sports car racing in the 1970s with the Tipo 33 series.)

The 1952 Championship was run for Formula 2 cars, on the basis that it would allow teams like Alfa to revitalise themselves, and cars could be fitted with larger engines when the rules reverted to the F1 formula in 1954. The Ferrari 500 – so numbered because each cylinder bore displaced 500cc – was an unsupercharged four cylinder in-line unit fed by a pair of twin choke Weber carbs, and produced 170bhp at 7000rpm. Its chassis was, typically for the time, a very simple twin-tube ladder frame, with its suspension consisting of transverse leaf springs at the front and rear, with wishbones at the front and de Dion back end. In other words, not terribly sophisticated. It was, nevertheless, a very effective machine from its debut at the Modena Grand Prix in 1951, and superior to everything else in the two years the F2 category held sway. The only times it was

Ascari's

nickname in

Italy was

Cicco,

meaning

'butch', or

'meaty'

beaten were at a non-championship F1 race at Rheims in 1952, when Béhra's Gordini triumphed, and at Syracuse, Sicily, in 1953 when a faulty batch of valve springs sidelined the works entries. And, of course, the 1953 Italian GP when Fangio's Maserati A6GS scooped the honours.

Ferrari's challenge

It could be argued that Ascari had an easy time of it, with no Alfas and Fangio, champion of 1951, out of the picture for seven races of the 1952 Grand Prix season, due to severe neck injuries sustained in a Maserati in a non-championship race at Monza. But Farina was still a force to be reckoned with, and team-mate Taruffi was also a potential challenger.

Indeed, Taruffi won the Bremgarten opener from Fischer in another Ferrari. The Formula 2 rules allowed onto the scene cars such as the Gordinis of Jean Béhra, Robert Manzon and Maurice Trintignant, H.W.M.s of Peter Collins and Paul Frére, with Alan Brown's and Mike Hawthorn's Cooper-Bristols, and Ken Wharton's Frazer-Nash.

Ascari won pretty much as he pleased at Spa-Francorchamps in Belgium, where Farina was two minutes behind him, followed by Manzon, Hawthorn and Frére in the Gordini, Cooper-Bristol and H.W.M. At Rouen-les-Essarts in France, Farina was a lap down on Ascari, with Taruffi a further lap in arrears, from Manzon, Trintignant and Collins. At the British Grand Prix at Silverstone, it was Taruffi's turn to follow Ascari past the chequered flag, with Farina a distant sixth behind Hawthorn and a pair of Connaughts driven by Poore and Thompson.

With the best four results counting towards his points tally, the Championship would be Ascari's if he won in Germany.

It has always been regular practice for drivers to walk round a circuit prior to practice, studying every nuance and undulation of the track surface, rather as a golfer surveys the green before making that decisive putt. At over 14 miles in length, however, the Nürburgring would have been something of a daunting prospect, so Ascari did his homework from his Fiat saloon. Set in the Eifel mountains, great rolling hill country, relatively remote, with great stands of pine forest, it was ideal for camping enthusiasts. But the Nürburgring had so many corners and varied challenges that it was difficult to learn. Whereas a GP at Silverstone might run to 85 laps, the German GP covered just 18 laps – at some ten minutes per lap – so each challenge wasn't encountered often enough to become completely familiar with it. It is just

Ascari's Ferrari 125 gets a push from the pits at the 1949 Italian GP.

for a rear tyre change on lap nine, Farina also pitted. But the latter stalled twice trying to get away again, and Ascari was soon half a minute ahead. That might have been an end of it. But as is frequently the case in motor racing, the unexpected can happen on the very last lap. At the end of the 16th tour, Ascari was overdue. He rushed into the pits clamouring for oil, which was swiftly poured into the Ferrari catch tank. It was enough for Farina to speed by. Ascari drove the race of his life, and pounded through the Nürburgring's myriad corners in pursuit of his colleague. The gap lessened all the time, and down the long, long finishing straight to the start-finish line, Ascari hauled him in.

Past the pits and he was through. The South Curve which followed allowed Farina to fight back, but Ascari held his ground. Farina's challenge faded, and Ascari was gone again. He took the flag 14.1 seconds ahead of Farina, averaging 82.2mph for 3hrs 6mins 13.3 secs, with a fastest lap of 84.4mph. Compounding Ascari's supremacy in a way, the Ferraris of Fischer and Taruffi filled the next two places, with Béhra fifth for Gordini and Laurent sixth, also in a Ferrari.

Ascari was just as dominant in 1953, winning the non-championship Pau Grand Prix, around the streets and park of the French town. Instead of addressing the crowd over the PA, as was customary, Ascari went off to check on the condition of Béhra who had crashed.

not possible to learn a circuit with such a short number of laps. Spectators at the old Nürburgring were spoiled for vantage points, but best of all was the Karusell, a tightly banked left-hand hairpin, which allowed you to watch the cars plunge in, travel all the way round in front of you, with the drivers clearly visible at work, and swoop out again.

Like Spa, the Nürburgring was subject to the vagaries of hill weather, so it might be raining on one side of the circuit and not on the other, and if encountered at high speed, a trip into the scenery, such as an earth bank or a stand of pines, was the likely outcome.

In 1952, Ascari led from the start, followed by Manzon, Farina and Bonetto in a Maserati. The rate of attrition was high, with cars breaking due to mechanical failure and burst tyres, and when Farina pitted on the fourth lap, for fresh goggles, Ascari's lead was extended. As he came in

Ascari was victorious at the first of the World Championship events, at Buenos Aires, in a 2.5-litre Ferrari – the regulations were Formule Libre for this event – with González, fellow countryman Oscar Gálvez and Mike Hawthorn all driving 2.0-litre Ferraris.

Another non-championship race followed, at Bordeaux on 3 May, and although Ascari won from Villoresi in another Ferrari benefit, the winner was tired and worn-out afterwards, stating that 123 laps were 'a little too much.' Surprisingly, Fangio drove a Gordini, and finished third, four laps behind.

In the dunes at Zandvoort in June it was Ascari again, from Farina, Gonzalez/Bonetto's Maserati, Hawthorn learning his trade in a Ferrari, and de Graffenreid's Maserati, two laps down. Trintignant's Gordini was sixth this time, and Villoresi set fastest lap for Ferrari. Fangio had been squeezed out of contention by the Ferraris on the first lap, and retired on lap 37. The most dramatic pursuit of Ascari was by Gonzalez, who earned the accolade of the crowd for his physical driving style. There was controversy about the track surface and, along with most of the front runners, Gonzalez's Maserati was to be seen with a fence of gauze ahead of the cockpit to protect the driver from flying gravel. Afterwards the FIA sought to ban the circuit for poor maintenance.

The Ferraris of Ascari and Villoresi were first and second at Spa, from Marimon and Baron de Graffenreid in Maseratis, with Trintignant's Gordini and Hawthorn's Ferrari next up.

Fields of glory

To the cornfields of Rheims-Geux next, hosting the 40th French Grand Prix and vying with Le Mans for spectator appeal – to the extent that a 12 hour sports car race was run as a curtain-raiser to the Grand Prix. In what turned out to be one of the closest finishes of all time, the field was led by a train of red cars – and therefore all Italian – comprising Gonzalez, Ascari, Villoresi, Bonetto, Hawthorn, Marimon and Farina, with Prince Bira's fuel-injected Connaught heading the rest of the field. Eventually the lead was contested by Fangio and Hawthorn, the pair running in tandem for lap after lap. As for Ascari, he was locked in combat with Gonzalez, and the Ferraris were able to make up on the Maseratis under braking what they lacked in straight-line speed. Both pairs came over the line to start their last lap absolutely neck and neck. The cars passed the chequered flag in a red blur – Hawthorn, Fangio, González and Ascari – with less than five seconds between them. The crowds surged on to the track in a frenzy of enthusiasm. It was the Englishman's first GP victory, and a well-deserved one too.

While Hawthorn and Farina were adding to Ferrari's tally of successes at the non-championship GP at Rouen-les-Essarts, Ascari and Villoresi were at Monza testing the new four- and twelve-cylinder 3-litre Ferrari sports cars prior to the Inter Europa Cup race. Ascari was sidelined in the first heat when he collided with another car while lapping it, and Villoresi emerged the winner of a fierce Ferrari-Lancia duel with Gonzalez; Bonetto's open 2.9-litre V8 Lancia finished second after the Argentinian retired, with Farina third. The second heat brought exactly the same result.

The sixth RAC British Grand Prix – sponsored by the *Daily Express* – was held on 18 July 1953. It was to be another Ferrari-Maserati stand-off, and Fangio, Hawthorn, Gonzalez and Ascari occupied the front row. Ascari and Gonzalez were soon trading fastest laps, until Gonzalez was brought in because the stewards suspected his rear axle was leaking oil onto the track. The six slice Ferrari/Maserati sandwich – as *Motor Sport* put it – consisted of Ascari, Fangio, Farina, Gonzalez and Hawthorn. They were all slowed only temporarily by a sudden hailstorm and deluge of rain, which sidelined a few further down the running order.

Although he completed a hat-trick of wins at the Nürburgring in 1952, Ascari was not to have the same share of good fortune in 1953. After Fangio led initially, Ascari was away, and apparently uncatchable. Then he lost his front off-side wheel, and coasted some distance to the pits on the remaining three. Not wanting to use the brakes lest he wear out the still functioning near-side one, he coasted the length of the pits until the car came to a standstill. A mechanic rushed down from the Ferrari pit with a trolley jack and steered the stricken Ascari backwards to his pit, where a new wheel was fitted. Ascari broke the lap record again and again in a bid to catch the leaders, Farina, Fangio and Hawthorn, but blew the Ferrari's engine in the process. Somewhat disconsolate, he packed helmet and goggles into his small blue case, donned his sports jacket and retired to his hotel.

It may have been some compensation that Ascari also won the Nürburgring 1000kms sports car race teamed with Farina. Sixty-five laps round the Bremgarten circuit at Berne saw Ascari finish first ahead of Farina and Hawthorn for a Ferrari 1-2-3, ahead of Fangio/Bonetto and Hermann Lang in Maseratis. Ascari set fastest lap at 101.1mph, and it was enough to secure him the 1953 title.

The controversial Italian Grand Prix ended with Ascari punted off, probably by Marimon's Maserati, but maybe with Farina's help too. Or was there oil on the corner, as the organisers stated? The Ferrari just about had the legs of the Maserati, but it had been a close-run contest. In the end it was Fangio who benefited. Ferrari was sufficiently miffed to withdraw from racing after Monza, missing the non-championship Modena GP the following week. Fangio and Marimon finished one-two.

A major error

In what must surely rank as one of the biggest motor racing mistakes of all-time, Ascari and Villoresi left Ferrari to join Lancia for the 1954 season. The D50s were not ready until the end of the season, which must have been incredibly frustrating for all concerned. Ascari took the honours in the Mille Miglia – not his favourite event by any means – in a 3.3-litre Lancia V6 sports car. His only race with the side-tank Lancia was the Spanish GP, which he led for ten laps before retiring.

Come 1955, Lancia was all set to race competitively, and Ascari won two non-championship events. At Turin – around the Valentino Park circuit – he led fellow Lancia drivers Villoresi and Castellotti home, with Mieres' Maserati second. He then won at Naples soon afterwards. The key opposition was Mercedes, in the hands of Moss and Fangio, and the pair led away at the start of the season's first Championship round, the Monaco Grand Prix. When the German cars retired, Ascari led for one lap, and his colleague Castellotti finished second in the other Lancia; the race was won by Maurice Trintignant in a Ferrari 625.

Strangely, what most people remember about Ascari is not so much his excellence as a driver but the fact that he was fished out of Monaco harbour when his Lancia slid sideways and crashed into the bales and sandbags at the entrance to the harbour section, and plunged into the sea in a cloud of steam. Such an incident is immortalised in John Frankenheimer's 1966 movie Grand Prix but in real life it only happened to one other driver – Paul Hawkins. Ascari, however, is the driver we remember suffering this most Monegasque of mishaps.

The Lancia had fallen into 15 feet of water, but Ascari emerged with nothing more than a cut nose and, as a number of frogmen swam to his aid he was picked up by a small motor boat. He was nevertheless kept under observation in Monte Carlo hospital for a couple of days.

Perhaps Ascari's one vulnerable spot was that he was susceptible to superstition. He always had a lucky helmet, lived by particular routines, and always at the back of his mind was the fact that his father Antonio was killed at Montlhery in 1925, aged 36; for Alberto that was not an age he relished attaining. He sought courage from St Anthony – who had also succumbed when aged 36. Incredibly, Alberto Ascari was to lose his life at exactly the same age.

Straight after being released from hospital in Monaco he went to Monza on 26 May 1955 to watch the 3.0-litre Ferrari sports cars testing. He asked to have a drive in the car he might be able to share with Castellotti in the following weekend's Supercortemaggiore event, and also to check how his back felt after the Monaco accident. Wearing a borrowed helmet, he set off, and completed four slow laps, only to lose control at the sweeping Curva Vialone left-hander. The car overturned and Ascari was killed. Two long skid marks led up to the scene of the impact, but no-one could say for sure why it happened.

Juan Manuel Fangio

(1911–1995) World Champion 1951, 1954, 1955, 1956, 1957

Juan Manuel Fangio, considered by many to be the greatest racing driver ever, remains the only man to have won the Formula 1 World Championship five times. He had a full and fruitful career. Almost every schoolboy who grew up in the 1950s idolised one racing driver or another. And the one who commanded most respect was undoubtedly Fangio.

He always appeared cool, calm and collected; there was none of the fiery brio of Ascari or the temperament of Farina or the boyish gaucheness of Collins and Hawthorn. Fangio was invariably self-assured and good-humoured. Out of a car in the pits or paddock, his crash hat perched on the back of his head, he could also appear to be one of the boys.

Slow of speech – taciturn even – he was the reverse in a car, his reactions quick and precise. His upbringing made him strong and tenacious, yet he frequently displayed masterful race-craft on the circuit. Fangio was a true professional, with virtually no interests outside motor racing.

These were also the days of sheer bravery, when there were no Armco barriers, tyres were narrow, mechanical failures commonplace, and no protection whatsoever was built into the cars; crash helmets only came in in 1952. Before that the vast majority wore cloth or linen helmets. There was an incessant trail of carnage as Fangio's contemporaries were killed – an attrition rate wholly unacceptable today, and all these factors have to be taken into account when assessing his achievements.

The early years of the World Championship are difficult to compare with today's crowded calendar, with scarcely a three month lay-off in the winter and Grands Prix more or less every fortnight at the height of the season. In the 1950s, there were only eight Grands Prix counting towards the Championship – other, smaller events called themselves Grand Prix of this or that, but lacked the international status of a full-blown GP.

Judging from the results, Fangio was the most accomplished driver of his era. It's impossible to say how he would have fared in a modern GP car were he a competitor today. But the innate driving talent, the physical aptitude and metabolism were all there. Keeping the car balanced under

braking and acceleration was his forté – perhaps reminiscent of Alain Prost in more recent times.

His rustic roots provided a surprising background for a future maestro. Early this century, the Argentine town of Balcarce, some 200 miles from Buenos Aires, was noted for its potatoes. That's a measure of the rural environment in which Fangio grew up.

Born in Balcarce on 24 June 1911, the son of Italian immigrants, Fangio was noted for his footballing skills and was nicknamed 'el chueco': bandy-legs. He learned his craft doing jobs for a local garage. Later on, his father found him work at Senor Viggiano's garage as an apprentice mechanic delivering customers' cars on the dirt roads between Balcarce and Buenos Aires. This stood him in good stead for the Argentinean Carretera city-to-city races, where competitors raced on public roads, few of which had tarmac surfaces.

Aged 17 and by now a qualified mechanic, Fangio was invited by Snr Ayerza, one of Viggiano's customers, to be his riding mechanic in a Model T Ford race. He was hooked. Despite a serious bout of pneumonia, from which he nearly died, Fangio was called up for national service. Having got that out of the way, he set up a garage in Balcarce in 1932 with a loan from his father, and with his friend José Duffard as partner.

In 1934 Fangio was able to compete in a borrowed Model T racer, but the big-ends failed and he was forced to repair the damage for nothing before returning the car. More races followed in a 1929 Ford Model A – a

Fangio won his second world title in 1954, driving the Mercedes W196. Here he is on his way to victory at Pedralbes, Barcelona.

**A relaxed Fangio with his constant companion
Andreina (centre).**

date 4CLT/48 he won the Mar del Plata Grand Prix – trouncing the visiting European drivers. It was no surprise when the Argentine club decided to send him to Europe the following year.

Fangio made his debut on the European scene in an F2 race at Rheims in 1949 when Amédée Gordini offered him a drive in the injured Trintignant's car. He was second fastest in practice, but retired in the race.

He had laid the foundations of an international career, but when participating in the 10,000-mile South American Grand Prix, a rare mistake cost the life of his co-driver Daniel Urrutia when the Chevrolet Coupé overturned. Fangio was sufficiently devastated to contemplate giving up racing for good.

Happily for the sport he didn't, and was back in Europe in 1949 to begin his climb to the top, driving the blue and yellow Maserati 4CLT/48, winning at San Remo, Pau, Perpignan and Marseilles. Things looked bleak financially when a piston failed on the first lap of the Belgian Grand Prix, but financial sponsorship from a textile manufacturer and an IOU from the Perón government enabled the team to acquire a V12 F2 Ferrari 166C from the factory. Fangio promptly saw off the three works cars in the Monza Autodrome Cup. The prize money enabled them to rebuild the Maserati engine, and he won at Albi, but the team packed up and went back to Argentina.

converted taxi with a two-seater body, powered by an 85bhp Ford V8 engine. Its first race was at Necochea, and Fangio managed to out-gun the Alfa 8C-35 Grand Prix car of Carlos Arzani. Power and experience told, however, and the Ford special was third.

Highlight of the Argentinian race calendar was the Gran Premio Nacional, a 6000-mile event for modified production cars, split into ten-hour stages. Acting as riding mechanic in 1938, Fangio crewed home the seventh-placed car and, the following year, his friends in Balcarce had a whip-round to buy him a Chevrolet Coupé. He finished fifth, in spite of an accident.

His first taste of success was driving in the official Chevrolet team in the 1940 Gran Premio del Norte, a Carretera event of nearly 3000 miles, over the Andes to Peru. During the next two years, Fangio consolidated his position as South American champion, driving the Chevrolet Coupé, which required continual refurbishment.

Wartime shortages came late to Argentina, and motor sport came to a standstill. Fangio filled in the time as a taxi driver. But after hostilities ceased, Fangio started racing again on dirt tracks with Chevrolet specials and a single-seater Model T Ford special. When the European circus came to Argentina for the Temporada series in 1947, Fangio entered a Chevrolet-engined 'bitsa' known as Negrita, and finished sixth behind some of the leading Grand Prix talent.

Under the auspices of Argentina's president Perón, a great fan of motor racing, the country's leading drivers were dispatched on an exploratory mission to Indianapolis and Europe in 1948.

The same year saw Fangio in a pre-war 4CL Maserati, lent by the Argentine Automobile Club, and a Simca Gordini, and with an up-to-

Alfa Romeo's three musketeers

Fangio won the first race in the newly-instituted Formula 1 series on 10 April 1950 at Pau, in south-west France, driving the Maserati 4CLT/48. The F2 Ferrari was also available, and he was placed third at Marseilles. But then he was signed up by Alfa Romeo to join Farina and Fagioli – the three Fs – to drive the fabulous Alfa 158 Alfettas and, after a poor start, he won the rain-soaked San Remo Grand Prix.

At Monaco he avoided a first-lap catastrophe by inches – simply by observing that the crowd was looking towards the scene of the accident as he approached it, rather than at him. Wins came at Spa, Rheims, the Grand Prix des Nations at Geneva, and Pescara. Fangio had lost none of his long-distance acumen. He took third place in his first attempt at the Mille Miglia sports car road-race when he drove an Alfa 6C/2500 Berlinetta. He could easily have been champion in 1950, as he was leading the series on points before the Italian Grand Prix. But his Alfa's engine blew in the race and, despite taking over Bonetto's car, he broke down again, leaving the honours to team-mate Farina. Thus, he finished second to Farina in the inaugural World Championship.

Back in Argentina prior to the 1951 World Championship, Fangio had a go in one of the pre-war Mercedes 'Silver Arrows' W163s, although it was something of an anti-climax. Naturally Alfa Romeo were only too pleased to have him on the strength for 1951, and wins came at Bremgarten, Rheims-Geux, and Pedralbes-Barcelona, with second places at Silverstone and the Nürburgring. With five fastest laps set – and a point for each – it was enough to earn him the Championship, with 31 points to Ascari's 25, and Gonzalez's 24.

Fangio also shared a Talbot-Lago with Rosier at the Le Mans 24-Hours in 1951, and at one point took two seconds off the lap record set by Moss' C-type Jaguar. After a dramatic carburettor fire in the pits, the Talbot was eventually sidelined. Fangio also drove an Alfa 6C 3.0-litre in other sports car events including the Spa 24 Hours.

With Alfa withdrawing at the end of the season, Fangio was contracted to drive for Maserati in the 1952 World Championship, to be run to Formula 2 regulations for the next couple of years. He also signed up with BRM to do a handful of non-championship events. The year began well, with no less than six victories in the Argentinian

Temporada series in the old Ferrari 166C, now fitted with a 2.0-litre supercharged engine.

He drove the P15 BRM at Albi and Dundrod – the most sensational car, he thought – and so it was, with its V16 engine of only 1496cc, blown by two-stage Rolls Royce superchargers and developing 500bhp – but the BRMs were desperately dogged by unreliability in their early years, and Fangio brought the car no better luck.

The day after Dundrod, Fangio was booked on a flight to Monza for the Grand Prix there on 8 June. The French leg of the flight was cancelled due to the weather, so he hired a car and drove through the

Fangio set a new lap record on the last lap at Monaco in 1956.

Fangio drove the V16 BRM P15 in non-championship races in 1953.

night, arriving at the circuit just two hours before the race. Not having practised, he started from the back of the grid and, as he carved his way through the field, he ran wide at Lesmo curve, clipped the straw bales and was thrown out as his Maserati A6GCM somersaulted. He was hospitalised for 42 days, and in plaster for a further five months. As a result, the title went fairly easily to Ascari.

Back in business

For 1953 Fangio was back behind the wheel of a Maserati, and had lost none of his old form. At Buenos Aires for the first Argentinian Grand Prix his Maserati A6GCM led until it was sidelined with transmission failure – typical of those cars, which were fast but fragile. Although he finished second at Rheims, Silverstone and the Nürburgring, the Ferraris of Ascari, Farina and Hawthorn were just too agile, and outright success eluded Fangio. It had been a tremendously close thing over the flat-out straights and tight hairpins of Rheims-Geux – almost a triangle of a circuit on closed-off public roads, and an epic 32-lap struggle finally went in Hawthorn's favour. Fangio set matters to rights at the Italian Grand Prix, taking advantage of the last lap crash in which his team-mate Marimon took out the leader Ascari and wrong-footed Farina.

In 1953's Mille Miglia, Fangio finished an incredible second, driving an Alfa Romeo Disco Volante Berlinetta with only one wheel steering after a chassis breakage. Driving a Lancia D24 sports-racer, he won the 1953 Carrera Panamericana.

In 1954 the World Championship reverted to Formula 1. Driving the new 2.5-litre Maserati 250F, Fangio won the Argentinian and Belgian Grands Prix. After the Nürburgring, Spa was probably his

favourite circuit, and as he shattered his own lap record set in the Alfa 159, onlookers were said – by *Motor Sport* – to be 'electrified'. There were two bends on the old circuit at Spa which gave all drivers pause for thought: the Masta kink – a right-hand twitch on the flat-out Masta straight – and the Eau Rouge at the bottom of the downhill run after the start-finish line. To get either of these right was said to give the greatest satisfaction. With the circuit's revision and abandonment of much of the old track, there is now a chip shop at the Masta kink.

Then came a sea change in Formula 1 with the arrival of a key player to shake up the Italian-dominated establishment. Mercedes-Benz had already made its presence felt in sports car racing, and its arrival on the GP scene was anticipated with a degree of unease by the other leading teams. Fangio threw his lot in with Mercedes, reappearing for the first time since their pre-war glory days and still led by the meticulous Alfred Neubauer and design engineer Rudi Uhlenhaut.

The regulations permitted the use of all-enveloping body styling in Formula 1 at that time, and the streamlined effect contributed to greater straight-line speed. Surprisingly, hardly anyone else bothered with it in single seater racing, with the exception of Maserati, Connaught and Cooper. At the French Grand Prix, on the fast Rheims-Geux circuit, Fangio drove the straight-eight-engined W196 to victory, with his team-mate and Mercedes test-driver Karl Kling only a second behind. Hans Hermann set fastest lap to establish that Mercedes was back with a vengeance. Fangio had set fastest lap in practice and the Automobile Club de Champagne awarded him 50 bottles of champagne. The crowd's applause was loudest for Fangio too, at the pre-race parade.

The W196 was based around a low-slung, space-frame chassis, not dissimilar to the 300SL sports car, with inboard massive drum brakes, front wishbone and torsion bar suspension and a kind of swing-axle arrangement and Watts linkage at the rear; telescopic dampers were fitted all round, and the cars were, typically, extremely well built. Apart from Mercedes and H.W.M., which used fuel injection, all other GP cars used Weber carburettors.

GP at Monza. With the Ferraris and Maseratis of Ascari, Gonzalez, Moss and Villoresi all within 1.8 seconds of the Mercedes times, a close race was promised. So it was that by half distance, Ascari led Fangio by a second, with Moss' and Villoresi's Maseratis sitting close behind. Soon Moss was ahead of both Fangio and Ascari, but the Englishman's Maserati succumbed to a massive oil leak. He had served notice on the establishment of greater things to come. Fangio, meanwhile had to stave off attacks from all the top names, even Gonzalez when he was lapping him, and it was a well-deserved win, securing the 1954 World title. The season closed with the Spanish Grand Prix at Barcelona. A number of 'new' names were coming to the fore – Maserati's team now consisted of Stirling Moss, Luigi Musso, Sergio Mantovani, Roberto Mieres and Harry Schell, while Peter Collins practised but damaged the new Vanwall. Alberto Ascari was set to launch the dramatic 2.5-litre double-overhead cam V8-engined Lancia

Fangio (left) and Moss dominated the Grand Prix scene in 1955.

The open-wheel cars were triumphant at Silverstone, however, with Gonzalez and Hawthorn finishing together in a Ferrari 1-2. Fangio was fourth in a very battered streamliner, and somewhat overcome by fumes. The faired-in wheels made it difficult to judge apexes on corners, and Fangio struck corner markers during the race. Heavy rain midway through left Kling foundering in seventh place.

At the Nürburgring on 1 August, the Mercedes front runners used new open-wheel bodywork: drivers could now see where they were placing the front wheels. Fangio, Hawthorn and Moss – running his own Maserati 250F with factory support – formed the front row of the grid. Fangio, like the majority present, had been upset by Marimon's fatal crash during practice. Gonzalez in particular found it hard going for this reason, although he stormed by the leaders briefly. Fangio and Kling ran side by side for a lap, but Kling damaged his suspension and Fangio won by some two minutes from Gonzalez and Hawthorn, sharing the same car. During a pit stop to attend to Kling's broken suspension, team manager Neubauer cleared the crowded pit area by threatening to beat the assorted photographers with his signalling flag.

Fangio won the Swiss GP at Bremgarten from Gonzalez and Hermann, and the penultimate race of the 1954 season was the Italian

D50, with its fuel tanks set lengthways between the wheels. He led for nine laps before retiring. This somewhat processional affair ended with Fangio in fourth place, his left side soaked in hot oil. Hawthorn was the winner in the new Ferrari Tipo 553, with Musso second. Hawthorn thus finished the year third in the Championship behind González.

While the Grand Prix season comprised just six events, compared with 16 today, it should be appreciated that racing was going on at many different levels, from rallying and club racing to non-championship F1 and domestic Formule Libre races, where top drivers often competed. Contracts forbade the likes of Fangio from getting involved in such things, but the Mercedes Benz sports car team also had a busy programme in 1955. In the legendary Mille Miglia, won by Stirling Moss/Denis Jenkinson – of *Motor Sport* fame – in a Mercedes 300SLR, Fangio drove solo to finish second, just over half an hour behind after 1597kms of demanding road racing.

At the Le Mans 24-Hours the Mercedes SLRs were fitted with hydraulic air-brakes to slow them down at the end of the 175mph Mulsanne Straight. It was a head-to-head contest with the Jaguar D-types, and a fierce duel was in progress between Fangio's Mercedes and Hawthorn's Jaguar. However, tragedy struck when the Mercedes of

Fangio drove like a man possessed to win the 1957 German GP in his Maserati 250F.

Frenchman Pierre Levegh collided with Lance Macklin's Austin-Healey and was launched into the earthworks opposite the pits. The disintegrating SLR sliced through the crowds, leaving 85 dead. In the wake of what was absolutely the worst accident in motor racing history, the Mercedes team withdrew, and the Hawthorn/Bueb Jaguar was the hollow victor. Fangio had been approaching Levegh at the time of his accident, and was fortunate not to have been involved.

Competition didn't stop for long, although after the Le Mans tragedy it was banned in Switzerland. Later in the year, Fangio and Moss dominated the Swedish sports car Grand Prix in their 300SLRs. The order was reversed in October's Targa Florio, when Moss/Collins won the tortuous Sicilian road-race from Fangio/Kling, ahead of the Castellotti/Manzon Ferrari 750S.

Meanwhile, back in the world of Formula 1, the 1955 season commenced with Fangio taking the laurels in Argentina, setting fastest lap at Monaco and winning at Spa, followed home by Moss. These two were often so closely matched and their cars running in such close company that they were known as 'the Train'. The same result was achieved at Zandvoort, Moss scarcely a second behind the maestro. At Aintree for the British Grand Prix it was a Mercedes whitewash, with the silver cars filling the first four places, now with Taruffi on the strength. Moss is still unsure whether Fangio allowed him to win, stating that he felt sure Fangio could have passed him at

any time during the race. In fact they crossed the line virtually as one car, and Moss insisted Fangio wore the laurel wreath – something we don't see today. A measure of Moss/Mercedes supremacy is that by half distance, he had twice lapped Macklin.

A new challenge

Monza 1955 was to be Mercedes' last race. They had announced that they would be pulling out at the end of the season, having achieved all they'd set out to do. They'd won ten races in just over a season and a half, only been beaten three times, and failed to finish but once. The Monza race was the first Grand Prix to use the new oval banked section which integrated uncomfortably with the original configuration. Cars passing off the south banking on to the outside of the finishing straight were travelling very fast and those on the inside were still relatively slow, accelerating out of the south corner. It was some drivers' only hope of ever overtaking the likes of Moss and Fangio. As it was, Fangio took the honours, while Moss' car broke its transmission. Fangio was World Champion again, with 40 points, and Moss was second with 23.

While sportsmanship ruled on the circuit, it was not always so back home, and in the wake of President Perón's downfall in 1955, Fangio was investigated by the new regime to see if his career was politically motivated. A proud Argentinian he certainly was, but he was a professional racer and not a political activist. However, he was not clear of the inquisition for four years.

For 1956, Fangio moved to Ferrari, and shared cars with Musso to take the Argentinian Grand Prix again, from Jean Béhra's Maserati.

Lancia had gone broke, and since their cars had been taken over by Ferrari, they were for most of the season referred to as Lancia-Ferraris. Fangio opened the European F1 season by winning the non-championship Syracuse GP from Musso and Collins in similar cars. The D50-based cars now had the pontoons faired-in with the main body of the car, and did not contain the fuel tanks; these were now inboard.

Taking the initiative

At Monaco, Stirling Moss led from the first corner and his Maserati 250F was never headed. Fangio, on the other hand, had to fight past Castellotti, Béhra and Collins in his Lancia-Ferrari. Clutch slip forced Fangio to retire his car, and Collins was brought in by the Ferrari management to lend his car. Although he set fastest lap in pursuit of Moss, he couldn't catch him, and Moss won his first 'classic' Grand Prix. Monaco also marked the Maserati renaissance.

With Fangio retiring from the Belgian race with failed transmission, the Championship was led by two Englishmen – Moss and Collins, the latter having won at Spa. Belgian motoring journalist Paul Frére was second, also in a Lancia-Ferrari, while Moss was third.

Collins was the victor at Rheims on 1 July, from Castellotti, also Lancia-Ferrari, and Béhra's 250F, with Fangio fourth and Moss fifth. It was Ferrari again at Silverstone, this time with Fangio ahead of Collins, sharing the Marquis de Portago's car. Béhra was third again, and Moss set the fastest lap.

Fangio's lone Lancia-Ferrari won the German Grand Prix, with Maseratis filling the next five places, headed by Moss, who was under a minute down on Fangio. Finally, the tables turned at Monza, with Moss leading Fangio by less than six seconds at the chequered flag. It was touch and go for Moss, as he ran out of fuel and was literally pushed 2.5km back to the pits by fellow Maserati driver Piotti, who used his own car like a tug pushing a barge. It was also a race largely dependent on tyres – Castellotti's Englebert shedding a tread and throwing his Ferrari into a violent spin. Moss' Pirellis on the other hand were not completely worn out at the end of the race.

Again, Collins' sportsmanship enabled Fangio to get to the finish. This time it clinched the Championship: Fangio beat Moss by just three points, with 30 to Moss' 27. Collins wasn't far behind, on 25.

Fangio moved to Maserati again in 1957 for what turned out to be his last full season in Formula 1. Despite stiff opposition from Ferrari and Vanwall, his 250F Lightweight was sufficiently successful to take the title yet again. It was a relatively clean-cut affair, with wins in Argentina, Monaco, Rouen-les-Essarts, and the Nürburgring, plus second at Pescara and Monza behind Moss' Vanwall. Otherwise his closest rivals that season were Musso, Hawthorn and Collins, all in Ferraris, and Tony Brooks, also driving for Vanwall. His tally at the season's end was 40 points, from Moss' 25, with Musso third in the ratings with 16. At Monaco in 1957, a certain Jack Brabham finished sixth in his rear-engined Cooper-Climax. It was the first sign of yet another sea change.

That was Fangio's fifth Championship and at 46 he was the oldest man in the game. He had sat on pole position for 29 Grands Prix, and won 24 of them. His best race – in which he did things he swore he would never do again – was the German GP at the Nürburgring. He decided not to risk the Maserati's rather delicate rear suspension by doing the race on full tanks, so he elected to make one pit-stop at half distance. He came in with a 27.8 second advantage, but the refuelling went awry, and he went out again with a 28 second deficit.

Driving an inspired race he overhauled the Ferraris of Hawthorn and Collins over the next nine laps, breaking the lap record each time, and they watched him go by, incredulous and seemingly powerless to prevent him. He led Hawthorn over the line by 3.6 seconds. Afterwards Fangio confirmed that the Nürburgring had always been his favourite circuit, but it was not until that day in 1957 that he actually managed to master it. 'It was as if I had screwed all the secrets out of it and got to know it once and for all.' He was trying out new things during those last laps, pushing himself further at the many blind spots where he had never previously had the courage to take it to the limit. He admitted afterwards that, 'Quite simply, I had always had faith in my own abilities and in the preparation of the machines I drove. Until that race, I had demanded nothing more of myself or the cars. But on that day, I made such demands on myself that I couldn't sleep for two days afterwards… for days I felt delayed-action apprehension at what I had done, which had never come over me after any other race.'

In the 1958 Argentinian Grand Prix, he was placed fourth with an ailing Maserati, but won the non-championship Buenos Aires Grand Prix a fortnight later. In Cuba for a sports car race, he was kidnapped by Fidel Castro's guerrillas, but was released unharmed after the event. He entered for the Indianapolis 500, but found his cars uncompetitive and withdrew the entry.

In a bid to see how American machines fared against the European-based Grand Prix circus, an Indy-type contest was set up at Monza, and Fangio posted some promising times in practice. Fuel pump failure put him out of the event. His last race was the French Grand Prix at Rheims, and he did well to finish fourth in a new Maserati 250F, running without a clutch.

> **'Like others who quit while the going was good, Fangio assumed the role of elder statesman'**

Partly influenced by the deaths of his friends and colleagues, Musso, Collins and Castellotti, Fangio decided to call it a day. Like others who quit while the going was good – Jackie Stewart, for instance – Fangio then assumed the role of elder statesman around the world's race circuits, and continued to oversee his Mercedes-Benz dealership in Buenos Aires. He lived contentedly in Argentina, surrounded by his family and his friends, until his death in August 1995 at the age of 83.

In his home country he remains as much a national hero as Moss and Clark here – matched by the kind of acclaim bestowed in recent years by Brazilians on Ayrton Senna. As well as Fangio, Argentina has had several international motor racing heroes to celebrate: Oscar Gálvez, Froilán González, Onofré Marimón, Carlos Menditeguy, and Carlos Reutemann, to name just six.

Today, Balcarce Town Hall houses the Fangio Museum. Fangio built up a collection of important racing cars after his retirement, including an Alfa Romeo 159 and Mercedes-Benz W196. Also present are some of his earlier mounts – the Carretera Chevrolet coupés and the Volpi-Chevrolet Mecanica Nacional car. Just up the road at Sierra La Barosa, a race circuit was opened in his honour in 1969.

Fangio's competition career spanned the thrilling period of post-war evolution, before the advent of the modern mid-engined racing car and the onset of commercialism, and the best tribute is to remember him as the man who won five World Championships against stalwart opposition, and who knew when to retire with dignity.

ALFA ROMEO 158/9 (1938–51)

The Alfa 158 belongs more with the generation of cars that preceded the World Championship; it was essentially the same car as seen in 1938. Five Alfettas were hidden away during the war, and because of a dearth of new cars complying with the new formula, it was still very much state-of-the-art when the Championship commenced. Designed by Chief Engineer Gioachino Columbo, it remains the most successful Grand Prix car of all time, with 47 wins from 54 Grands Prix entered.

The new Tipo 158 Alfa Romeos debuted at Livorno in 1938, where they finished first and second, run by Enzo Ferrari's team. The Alfetta was powered by a 1.5-litre straight-eight with a triple-choke up-draught Weber carburettor and a twin-stage supercharger.

After the war, development continued under Orazio Satta Puliga with changes to the exhaust system and magneto. The gearlever was on the left, and, alarmingly, the transmission passed between the driver's legs. While Farina drove a 158 to win the inaugural World Championship, Fangio's was won in the Tipo 159. The bodywork was identical, but the more powerful 420bhp motor had a prodigious thirst for methanol fuel,

drinking 1.5 gallons a mile. The fuel tank was enlarged accordingly, and the extra weight affected the handling adversely. Nevertheless it was still able to attain speeds of 170mph at Rheims and Silverstone.

MASERATI 250F   (1954–1960)

Not so much a technological trendsetter as the yardstick of the front-engined era of the 1950s. The mainstay of privateers during the latter half of the decade, the 250F saw action in the first race of the 2.5-litre Formula 1 in 1954, and the last in 1960. By 1965, they were being raced in historic events. The mysteries of 250F development and individual

chassis are the subject of much scholarship and debate. For example, of the 28 cars built in five years, 17 appear to have been given new chassis numbers at some point.

The 250F was principally the work of Columbo and Alberto Massimino. The 2493cc straight-six engine produced over 220bhp, and the suspension was transverse leaf rear and twin wishbone front, with tubular spaceframe chassis clad in aluminium panels.

Maserati ran a works team in 1954, starting with two cars and ending with five, which was the number they raced in 1955, with Béhra as leader. Moss was his successor in 1956, followed by Fangio in 1957. In 1960 the trident of Bologna's finest was still going strong, and the 250F is now raced extensively in historic racing.

COOPER T51 Mk IV (1959–60)

The instigator of the rear-engined revolution, Charles and son John Cooper had been producing racing cars with this layout since the late 1940s for the 500cc F3. The Surbiton-based marque debuted in Formula 1 in 1957, essentially with an F2 car, and Moss won Cooper's first Grand Prix in 1958 in Buenos Aires. Essentially, the simple tubular space-frame chassis with coil-spring and wishbone front suspension Cooper was more nimble and could be cornered faster than the relatively large front-engined Ferraris, Maseratis and Vanwalls. Having only a 2.2-litre Coventry-Climax FPF engine, however, it was slower in a straight line.

The 1959 car had much cleaner lines, and later in the season was powered by the new 2495cc Coventry-Climax FPF twin-cam engine, developing 240bhp. Jack Brabham took the Championship with it.

Other drivers to be successful with Coopers were Roy Salvadori, Bruce McLaren, Stirling Moss and Maurice Trintignant. With Cooper's success – in tandem with that of the Lotus 18 – there was no going back for the evolution of the Grand Prix car.

LOTUS 25 (1962–1965)

The Lotus 25 was revolutionary by F1 standards in being the first monocoque single seater racing car – sometimes known as a 'bath-tub'. (The D-type Jaguar sports car of 1954 featured a monocoque centre section). Chapman introduced the spaceframe 24 for 1962, but almost immediately replaced it with the Lotus 25. The new car's construction consisted of twin pontoons either side of an undertray, with front and rear bulkheads, while a stressed panel incorporated the instrument dash.

Front suspension was by upper cantilever rocking arms, lower wishbones and inboard coil springs and dampers; rear suspension was by upper links, twin radius rods, reversed lower wishbones and outboard coil springs and dampers. The 25 was powered by the Coventry Climax FMWV V8 engine, and along with its successor the Lotus 33 and the V8 BRM, it was the most successful car of the 1500cc Formula 1 period, giving Jim Clark the Championship in 1963. For much of 1964, Clark and Arundell used the 25B with revised rear suspension, and after Lotus began using the 33 in 1965, privateers continued to race the 25. The 33 was raced by the works into 1967.

Mike Hawthorn
(1929–1959) World Champion 1958

John Michael Hawthorn was born on 10 April 1929 at Mexborough, Yorkshire. He lived there only two years, as his father Leslie Hawthorn, a keen racer on two wheels, bought a partnership in the TT Garage business at Farnham, Surrey. He was thus ideally placed for action at Brooklands race track, Weybridge. It wasn't long before the young Mike was a regular spectator at Brooklands, and, indeed, his first taste of motoring was aged eight, behind the wheel of a customer's Jowett in the paddock behind the family garage.

During the war years, Hawthorn senior was a pilot, ferrying aircraft from one base to another, and Mike was a pupil not too far away at Ardingly College, Sussex. It was here that Mike got hooked on motor cycling, and he proved very successful at trials and scramble riding.

On leaving school, the young Hawthorn became apprenticed to truck manufacturers Dennis Bros., handily based at Guildford. With an eye to his son taking over the business, Leslie Hawthorn steered Mike towards gaining an education in engineering theory and practice, and he was sent to Kingston Tech and then the College of Automobile Engineering in Chelsea.

One of the perks of a family garage business is access to cars, and Mike was seen hustling a diminutive Fiat 500 around the Surrey lanes. It just wasn't fast enough, and he was given an old Riley 9 for a while. The arrival of a Lancia Aprilia was just what he needed, and it boosted his ambition to take up motor racing.

Mike Hawthorn's competitive debut was at the 1950 Brighton Speed Trials, driving an 1100cc pre-war Riley Ulster Imp on the sea-front promenade. The car had been completely overhauled for the occasion, and Hawthorn won his class. Soon afterwards he was second in class at the Gosport Speed Trials.

In 1951 he took to the circuits, entering the Riley Imp and a 1.5-litre Riley TT Sprite at events like the support race for the Ulster TT at Dundrod, which he won easily due to a favourable handicap system. Victory followed in the Leinster Trophy at Wicklow.

Just as today, there was a recognised route to the top of the tree in motor racing which tended to ignore anything except single seaters, so Hawthorn recognised that he needed to get into formula racing cars in order to advance his career. He had unsuccessful test drives for Connaught and H.W.M. at Goodwood, spinning the Connaught and losing out on the H.W.M. drive to Peter Collins. But the Hawthorns' family friend Bob Chase came to the rescue with the offer of a Cooper-Bristol, providing TT Garage would prepare and run the car.

His first outing with the silver Formula 2 Cooper-Bristol was the 1952 Easter Monday meeting, attended by 50,000 race fans, with stars like Fangio and Gonzalez present. The meeting also featured a duel between Stirling Moss and motor cycle champion Geoff Duke in the sports car race – Aston Martin versus Jaguar – which Duke won. Hawthorn led all the way in the Levant Cup race, blowing off Abecassis' H.W.M. In the Formule Libre event, Hawthorn beat some strong opposition, including Fangio, who was also driving a Cooper-Bristol. More remarkably, in the day's Richmond Trophy race for F1 cars, he was second to Gonzalez's Ferrari. The press latched on to the fact that here was Britain's great hope.

Some drivers stand out from the rest because of some sartorial idiosyncrasy. Hawthorn's was the bow-tie he invariably wore, even during races. In the paddock he smoked a pipe and wore a battered cap. These weren't gimmicks, they were accoutrements of the man. For many he encapsulated the spirit and aspirations of post-war Britain.

Home wins

Further successes in 1952 included the Ibsley club races at Goodwood, a heat of the Daily Express International Trophy races at Silverstone – again facing top-class opposition; as was often the case, he drove the Cooper Bristol hard, and usually won unless it broke down, which it did in the second heat at Silverstone.

Two fourth places followed at Spa and Zandvoort in the Belgian and Dutch Grands Prix. Third in the British Grand Prix, he added a Coupe des Alpes to his successes, was first at the Goodwood Whitsun meeting, third in the British Empire Trophy on the Isle of Man, second in the TT at Dundrod, and Formula 2 class winner at the Daily Mail festival of Motor Sport at Boreham. Motor Sport credited the win to the preparation of the car, as well as Hawthorn's driving abilities. On the strength of these performances, he was invited to Modena for a try-out later in the year. After driving the Ferrari, he took out his Cooper Bristol as a comparison, but hit some straw bales and was laid up in hospital for a while.

It didn't matter to Enzo Ferrari. Il Commendatore knew that a driver who never crashed wasn't trying hard enough, and Hawthorn was hired for the 1953 season. He duly rewarded Ferrari's confidence with wins in the non-championship Pescara grand prix, the Ulster Tourist Trophy, the *Daily Express* Trophy at Silverstone, and the legendary French Grand Prix at Rheims, at which he beat Fangio by one second. At Silverstone he was fifth, then third at the Nürburgring behind Farina and Fangio, third again behind Ascari and Farina at Bremgarten, and fourth at Monza.

Hawthorn's reputation was made, and it demonstrated also that a British driver could actually beat the rest of the world in Grands Prix and not just sports car racing. The only chink in his halo was that kidney trouble prevented him from doing national service, which the cynics in the press and certain MPs seized on. This was not a happy period for Hawthorn. A crash in the 1954 Syracuse Grand Prix burned him quite badly – he was rescued from the blazing Ferrari by team-mate Gonzalez, whose own car became engulfed in the flames. Hawthorn missed the first World Championship round at Buenos Aires while recuperating. Then his father died in a road accident, and he was forced to take control of the TT Garage rather sooner than he'd expected.

The second round of the 1954 Championship – run to 2.5-litre Formula 1 (or 750cc supercharged) rules – wasn't until 20 June at Spa, and he came back with fourth place, shared with Gonzalez. Spa-Francorchamps was one of the most spectacular circuits on the scene: featuring eight miles of sweeping, undulating public roads among the wooded Ardennes hills. It was, and to an extent remains, despite modernisation, the circuit that separates the best from the rest.

Competing with the best

Hawthorn was second at Silverstone behind Gonzalez's Ferrari and ahead of Marimon's Maserati, and again runner-up to Fangio at the Nürburgring in a shared car with the despondent Gonzalez, whose friend Marimon had been killed in practice; now the Ferrari squad faced the growing might of the Mercedes W196s. It was the same story at Monza: a second place, one lap down on Fangio's Mercedes, in a race which had been dominated by Moss' Maserati. The tables were turned on the road circuit at Pedralbes, Barcelona, for the final GP of the season, and Hawthorn's Ferrari Squalo 625, now running coil-spring front suspension, was the winner after playing a waiting game behind Schell's Maserati and Trintignant's Ferrari. He took them on lap 27, and Musso slipped past

Fangio's Mercedes, overheating because of some paper that had become stuck in its air intake. This was partly a legacy of the environment: the streets of Barcelona at that time were strewn with rubbish.

Hawthorn finished the season in third place in the Championship behind Fangio and Gonzalez. He had also won the Supercortemaggiore event at Monza and was placed second in the TT at Dundrod.

The following year, 1955, was not a happy one for Ferrari and Maserati, since every Grand Prix was won by Mercedes. But it was not so much the Teutonic supremacy as the need to spend more time in England, attending to the Farnham business, which prompted Hawthorn to sign for the emergent Vanwall team. He would also drive the Jaguar D-types in long-distance sports car races, winning the Sebring 12-Hours, and it was while disputing the lead at Le Mans with Fangio that Hawthorn was involved in the appalling tragedy which blighted motor sport as a whole. Hawthorn seemed to have decided to head for the Jaguar pit as a last minute decision, causing Lance Macklin's Healey to swerve into the path of Levegh's Mercedes 300SLR, itself pursued by Fangio's similar car. The Frenchman's car was launched into the barrier opposite the pits, and disintegrated among the spectators, killing 85 and injuring hundreds more. In the wake of the accident, the French, German, Swiss and Spanish Grands Prix were cancelled and, despite winning the 24-Hours with Ivor Bueb, Hawthorn was devastated. It was a racing accident, however, and no-one in particular was to blame.

Hawthorn's winning V6 Dino 246 at the Goodwood chicane in 1958.

Only a week after Le Mans came the Dutch Grand Prix, with a reduced entry of 16 cars, and, with Vanwall absent, Hawthorn rejoined Ferrari to finish a lowly seventh. Driving Stirling Moss' own Maserati 250F, Hawthorn beat Schell's Vanwall at South London's Crystal Palace circuit in a minor F1 event, but the Ferrari was simply not on the pace. Sixth at Aintree was the best he could do.

Hawthorn expressed the wish to stay with Ferrari for 1956, but Maranello refused to release him to race Jaguars in sports car events – fairly reasonably since they had a vested interest in that area. So he decided to give BRM a try. In the Argentine he was third in a Maserati 250F – owned by BRM. First inkling of the potential of the new British cars was at Silverstone, where Brooks' and Hawthorn's P25s led initially

in a race won by the Lancia-Ferraris of Fangio and Collins. Brooks was lucky to escape with burns and a broken jaw from an end-over-end roll when he crashed as the BRM's throttle jammed open.

It was a disastrous season, with races punctuated by accidents and mechanical failures, and BRM's reputation sank lower than ever. Even the Jaguars rewarded him with a mere second place at Rheims. In 1957 he made what looked like another bad move, signing for Ferrari, who were still using the now elderly Lancia D50-based 801 cars. The year began auspiciously enough with Collins and Hawthorn doing a 1-2 at Naples. But in a year which saw Fangio dominant yet again for Maserati, and the rise of the Vanwall – and being an ardent patriot, it would have been fitting for Hawthorn to have driven one – we find Hawthorn coming fourth at Rouen-les-Essarts, third at Aintree, and losing out to Fangio at the Nürburgring.

Meanwhile Moss was busy winning at Pescara and Monza for Vanwall, and Hawthorn managed only sixth at Monza. There was some compensation in finishing third at Sebring in a D-type Jaguar. Successes in the 3.4-litre Jaguar saloon included the support race for the *Daily Express* Trophy at Silverstone.

Dicing with danger

In those days of tall, narrow tyres, on wire-spoke wheels more often than not, the art of racing centred around how well a driver could corner in immense power slides. Sweeping, flat-out bends were taken with the cars virtually sideways, the driver grappling the steering wheel from lock to lock, driving it on the throttle and promoting lift-off understeer. Consequently, tyre wear was enormously significant: the tyres took a thrashing at the rear because these were the driven wheels, and at the front too, with the opposite locking. Tyres were all too vulnerable to debris from accidents and spin-offs, and Hawthorn was unlucky in this respect at Aintree; he might otherwise have won. The fatal accident to the Marquis de Portago and several spectators in the Mille Miglia that year, which caused the event to be banned, was thought to have been down to the failure of the Ferrari's Englebert tyres.

Vanwall's ascendancy in 1957 marked the rise of Britain as a world-class producer of F1 racing cars, which, in spite of Hawthorn's success with Ferrari in the Championship in 1958, was never seriously challenged thereafter. The team's breakthrough had come in the 1957 British GP at Aintree, where Moss had taken over Tony Brooks' car to work his way through the field and eventually take the lead. It was the first all-British GP win since Henry Segrave took the French GP in 1923.

For 1958, the FIA ruled that cars were to run on Av-gas aviation fuel of 100/130 octane rating. This was a move to placate the oil companies who supported the sport quite handsomely, yet saw little benefit in practice because teams used quite exotic concoctions to fuel their cars. Regular pump fuel was quite unacceptable, so Av-gas was

Hawthorn's BRM (23) leads at the start of the 1956 British GP at Silverstone.

the compromise. This decision affected Vanwall, who had problems getting their engine to run on it. The four-cylinder power-plant was based on Norton motor cycle engines, and the spaceframe chassis was designed by Colin Chapman. Meanwhile the tail of the large, high-sided bulbous car was re-profiled by aerodynamicist Frank Costin.

English domination

Ferrari came back with the new Dino V6 cars for Hawthorn, Musso, Collins, Wolfgang von Trips and the American Phil Hill. It proved to be a season-long battle between the two Englishmen, Moss and Hawthorn.

Moss opened the scoring in Argentina, driving a rear-engined 2.0-litre Cooper-Climax, from Musso and Hawthorn. Moss conserved his tyres by deliberately driving through oil and on the grass. At Monaco all three Vanwalls retired, leaving the laurels to Trintignant's Cooper-Climax, with Musso and Collins next up. Hawthorn set fastest lap.

At Zandvoort, Moss led from start to finish, the Vanwalls now shod with wire spoke wheels at the front and 'wobbly-web' alloys at the rear. Remarkably, the BRMs of Schell and Béhra were second and third, with Hawthorn fifth behind Roy Salvadori's Cooper-Climax.

The Belgian race at Spa-Francorchamps looked as though it would go Moss' way, but a missed gear change sent the revs sky high and the car was out with bent valves. Instead, Tony Brooks' Vanwall took the win, from the other Vanwall of Stuart Lewis-Evans. Hawthorn's Dino-Ferrari expired just before the line.

Hawthorn won the French Grand Prix at Rheims, but the team was stunned by the death of Luigi Musso during the race. Moss finished second with von Trips third. At Silverstone, Moss was on pole but retired with engine trouble. The Ferraris were on form again and Collins led Hawthorn home with Salvadori third.

Vanwall had sorted out its suspension settings for the Nürburgring, and Moss led until magneto failure put him out on lap four. Brooks tailed the Ferraris of Hawthorn and Collins, passing them on lap 10. In his efforts to recover the place, Collins crashed on the following lap, and died almost instantly. Hawthorn's clutch failed, and Brooks won at his

ease from the Cooper-Climaxes of Salvadori and Trintignant, with von Trips fourth. It was a solemn day for Britain and for motor sport in general. Collins had exemplified the true British sportsman and he was much liked by everyone on the Grand Prix circuit.

To Oporto next for the Portuguese Grand Prix around the tram-lined streets of the port-producing capital. Moss took the lead from Hawthorn early in the race, and that was how the race finished. Hawthorn's second place was achieved with some controversy: he had spun off and stalled on an up-hill section of the course and it was against the rules to re-start a car against the direction of the race. However, Moss, seeing Hawthorn's plight, advised him to push the car down the pavement to fire-up the engine, then turn it around. At the post-race stewards' inquiry, Moss testified that Hawthorn had not actually driven on the circuit against the flow of traffic, so Hawthorn's second place was allowed to stand. That eventually would clinch him the Championship.

A showdown in Morocco

At Monza the front row of the grid featured all three Vanwalls, plus Hawthorn's Ferrari. Brooks took the lead from Hawthorn when the Dino engine went off-song. The Championship would actually be settled by the final race, the Moroccan Grand Prix at Casablanca. Hawthorn's tally stood at 40 points from six events; Moss had 32 from five races. Only six races could count towards the title, plus one point for each fastest lap set. Moss thus needed to win and make fastest lap, while Hawthorn needed to finish at least second for six points.

Moss set fastest lap on his way to victory. Hawthorn managed second place however, being led through by his team-mate Phil Hill. But there was a bitter pill for Vanwall to swallow with its sixth win that season and the first Manufacturers' Championship award: Lewis-Evans crashed heavily when his engine seized, and he died of burns received in the ensuing conflagration. Vanwall's chief, Tony Vandervell, announced the team would be withdrawing from competition.

The accident to Lewis-Evans and the deaths of Musso and Collins (whom he called 'mon ami mate') led Hawthorn to announce his retirement. There was no fun in a game where the mortality rate was so high. He turned his attentions to the Jaguar dealership at Farnham, and set about restoring a 2.3-litre Alfa Romeo and the Riley Sprite.

Unless they had substantial private incomes, racing drivers of the period were paupers compared to today's sponsored-to-the-hilt brigade; Stirling Moss and Fangio drove Mercedes 220 saloons, Luigi Musso a more glamorous Alfa Giullietta Sprint GT, Peter Collins a Ford Zephyr, Jean Behra and Maurice Trintignant had Renault Dauphines, while Mike Hawthorn used a 3.8 Jaguar. He also owned and flew his own aircraft.

On a gloomy January day in 1959, Hawthorn drove towards London along the Hog's Back Guildford by-pass. He passed erstwhile racer Rob Walker's Mercedes 300SL at high speed, and Walker came upon the Jaguar halfway down the hill into Guildford sliced apart by a tree at the side of the road. Hawthorn was dead. No-one could say for sure what had happened – a slippery road caught him out, perhaps. He could have been driving in the Monte Carlo Rally at the time, but had turned down the offer on the grounds that it was too dangerous.

Jack Brabham

(1926–) World Champion 1959, 1960, 1966

Jack Brabham – christened John Arthur Brabham – was born in Sydney on 2 April 1926. His grandfather had emigrated to Australia from the East End of London in 1885, and father Brabham was a greengrocer. Jack excelled at technical subjects in school, and aged 15 began working in a garage. He was just old enough to see military service in World War II, and spent two years maintaining twin-engined Beaufighter fighter-bombers. After the war he set up a car servicing business from a workshop at his grandfather's Hurstville home.

A friendship with an American midget-car racer, Johnny Schonberg, led to Brabham building his own car for Schonberg. Broadsiding around a cinder-surfaced quarter-mile oval track – a specialised form of competition – called for a particular skill in car control. Brabham effectively manufactured the parts to make the strong, powerful 1350cc engine that gave the American a successful season. When his friend retired, Brabham took over. After some hard lessons learning the ropes, he emerged New South Wales Champion in his first season.

This chapter in his life lasted six years and Brabham was on the point of joining his father in the greengrocers when he became involved with hill-climbing. The entrée was provided by Ron Tauranac, destined to become Brabham's chief designer. Brabham entered the midget-racer in a hill-climb and proved much faster than the competition, so he stayed for more, using a 500cc Cooper Mk IV and a 1000cc Mk V Cooper-Vincent.

Ambitious moves

When Brabham bought a new Formula 2 Cooper-Bristol for a knock-down price, he looked all set for a move into the big-time. He was sponsored by Red-Ex, engine additive manufacturers, and proposed to enter the car as the Red-Ex special. The Australian governing body vetoed the scheme and Jack went off to race in New Zealand. Entered for the 1954 New Zealand Grand Prix he rubbed shoulders with the big names of the day, and showed promise by finishing sixth. The following year, having raced extensively in Australia and New Zealand, he finished fourth in the New Zealand GP. In conversation with Dean Delamont, then RAC Competitions Director, he was enthused by the notion of trying his hand at racing in Europe. Jack was the first of the antipodean invasion to hit the European scene with any serious intent on breaking into Grand Prix racing.

On his arrival in Britain, Jack Brabham bought Peter Whitehead's Mk II Cooper-Alta, but its engine proved unreliable and it was quickly swapped for a Bristol unit. He soon became noticed on British circuits, not so much because of his nationality but because of his tail-out driving style, a legacy of the midget-racer days. It was inevitable that he would meet up with the Coopers, and he and John Cooper became firm friends. Brabham and his wife Betty were virtually adopted by the Cooper fold. Brabham quickly gained the nickname 'Black Jack' because of his permanent 'five-o'clock shadow'.

In the early postwar years Charles and son John Cooper made a name for themselves as manufacturers of 500cc motorcycle-engined machines, which gained international recognition as Formula 3 cars in 1950. Although some of their sports cars and Cooper-Bristol F2 cars of 1952 were front-engined, their reputation was made with the rear- or, more correctly, mid-engined layout.

From 1955, Jack Brabham worked in the Cooper factory at Surbiton, Surrey, and was allowed to build his own car in lieu of a wage. This was a rear-engined special, powered by a 1971cc Bristol engine, and was known as the 'bob-tail' Cooper. It was entered for the 1955 British Grand Prix at Aintree, as a 2.2-litre engined car in order to side-step the organisers' reluctance to admit any F2 cars. Its clutch failed, but in an F1 race at Snetterton, Brabham was placed fourth behind a pair of Vanwalls and Stirling Moss' Maserati 250F. That winter, the 'bob-tail' Cooper was sold in Australia, having won the Australian GP for Brabham, and a replica built up as a sports racing car – later written off in a fatal crash at Goodwood. Although it was a portent of things to come, it would be another two years before Cooper's made a serious impression on Grand Prix racing.

After Brabham arrived on the scene he became inseparably linked with the Coopers, to such an extent that he acted as a catalyst to motivate the team to its pinnacle at the end of the decade. Brabham was

Black Jack – pictured in 1959 – was never without a 'five o'clock shadow'.

indefatigable, a slogger and an innovator, as well as being perfectly well qualified as an engineer. He was a force to be reckoned with as a test driver and was full of creative solutions to mechanical problems. He was also a tough competitor on the circuit, which, bearing in mind the new ground being covered by the mid-engined Coopers, was not a bad thing.

The three-year period between 1957 and 1960 witnessed the demise of the traditional conception of Formula 1 and the inexorable rise of the modern racing car. The Coopers and Colin Chapman of Lotus were responsible for this turnaround, the latter picking up on the Coopers' groundwork and refining it. It soon became clear that his more sophisticated F2 Mk 12 design was no match for the cruder rear-engined cars from Surbiton, so he changed direction accordingly.

The original basis for the Cooper-Climax was a curved-tube spaceframe chassis, transverse leaf suspension front and rear, powered by the Coventry Climax FWB twin-cam engine linked, at first, to a Citroën gearbox. Lotus also used this engine, originally designed as a wartime fire-pump engine for fire-fighting.

Brabham takes the chequered flag for victory in the Silver City Trophy in 1961.

Brabham, meanwhile, had bought a second-hand Maserati 250F – the privateers' delight – with the proceeds of the Cooper 'bob-tail' sale, but it was grossly unreliable in the 1956 season and burned up much of his resources. In 1957 the MkII T43 Cooper came out with a longer wheelbase and the more developed 1475cc FPF Climax unit, and John Cooper invited Brabham to drive it. His first taste of Grand Prix racing on the continent was the 1957 Monaco event, where the much more nimble Cooper, now running a 2.0-litre Climax engine and the distinctive alloy-spoked 'Minilite' style wheels, was ideally suited to the myriad hairpins and curves. Brabham was running third when the fuel pump mounting failed with three laps to go, and he managed to push the car over the line to claim sixth place. It was his – and Cooper's – first World Championship point in the 2.5-litre Formula 1. The remainder of the season was spent in F2 events, and early in 1958 Brabham took the Cooper to New Zealand and won the Grand Prix.

With the FIA directive that F1 cars would run on Av-Gas aviation fuel in 1958, the Coopers were again at an advantage, since cars would be more economical and therefore need to carry less fuel, particularly as race distances were being reduced. Smaller, lighter cars were the way of the future. The Climax engine could manage 180bhp on Av-Gas, which wasn't much less than the alcohol-based solvents used previously. Stretched to 2.2-litres, 194bhp was possible. Stirling Moss proved it was possible to win with the Cooper-Climax in the Argentinian GP, and Brabham finished second to Hawthorn's Ferrari at the Richmond Trophy race at Goodwood, with team-mate Roy Salvadori third. Brabham was fourth this time at Monaco in the usual race of attrition which saw three Vanwalls and Hawthorn's Ferrari retire to give the win to Trintignant's Cooper Climax. Brabham was sixth at both Rheims and Silverstone, where Salvadori was third behind the Ferrari Dinos of Collins and Hawthorn, but in general the cars were still out-classed. Salvadori generally finished better than Brabham.

New technology

Two major factors led to the Coopers' rise to prominence in 1959. One was the disappearance of the previously all-conquering Vanwall team, and the second was the introduction of the Coventry Climax 2.5-litre unit, which developed 250bhp.

The new Cooper T51 Mk IV appeared at Silverstone for the *Daily Express* Trophy race, and Brabham's team-mates were bespectacled American Masten Gregory and Bruce McLaren, fresh from New Zealand. Cooper sought sponsorship from Esso to secure Brabham's services, since it was likely that he would move to Aston Martin's fledgling F1 team with Salvadori – not, as it transpired, a good move. Brabham was the Silverstone winner, and as Moss' Rob-Walker-entered Cooper failed when leading at Monaco, Brabham took first place in the Principality, ahead of Brooks' Ferrari – now something of a dinosaur – and second place at Zandvoort to Jo Bonnier's BRM after a race-long struggle. Gregory was third. At Rheims-Geux, the Ferraris could stretch their legs, and their straight-line speed told against the little Cooper Climaxes. Still, Brabham was third to Brooks and Phil Hill, and McLaren was fifth behind Olivier Gendebien's Ferrari.

Brabham took the glory at Aintree, ahead of Moss, in a BRM, and McLaren. Brabham had tested a more streamlined Cooper in practice, but discovered the aerodynamics didn't work on the straight, where they really mattered. Where Moss had to make tyre stops in the heavier, front-engined BRM, Brabham drove without a stop.

There was some speculation that the organisers had designated the Avus circuit in Berlin as the venue for the 1959 German Grand Prix because it favoured the more powerful front-engined establishment. Virtually two lengths of a dual carriageway – up one leg, back down the other, with a vast banked corner at one end and a large-radius hairpin at the other (the pre-war banking at this end was now inside the East Berlin sector) –it was decidedly an odd-ball track. There were to be two 155-mile heats, and although the Coopers were at times locked in with the Ferraris at close on 180mph, the Italian cars of Brooks, Dan Gurney and Phil Hill won both heats. Trintignant's Cooper was fourth.

At the fast Monsanto road circuit in Lisbon, Brabham was knocked off by a slower car. Moss and Gregory were first and second in Cooper Climaxes, Gurney third for Ferrari and Trintignant fourth in a Cooper. Stirling Moss was also the victor at Monza, starting from pole and conserving his tyres well to win from Phil Hill and Brabham. This was enough to give Cooper the Manufacturers' Championship.

A couple of non-championship races followed; the Gold Cup at Oulton Park, which Moss won from Brabham – who jumped the start – and young hopeful Chris Bristow, third in his F1 debut. At Snetterton for the Silver City Airlines' Trophy, Ron Flockhart's BRM bested Brabham's 2.2-litre Cooper.

The Drivers' Championship depended on the American Grand Prix, held on the Sebring airfield track in Florida, 42 laps of a 5.2-mile circuit. Brabham had driven in the Nassau Speed Week just before the American GP and a stone had shattered his goggles, threatening the sight in one eye. He passed a last-minute medical. After an argument over practice times and grid positions between Schell and Brooks, accompanied by the Sebring girl's band, the race was on.

A final push

Moss, Brabham and McLaren sped away from the start, while Brooks was shunted by team-mate von Trips, effectively putting an end to his Championship hopes. Moss'

Brabham leads down the main straight at Rheims-Geux.

Ireland's Lotus 18 won at Goodwood and Silverstone's non-championship events, and Stirling Moss showed the writing was definitely on the wall at Monaco, winning the Grand Prix in Rob Walker's Lotus 18. Brabham had passed Moss as rain began to fall, but crashed at Ste Devote hairpin. Sixth, in the new rear-engined Dino 246-powered Ferrari, was American Richie Ginther. Brabham's luck changed for the better at Zandvoort, where a battle between him and Moss was settled when the Australian's Cooper flicked up a small piece of concrete kerbing into Moss' Lotus, damaging a wheel. Moss finished fourth after pitting for a new wheel, behind Ireland's Lotus and Graham Hill's BRM.

The 1960 Belgian Grand Prix was a tragic one for British fans, for Lotus works driver Alan Stacey was killed as he lost control after being

recurring gearbox nightmare struck again and he was eliminated, and a surprised McLaren took the win as Brabham's car expired with fuel starvation. Brooks came third behind Trintignant, and Brabham gamely pushed his car over the line to finish fourth. Remarkably, Brabham – a bashful man in the face of the attendant publicity – had won the title with 31 points to Brooks' 27, and Moss' 25.5.

For 1960, Lotus, BRM, Ferrari and Aston Martin had plans to go rear-engined, although Aston's project foundered at the chassis stage. The BRM P48 had been seen in practice at the previous year's Italian GP, but it was not ready by the time of the Argentinian Grand Prix. McLaren took his second World Championship victory here in a Cooper Climax, with Cliff Allison second for Ferrari, and the Moss/Trintignant Cooper third. Lotus debuted the new 18 here and Innes Ireland came home in sixth place, having led at one point until he spun. The beauty of the Lotus 18 was that the chassis was simple while being versatile enough to be used in Formula Junior (which was the Formula Ford/F3 of its day) as well as in F1 and F2.

At the non-championship formule libre race at Cordoba, 500 miles from Buenos Aires, Brabham and McLaren both led, only to become sidelined with problems, allowing Trintignant to win.

By May, the new low-line Cooper was ready, with straight tube spaceframe chassis and double wishbone and coil spring rear suspension, plus a five-speed gearbox. Several private teams were by now running Coopers, like Roy Salvadori's Maserati-engined car and Ferrari's own experimental Super-Squalo engined Cooper.

hit in the face by a bird. Bristow misjudged his line through Burnenville corner and crashed fatally. Stirling Moss' Lotus had a hub failure, and his injuries put him out of action for two months. Another 18, driven by privateer Mike Taylor, also crashed badly as a steering column weld fractured – for which he received substantial damages. Lotus had a reputation of being built down to the minimum tolerances: Chapman's ideal racing car was one which crossed the finishing line and then fell apart. When they held together, they were invariably quick. Accidents aside, Spa was a good result for Cooper. Brabham led McLaren home.

Brabham won his third consecutive World Championship race at Rheims, having battled it out with the front-engined Dino-Ferraris of Phil Hill and von Trips for 29 laps. Both Ferraris retired and the Coopers of Gendebien, McLaren and Henry Taylor followed Brabham across the line. Fifth was the newcomer Jim Clark in a Lotus 18.

Coopers were now in top form, and Brabham sat on pole position for the British GP at Silverstone, with Graham Hill alongside in the BRM. Hill stalled on the line, but caught up by two-thirds distance to pass Brabham for the lead. As Hill spun off at Copse while lapping a slower car, Brabham re-took the initiative, and took the chequered flag ahead of the Lotus 18s of John Surtees and Ireland, and McLaren and Brooks in Coopers. Von Trips' Ferrari was sixth.

Brabham then won the Silver City Trophy at Brands Hatch, before the circus moved to Oporto at the mouth of the River Douro for the Portuguese Grand Prix. Brabham took the honours, from McLaren, then Clark, von Trips, Brooks and Ireland. Surtees had set fastest lap.

As it looked likely that Brabham had done enough to clinch the title, Cooper decided not to go to Monza. The other British teams also didn't contest the Italian Grand Prix because they felt that they wouldn't be able to match the Ferraris for speed around the banked section. It proved a Ferrari benefit, with Phil Hill winning from Ginther and Willy Mairesse in front-engined Dino-Ferraris, Cabianca in the Cooper Ferrari, and von Trips in the rear-engined F2 Ferrari. Sixth was Hans Hermann in the F2 Porsche.

The final event was the American Grand Prix at the Riverside Raceway in California. It was Ferrari's turn to stay away for the same reasons that British teams had been absent at Monza. Moss led all the way from pole position, from Ireland, with the Coopers of McLaren and Brabham third and fourth, then Bonnier's BRM, and Phil Hill, in a Cooper, sixth. Brabham experienced some fuel feed problems and two pit stops accounted for his relatively lowly position. It was nevertheless good enough to secure the 1960 Championship for him and the Manufacturers' title for Cooper.

After he left Cooper in 1961 to set up on his own, Cooper went into a sad decline – on the Formula 1 front at least. The team was taken over following Charles Cooper's death in October 1964. John Cooper's reputation was really forged in the public's mind by his association with the Mini Cooper, a model he developed and BMC ran with until 1971 – relaunching it in 1990 on a wave of classic nostalgia.

Garlanded for victory in the 1965 Tasman Series at Sandown Park, Australia.

The change of Formula 1 rules to a 1.5-litre capacity was not at all popular with constructors, and in Britain a series was run called the Intercontinental Formula with a 3.0-litre maximum capacity limit. By the end of the year, most teams had sorted out their F1 engines, and the stop-gap series fizzled out.

The new Coventry Climax V8 unit first appeared at the German GP in Brabham's Cooper, and BRM's V8 wasn't seen until Monza. Thus 1961 was a walkover for the new rear-engined Ferrari 156 'nostril' nose cars. Pump fuel was specified, with no oil refills during races, and cars had to have self-starters.

At Monaco Moss drove one of the most accomplished races of his career in the Rob Walker Lotus 18 and dictated the pace to win from Ginther, Phil Hill and von Trips in the Ferraris, Gurney in a Porsche and McLaren five laps in arrears in a Cooper.

Straight-line aces

At the Dutch seaside resort of Zandvoort, the Ferraris' straight-line speed told on the long straight past the pits-grandstand. Although the Lotuses of Clark and Moss harried them in the turns, von Trips won from Phil Hill, with Clark third. Moss managed to hold off Ginther's Ferrari for fourth, while Brabham picked up sixth place a minute and a half behind.

Ferraris ruled at Spa and Rheims, although in the French Grand Prix only Maranello's new boy Giancarlo Baghetti kept his car intact – to win by a car's length from Gurney's Porsche for a first-time victory.

Brabham followed three Ferraris home at spray-drenched Aintree, but after practising in second fastest place at the Nürburgring in the Cooper with the new Coventry Climax V8, he ended up in a ditch.

The death of von Trips at Monza – and the involvement of Jim Clark, and, by implication, Lotus boss Colin Chapman, in the accident in which the German Count lost his life – cast a shadow over the race. Brabham didn't feature in the Italian race. He rounded off the season with fastest lap at the American GP at Watkins Glen – where Ferrari was absent – but retired with overheating after a 44-lap dice with Moss. The popular Englishman's own career as a Grand Prix star and potential Champion would end in an unexplained crash at Goodwood the following Easter Monday. Happily, Moss is still on the historic scene today driving a variety of machinery, including a Healey 3000.

Brabham decided he would do just as well building his own cars, and could afford to go it alone due to his successful garage and tuning business at Chessington – the Brabham Viva of the mid-1960s was a rather half-hearted attempt to emulate the Mini Cooper. He had one outing in a Lotus Climax and finished sixth at Spa, two laps down – the race which gave Jimmy Clark his first GP win.

His pal Phil Kerr came over from Australia to manage the garage, and Ron Tauranac joined him to design the new car. Eventually Brabham was persuaded to give his name to the project.

The first Brabham-Climax V8 raced at the Nürburgring in 1962, where its maker retired from the race. At the American GP late in the season Brabham was fourth in his new car, and got the same result at the South African Grand Prix at East London at the end of December. The 1962 series was decided here, and when Clark retired with a blown engine after leading, Graham Hill won the race and the Championship.

In 1963 Brabham won the Australian, Solitude, and Austrian non-championship Grands Prix, was fourth at Rheims, fifth at Monza and fourth at Watkins Glen. His best result was second place at Mexico

City. In those days it seemed the cars were particularly fragile – perhaps more than usual for highly strung F1 machines – and it was more than ever a matter of luck whether the cars held together or broke.

For 1964, Brabham had Dan Gurney driving one of his cars, and the tall American was as much a potential front runner as anyone. Strangest race was the Belgian Grand Prix, with all the Climax-powered cars – Lotus, Brabham and Cooper – plus Graham Hill's BRM, all slipstreaming each other through the fast forested sweeps of Spa. At the end of the last lap but one, it was Hill, McLaren, Gurney, Clark, Brabham and Arundel, but all apart from Clark, McLaren and Brabham ran out of fuel on the last lap.

Power struggles

For the remainder of the 1500cc formula, Brabham had very little success, picking up fourth places here and there. With the return to 3.0-litre engines in 1966, old team loyalties to particular engine builders – mainly Coventry Climax – were blown away. McLaren and Gurney set up on their own and the New Zealander chose the Ford V8, while the American settled for the Weslake V12 unit for his Eagle. Cooper went to Maserati, BRM made an H-16 engine, which they loaned to Lotus for a while, and Honda appeared with a V12. Brabham out-played them all, picking a GM-based V8 built in Australia by specialists Repco.

Having come fourth at a rain-drenched Spa, Brabham won at Rheims to become the first person to win the title in a car bearing his own name. He won at Brands Hatch, Zandvoort and the Nürburgring, but at Monza it looked as if Surtees could also take the title. Brabham's short-lived lead ended with a blown engine but the Ferraris of Ludovico Scarfiotti and Mike Parkes took a popular 1-2 after Surtees' fuel tank had split. Brabham's second title was thus secure. Surtees gained a measure of satisfaction by leading Brabham home at the Mexican Grand Prix at the end of the season.

At the 1970 Mexican GP – Brabham's last race – he was third when his engine blew.

In an extraordinarily close title race, team-mates Brabham and New Zealander Denny Hulme vied with one another during 1967, with Hulme – the Bear – coming out on top more often than Black Jack. Brabham still managed to win well at the Le Mans Bugatti Circuit, Canada's Mosport Park, and he was second in the Championship with 46 points to Hulme's 51.

Not until 1969 would Brabham stand on the podium again – at Mosport Park with second place behind team-mate Jacky Ickx – and Brabhams had now joined almost every other marque in using Cosworth Ford engines. In Mexico, Hulme won in a McLaren from Ickx and Brabham, and Ickx, the young Belgian, had accumulated enough points for second place in the Championship albeit finishing a long distance off winner Jackie Stewart.

In 1970, a grim year in which Formula 1 lost Bruce McLaren, Jochen Rindt and Piers Courage, Brabham started off promisingly with a win at Kyalami, South Africa. In a dramatic last lap dice with Rindt, Brabham narrowly lost the Monaco GP after stuffing his Brabham Ford on the final corner of the last lap. Third at Clermont-Ferrand and second to Rindt at Brands Hatch, where he ran out of fuel, were his only successes. After the Mexican GP, he declared his retirement. The 44-year old returned to Australia, having sold off his team to Bernie Ecclestone, now FIA supremo. The Brabham team continued to race under different individuals' management until the early 1990s.

Jack was knighted in the 1979 New Year Honours, at the behest of Australian Prime Minister Malcolm Fraser, having notched up 14 wins out of 127 World Championship events, winning the title three times. Meanwhile, Jack's three sons are pretty successful racing drivers in the upper echelons of the sport. ■

The Sixties
Rear-engine Revolution

The 1960s witnessed the rise of the small team and the driver turned constructor, exemplified by Jack Brabham, Bruce McLaren and John Surtees. Alfa Romeo, Maserati and Lancia were long-gone.

Traditionally, the majority of racing cars had been of a front-engine, rear-drive layout. The first of the successful rear-engined builders of the modern era was Cooper, father and son Charles and John having been crucially involved with the 500cc F3 since 1949. There were two major changes of engine capacity during the 1960s. The 1.5-litre Formula 1 took effect from 1961. Then from 1966 all the way to 1987 the formula was for 3.0-litres normally aspirated, or 1.5-litres supercharged.

In 1967 the Cosworth-Ford DFV was harnessed to the Lotus 49 – the first F1 car in which the engine was treated as an integral part of the chassis – and a new era dawned. This engine was the most successful F1 unit of all time, powering 157 cars to Grands Prix victories between 1967 and 1983. Commercial pump fuel with a maximum 100 octane rating had to be used. No oil could be added during a pit stop. There was a minimum weight limit of 450kg.

From 1966, it also became the decade of the aerofoil in F1, when wings started to sprout from rear suspension uprights and atop engines in the quest for greater downforce in the corners. This was clearly at the expense of outright speed when travelling down the straight, but on balance the wing made for faster lap times.

Phil Hill

(1927–) World Champion 1961

Phil Hill was one of Ferrari's star drivers in the early 1960s.

Before World War II, Americans weren't bothered about racing in Europe. Indeed, the majority aren't today, as F1 is still a minority interest compared with Indycar racing. Pre-war, it was mostly carried out on banked ovals like Indianapolis or cinder-track ovals. However, as many GIs returned to the USA after the war, they took with them European sports cars like the MG T-type Midgets and, more importantly, the ethos of sports car racing. It wasn't long before a network of events got going, organised by the Sports Car Club of America (SCCA), and these tended to be on road circuits or disused airfields like Sebring.

One of the first American drivers to break the mould was Phil Hill, and his career is linked mainly with Ferrari. Among the others of his countrymen who opted for the European scene, Hill always had an impish, almost bemused demeanour, compared with the laconic, lanky Gurney, or the crew-cut, boyish Ginther, or the bookish, bespectacled Masten Gregory. Invariably softly-spoken and erudite, Hill always behaved with dignity when confronted by adversity, particularly under the gloomy circumstances which prevailed when he won the Championship.

Hill was born in Miami, Florida on 20 April 1927, moving soon to Santa Monica, California, where his father was head postmaster. He became immersed in the car culture which pervaded all west coast life in the post war period, and Phil started competing with an MG TC. Even at this early stage in his career, Hill had obtained sponsorship to pay for his racing, because the importers realised the importance of success in competition to help sell cars.

His first win was at Pebble Beach, Monterey in 1952, and the following year he teamed up with Richie Ginther to drive the arduous Carrera Panamericana in a Ferrari. Their attempt ended with a crashed car – Hill was driving – but in the 1954 event the same pairing came second to the works Ferrari of Umberto Maglioli. Hill owned a Ferrari himself – a 212 Barchetta, the very car which had been the first Tour de France winner.

The same year he went to Le Mans with Fred Wacker to drive an OSCA, although the car broke when leading its class. In 1955 Hill and Carroll Shelby were placed second in the Sebring 12-hours race driving a privately entered 3.0-litre Ferrari Monza, and he and Ginther were set to drive Texan Alan Guiberson's Ferrari. Hill's success had attracted the attention of American Ferrari concessionaire and former racer Luigi Chinetti, who prevailed upon Enzo Ferrari to give Hill a chance in the works cars. He was summoned to the factory and told he would do the 1955 Le Mans with Maglioli. They retired when running third.

Teamed with Olivier Gendebien, they were second in the Buenos Aires 1000kms, third in the Nürburgring 1000kms, first in the Messina five hours, and second in the Oporto Grand Prix. At Le Mans he drove one of the works' 625LMs with André Simon, but retired after ten hours. Paired with Maurice Trintignant in a 3.5-litre Ferrari, Hill won the end-of-season Swedish sports car Grand Prix.

Serious victories

For 1957, Hill remained on the strength at Ferrari, and, because of his growing maturity as a long distance expert, able to nurse a car along if necessary, he stayed driving sports cars. Paired with Peter Collins, he won the Venezuelan Grand Prix in a 4.1-litre car, came second in the Rheims 12-hours, second in Sweden, and first at Palm Springs, California.

He was brought into the Ferrari Formula 1 squad in 1958, and finished third at Monza behind Brooks' Vanwall and Hawthorn's Ferrari, and third at Casablanca behind Stirling Moss' Vanwall and Hawthorn again. These excellent results for a Grand Prix debutant were nevertheless shaded by Hill's endurance victories at Buenos Aires, Sebring, and, more especially, the Le Mans 24-hours. It was Ferrari's third consecutive win at the Sarthe circuit, and Hill and Gendebien beat an Aston Martin in their 250 Testa Rossa. Third was a 1600cc Porsche; the German firm was at that time still on the lower rungs of the competition ladder. Ferrari thus took the World Sports Car Championship for the third consecutive year.

In Formula 1 the tide had begun turning against the big front-engined cars in favour of lighter and more nimble mid-engined machines by 1959, but Ferrari stuck with its old F1 Dino 246. Hill managed fourth at Monaco, sixth at Zandvoort, second at Rheims behind Brooks' Ferrari, third at the Avus in Berlin in a Ferrari 1-2-3, and second at Monza, sandwiched between the Cooper Climaxes of Moss and Brabham. The sports car championship was dominated in 1959 by Aston Martin, and Ferrari successes were few; Hill won at Riverside raceway, and he and Olivier Gendebien won the Sebring 12-hours and were second in the Nürburgring 1000kms. Their 250 Testa Rossa sports retired in the 20th hour while leading at Le Mans. In 1960, his only sports car victory was at Buenos Aires in a TRI/60 sports, partnered by Cliff Allison. Second place with von Trips in the Targa Florio round the Sicilian mountain roads was no mean achievement – drivers often ended their races against stray dogs, bridge parapets or other roadside hazards.

In Grands Prix, however, the 1960 season saw Phil Hill score his first World Championship victory. It came on the banked circuit at Monza when he headed a Ferrari 1-2-3 with Ginther and Mairesse. The season started off less auspiciously, with third at Monaco behind the Lotus 18 of Moss and Cooper Climax of McLaren. Hill was fourth at Spa and sixth at Riverside.

The 1961 French GP began with Hill in the lead but he later spun off.

From 1961 to the end of 1965, F1 was for 1.5-litre cars, and Phil Hill, Ginther and von Trips arrived at Monaco with new V6-engined shark-nosed 156s, against no fewer than eight new Coventry Climax engined cars. Two of the Ferraris had 90-degree V6s, with a single gauze blister over the carburettors, and one car had a 120-degree V6 with twin gauze blisters. Getting the engine in the right place was a revelation, according to Hill. As well as being one of the neatest Grand Prix designs of all time, the Ferraris also had about a 30bhp advantage, but Moss drove a truly outstanding race to beat Ginther, Hill and von Trips. These were the days when it was feasible to overtake easily and the Ferraris' power advantage was such that the drivers could pass most other cars at will. Moss and Ginther both set fastest lap.

At Zandvoort it was von Trips' turn to win. The main action was between Jim Clark and Phil Hill, with the Scot having the advantage in the corners, and the Ferrari retaking the Lotus on the straights. Moss reached the line a mere second ahead of Ginther's Ferrari.

A solid win

At the front, the Belgian GP was a relatively dull affair, with Phil Hill winning the Ferrari train from von Trips, Ginther and Gendebien's yellow Ecurie Belge car. After Spa the circus moved to Rheims, and what ought to have been another Ferrari walkover – bearing in mind the speed advantage – ended up a race of attrition, with new boy Giancarlo Baghetti's Ferrari taking the flag just a fraction of a second ahead of Dan Gurney's Porsche.

The spray-hazard proved Moss' undoing at Aintree for the British GP when his prowess in adverse conditions couldn't save him from spinning on a sheet of water, and von Trips led the way home from Hill and Ginther. After abandoning his Lotus, Moss returned to the fray in the new Ferguson four-wheel-drive car – a short-lived project.

Phil Hill is on record as saying that Stirling Moss is the greatest driver of all in the modern period, because he was self-reliant, and because of his ability to wring the best out of any car, no matter its shortcomings. Indeed, to many, Moss is the great uncrowned champion.

No one could catch Moss at the Nürburgring, and the more it rained the further ahead he went. The battle for second place between von Trips and Hill, which saw them frequently sideways in unison, was ultimately resolved in the German's favour with less than two seconds splitting them at the end of the race.

Sadly, it was to be von Trips' swan-song, for an accidental brush with Clark's Lotus at the next round at Monza pitched the Ferrari into the crowd, killing the personable German count and six spectators. Von Trips had been leading the Championship as they went to Monza, just four points ahead of Hill. So it was an unfortunate way for Phil Hill, who won the race, to clinch the Championship. The event itself had begun with new Ferrari recruit 20-year-old Ricardo Rodriguez jumping the start, then waiting for Hill, and the pair of them surging off. There were 32 cars on the grid – perhaps 10 more than usual – and there was much slipstreaming. This technique involves one car following another very closely down the straight, using the one in front to break the air, and it allows the following driver to back off the accelerator, until he has amassed enough spare revs to pull out of the tow and blast past his rival. Always a fast circuit – and the banked section was literally flat-out all the way round – Monza was a slipstreaming circuit. Ginther traded places with Hill, with Baghetti and Rodriguez hanging on, and Brabham in there too. In fact, just before the accident he was separating Clark and von Trips so he was lucky not to be involved. As the Ferraris fell out, one by one, Gurney and Moss caught up with Hill. But it was to be Hill's race.

Hill partnered Mike Spence in the winged Chaparral 2F in 1967.

At the time of an accident – and such incidents were relatively common then – most drivers try not to dwell on what they have seen, maybe out of the corner of their eye, and Hill was no exception. He made a mental note as he passed the pits on subsequent laps that von Trips' pit signals were no longer being made, but he had no idea of the extent of the casualties. He could tell from the pained manner of race engineer Dr Carlo Chiti that the news was bad, and the victory celebrations were therefore somewhat muted. Hill has since said that he believes drivers deliberately hid from the most dangerous aspects of racing, in a kind of self-denial. Some, like Luigi Musso, developed an accident pattern, yet were in such self-denial that they eventually killed themselves trying too hard.

The narrowest winning margin

The final tally for the 1961 season was Phil Hill, 34 points, von Trips second on 33, from Moss and Gurney on 21 points. Ferrari pulled out of the final race at Watkins Glen as a mark of respect to von Trips; besides, they had secured the title, so there wasn't much to be gained by racing there. Apart from being Hill's and Ferrari's year – Hill also won at Sebring and at Le Mans with Gendebien in the magnificent Tipo 250 TRI/61 – 1961 was also the year the Grand Prix points awards changed. Now it was 9-6-4-3-2-1 for the top six placings, with drivers counting their five best scores towards the final standings.

With Moss sidelined more or less permanently through his Goodwood accident, the way was clear for a new generation led by Graham Hill and Jimmy Clark to take over. In the early races of 1962, Phil Hill was third at Zandvoort behind Graham Hill's BRM and Trevor Taylor's Lotus-Climax. Phil came through a first corner multiple pile-up at Monaco to take second place behind McLaren's Cooper Climax.

The Spa round get off to a good start with the Lotuses of Clark and Taylor swapping the lead with Willy Mairesse's Ferrari. But when Taylor's Lotus jumped out of gear, Mairesse rammed him, the Ferrari rolling and bursting into flames. The brave Belgian was out of racing for three months. The Belgian race, meanwhile, was won by Clark from Graham Hill then Phil Hill.

Industrial action in Italy scuppered Ferrari's entry at Rouen, and they sent only one car for Phil Hill to Aintree. At this point Phil was only two points behind namesake Graham. But it was to be Clark's race again. In fact the Ferrari challenge faded away almost completely on the Grand Prix front. It was a different matter in the World Sports Car Championship, with Hill and Gendebien winning Le Mans again in a Tipo 330 LM – the last win for a front-engined car – in one of the most successful partnerships ever. Gendebien won the race four times and Hill three times. In 1962 they also won at the Nürburgring and were second at Sebring in a Ferrari GTO, which gave the Maranello concern another sports car world championship.

Times were changing at Ferrari. Team manager Dragoni sought a scapegoat for the team's lack of success with its basically out-dated cars, and bad-mouthed Hill to Enzo Ferrari, il Commendatore. A number of key figures were at that moment planning to leave, including race engineer Carlo Chiti, and Hill decided to quit Ferrari at the end of 1962. He elected to go with Dr Chiti's new Bologna-based ATS team for 1963, but the car wasn't ready until the Belgian GP. In any case it was poorly put together, and its engine unreliable, and Hill did well to finish at all. ATS was basically strapped for cash, struggling in an Italian recession to build a factory and foundry. So Hill moved to Cooper for 1964, but

this was not to bring him any better luck. The best he managed was sixth place at Brands Hatch in the British Grand Prix, two laps down on Clark's winning Lotus Climax.

It was a period of changing fortunes for Hill, who was now beginning to feel concern over the dangers inherent in the sport. He was also coming to wonder whether he was maybe getting too old to be truly effective in F1. But he still had a starring role in sports car racing, proven with victory in the 1964 Daytona 2000kms with rising Mexican star Pedro Rodriguez. Hill then drove Carroll Shelby's Daytona Cobras, which came close to stealing the GT Championship from Ferrari. Inevitably he was wooed by Ford to join the company's assault on the World Sports Car Championship. This began in 1965, and Ford began by winning at Daytona, although they failed at Le Mans with 7.0-litre Mk IIs. Instead Masten Gregory and young Jochen Rindt stole the show in a 250LM. Phil Hill retired in all but one event.

One success which sticks in Hill's mind as significant is his victory over Clark in the 1965 Tasman Series Australian GP at Longford, driving Bruce McLaren's 2.5-litre Cooper. It was a race-long contest between the two, and is perhaps all the more satisfying because it was to be one of Hill's last outings in a single-seater.

In 1966 the sports car championship included categories for Group 6 prototypes and Group 4 quasi-production cars (50 units) and Hill joined Jim Hall's team to drive the Chevrolet-powered Chaparral 2D. Paired with Jo Bonnier (Grand Prix Drivers' Association President), Hill took the Chaparral to victory at the Nürburgring. Le Mans was to be a Ford benefit, the Detroit cars scoring a 1-2-3. Phil also competed with an open-cockpit version of the Chaparral in the thundering CanAm series, winning at Laguna Seca, second at Mosport, and seventh at Las Vegas – earning enough points to be placed fourth in the inaugural CanAm championship.

Possibly the most popular competitors in the World Sports Car series in 1967, because they were the underdogs, Hill and Mike Spence drove the Chaparral 2F to victory in the BOAC 500 at Brands Hatch. Not only did the car have automatic transmission – which was virtually unheard of in a racing car – it also had a high, strut-mounted aerofoil, at least a season ahead of anyone else. The sight of the white winged wonder running like clockwork as Ferrari P4s and Porsche 908s fell by the wayside lifted the spirits.

After retiring at the end of 1967, Phil had an operation to get rid of stomach ulcers, which had undoubtedly affected his performance at the wheel. He was a TV commentator for a while, and is today involved in the restoration side. He remains an interested figure on the historic racing scene – and was to be seen reminiscing at the classic Goodwood Festival of Speed event in ■ June 1995.

Graham Hill

(1929–1975) World Champion 1962, 1968

I f anyone championed the cause of motor racing during the 1960s, it was Graham Hill. Debonair, charming, witty, he always had some dry quip at the ready for pressmen. With slicked-back hair and thin moustache, he appeared equally at home in a dinner jacket at the British Racing Drivers' Club dinner as in race overalls in the paddock. As an ambassador for the sport, he had no peers then or since.

There have been drivers with more innate talent, and more professionalism, but Graham Hill got to the top by sheer gritty determination. It took him five years to climb the ladder, which was a relatively long time then.

Graham Hill was born in London on 15 February 1929, the son of a successful stockbroker. His father never drove a car, so the young Hill was not introduced to motoring in what today might be considered the normal way. After a schooling at Hendon Tech, during which Hill excelled more on the playing field than in the classroom, he was taken on as an apprentice at Smith's instruments at Cricklewood, also in north London. His spare time was spent with the London Rowing Club, whose distinctive white and blue flashes decorated his black crash helmet. In the days before sponsorship and flashy full-face Bell Stars, only a few drivers bothered to personalise their helmets: Jean Béhra had a chequered band, Brabham's was usually silver, and Stewart's had a tartan band.

Smith's sent Hill off to its Birmingham factory, and he acquired a motorcycle to get himself there and back, and went scrambling on it at weekends. A road accident injured his legs sufficiently badly to leave him with a permanent limp, and gave a bow-legged impression.

In 1950 Hill did two years' national service in the navy, but as engine room artificer his rowing skills weren't greatly in demand. However as stroke in the LRC's first-class eight, Hill was instrumental in winning Henley Regatta's Grand Challenge Cup.

He bought his first car in 1953, a 19-year old Morris 8 Tourer. That he had neither licence nor driving lessons to his name was no deterrent. Coincidentally, he was attracted by an advert offering race-driving lessons at Brands Hatch, and bought himself four laps-worth for a pound. Hill was smitten. In exchange for the promise of some motor racing, he became an instructor-cum-mechanic, despite his almost total lack of experience behind a wheel. He must have been convincing, even then. When the Morris was written off, Hill commuted the 25 miles from London by train and bus and soon enough was given his chance to shine.

Learning the basics

On 27 April 1954, Hill drove a Mk IV Cooper-JAP to second place – having actually led at one point – in his first race. Home was somewhat closer to North London, where Colin Chapman was starting to make a name with his Lotus stable, and Hill was taken on as a mechanic for £1 a day. He would be involved both in building new cars, preparing others, or would have his services hired out by the entrepreneurial Chapman. Hill worked for some of the key racing entrants and owners including Danny Margulies, Dickie Steed, Peter Lumsden and Jack Richards. He was able to have an occasional outing in a C-type Jaguar and Lotus Elites. At a Lotus test day for prospective customers, Hill made second fastest time of the day in the Lotus Mk 9 demonstrator, after which Chapman offered him a permanent job for £9 a week, working on transmissions.

During his first year at Lotus, Hill built up an Eleven for himself, which was christened the yellow peril. In 1956 he won a number of club races with it. Anyone seriously ambitious about their racing in those days drove an Eleven, whereas if they were simply a club racer, they had a Lotus Mk 6 – forerunner of the illustrious Seven. Hill's earliest claim to fame as a racing driver was a series of spins on four consecutive laps during a wet Brands Hatch clubbie, resulting in the black flag and a stern reprimand from the Clerk of the Course.

Although there was never a dull moment at Lotus, Hill wasn't progressing on the driving front – he was after a works' drive – and left Chapman to join performance tuners Speedwell Engineering. He was later to become company chairman, and drove a 'souped-up' Austin A35 in saloon car races at weekends. It was exactly the sort of vehicle Speedwell's products catered for.

Chapman's F2 car was the Lotus 12, derived from the Eleven sports-racer, which handled well for a front-engined car, but in 1957 it was starting to look old-fashioned against the mid-engined Coopers. After seeing Hill racing a works Cooper, Chapman invited him back to drive the new F2 car, the pretty but anachronistic Lotus 16 – sometimes known as the 'mini-Vanwall'. Hill debuted the car at the 1958 French Grand Prix at Rheims, and came an amazing fifth – for an F2 car – in the Italian Grand Prix. The 16 may have looked good, but it was hopelessly outclassed in both F1 and F2 during 1959, when Hill and Ireland were the works drivers. One good placing for Hill was fifth in the Oulton Park Gold Cup.

For the 1960 season Hill was lured away to drive for BRM in their new rear-engined car, and at Silverstone, for the British GP, he came through to lead after stalling on the grid, only to spin off into retirement.

At Zandvoort Hill finished third in the BRM behind Brabham and Ireland, and at the ill-fated Spa race he was having a good tussle with McLaren, Gendebien and Bonnier for third place until the BRM engine blew all its oil out. There was a real debacle at the French Grand Prix when Hill's BRM wouldn't go into gear, and he sat helpless on the front row of the grid as the rest of the field took off around him. In the mist of oil and tyre smoke, he was rammed by the unfortunate Trintignant, and that was the race over for both of them.

In 1960 the Germans decided to run their Grand Prix for F2 cars, so it didn't count as a World Championship event. Perhaps the excellence of the F2 Porsche had something to do with it. At any rate, Graham finished fourth at a wet and foggy Nürburgring driving a Porsche, behind the similar cars of Bonnier and von Trips, and Brabham's Cooper Climax.

At the Solitude circuit near Stuttgart, Hill was placed fourth in the F2 Porsche, swapping places with the evenly-matched car of Gurney. The F2 Porsche had the beating of the Lotus-Climax and Cooper-Maseratis, although von Trips won in a Ferrari F2/60 from Hermann and Bonnier, who were also in Porsches.

Graham Hill joined BRM in 1960 and briefly led the British GP before spinning off.

In non-championship events, Hill was third driving the BRM in the BRDC International Trophy race behind Ireland's Lotus and Brabham's Cooper; the meeting had been saddened by the death in practice of Harry Schell in a Cooper. He was third again in the Aintree 200, a qualifying round of the F2 Manufacturers' Cup series, driving a Porsche. Also driving Porsche F2s, Moss won the race from Bonnier.

Hill picked up second place to Brabham in the Silver City Trophy race at the August Bank Holiday Brands Hatch meeting – the first meeting on the full Grand Prix circuit – with most of the stars present including Phil Hill and Jim Clark.

Hill was equally active in sports car racing, sharing a Porsche RS60 with Jo Bonnier at Le Mans, retiring with engine failure, and driving a battered Porsche 356 Carrera to a class win in the Tourist Trophy at Goodwood. He shared a Porsche RS60 with Edgar Barth in the Targa Florio, finishing a class-winning fifth.

At Zandvoort in 1961, Hill's sparring partner was Clark, but he slipped back after an excursion on to the grass, finishing eighth. In the Belgian GP, Hill shot into the lead from the third row of the grid, but soon lost the place to his American namesake in the Ferrari. After a duel with Surtees, Graham's engine failed on lap 19.

Hill's BRM-Climax ran with a huge gaggle of cars competing for third place for much of the race at Rheims, including Baghetti, Ireland, Clark, McLaren and Bonnier, resolved with Hill finishing sixth. Graham's BRM didn't feature in the results until Watkins Glen, when he came fifth.

Typically, Hill drove anything from F1 machines to saloon cars, and he was equally active in sports car racing. At the 1961 Le Mans, Hill was teamed with Moss in the Rob Walker-entered Ferrari 250 GT, which did well until its engine failed.

During 1962, the BRM V8 was the overriding force in Grand Prix racing, and Graham Hill was the dominant driver. The combination won four out of nine World Championship events, with Clark on three and McLaren, still with Cooper, scoring one win, and Gurney in the new flat-8 Porsche also on one win.

Hill's rampage started with a win in the *Daily Express* International Trophy at Silverstone, snatching victory by inches from an astonished Jim Clark. At Zandvoort, Clark debuted the new monocoque Lotus 25, rushing away from the BRM at the start, only to finish last. Graham Hill won from Trevor Taylor's Lotus-Climax and Phil Hill's Ferrari.

Gradual improvement

A first lap mêlée upset the form at Monaco, and McLaren took the honours, with Graham a lowly sixth, eight laps behind. Although Graham took pole position at Spa-Francorchamps and led initially, Clark was by on lap 9 and set a new lap record of 133.9mph in the process. It was Clark's first Grand Prix win, and he was well clear of Graham, who finished second ahead of the Ferraris of Phil Hill and Ricardo Rodriguez.

The French GP was held at Rouen-les-Essarts in 1962, and Graham took an early lead which he held for 29 laps until he was touched by Lewis' Cooper. After recovering from a spin, he set fastest lap in his pursuit of Clark, who had taken advantage of his 'moment', only to retire with fuel injection failure when leading on lap 42. The race went to Gurney in a Porsche.

At Aintree only two points separated the Hills, Graham and Phil, in the Championship standings, but, for the first race that season, Graham failed to make the front row. Instead Clark and Surtees were the front-runners, with McLaren also outpacing Graham.

His adventures continued in practice at the Nürburgring when he ran over a camera which had fallen off Carel Godin de Beaufort's Porsche. It severed an oil pipe and the BRM slithered off the track at the downhill Foxhole section. Hill was lucky to escape unharmed. Cooper driver Tony Maggs went off at 140mph on the same oil slick. The fight for the lead was between Gurney's Porsche, Surtees' Lola and Hill, with a recovering Clark catching up all the time. A mere four seconds separated Hill, Surtees and Gurney at the end of the rain-sodden epic.

BRMs showed everyone the way at Monza, as Clark retired with gearbox and electrical problems. Ginther in the second BRM was harried by Surtees' Lola, but the Climax engine broke a piston, and Hill and Ginther knotched up the Bourne team's first one-two victory.

By now only Clark – on 21 points – could catch Hill – on 36 – for the title. Clark had to win in Canada and South Africa to do it, so Graham's position looked invincible. Stranger things happen in motor racing, and when the Scot took the win at Mosport despite having to nurse an ailing clutch, the Championship was suddenly wide open again.

This added excitement may well have swelled the 90,000 crowd which flocked to the East London circuit for the first South African World Championship round. In the pre-race driver walkabout, Hill recalled being given such a rapturous welcome by the black section of the segregated spectator enclosure that he was left quite bruised.

Clark dominated practice, while BRM mechanics feverishly pared weight from the BRM in a bid to get him on equal terms with the Lotus. Basically Clark went too hard, although he set such a blistering pace that Hill was unable to match it, on lap 59 his Lotus' engine cried enough; it was only that a tiny bolt securing the distributor drive housing had worked loose. But it was enough to lose Clark the race, and hand the title on a plate to Graham Hill, who had been soldiering on in second place. He was thus the first Englishman to win the Championship in a

British car. Perhaps the most remarkable thing is that prior to the 1962 season, Hill had never won a Grand Prix, and had but one Championship point to his name. His finished the season with 52 points.

Monaco's main man

Hill became the undisputed expert at Monaco. More post-race glasses have been raised to him in the Tip-Top bar than to any other driver. His run of Monaco wins began in 1963. He and Ginther put their BRMs at the head of the field to beat McLaren and Surtees. Clark had led until lap 79 when his gearbox jammed. At this race of many thousand gear changes his position was hopeless. Hill had pole at Spa but Clark took an unassailable lead. Weather conditions were so appalling that Tony Rudd of BRM and Colin Chapman asked the organisers to stop the race. They declined. Many cars were wrecked and only six out of 20 starters finished. Hill's race had ended on lap 17 when his gearbox gave up.

Zandvoort was another disaster for Hill due to overheating problems. He lost places getting the new BRM's radiator topped up. The

Hill, the master of Monaco, rounds the Station hairpin en route to victory.

monocoque BRM, which carried its coil springs inboard, blew its engine as Hill struggled with Gurney's Brabham and Surtees' Ferrari.

Officialdom did for Graham's chances at Rheims, as he was docked a minute penalty after stewards ordered a push-start when he stalled on the grid before the 'off'. It wouldn't have mattered, as he came third in the BRM, more than a minute behind Tony Maggs' Cooper and two minutes behind Clark's winning Lotus. In fact, Clark's closest challenger had been Ginther in BRM number two, but a stone holed his radiator.

Clark was uncatchable at Silverstone after sweeping into the lead on

the fourth lap. Hill ran out of fuel at Woodcote bend on the last lap. At the Nürburgring, Hill retired with a broken gearbox.

A frazzled exit

The controversial banking at Monza was banned after several cars went off due to the concrete surface breaking up. In another slipstreaming epic, Surtees, Clark, Hill and Gurney contested the lead inches apart. But on lap 50 Hill's race was ended, his clutch burned out.

It was Clark's turn to be disappointed at Watkins Glen, as his car refused to start. This allowed Hill and Ginther to take the initiative, but Surtees challenged successfully, and Hill found it difficult to resist because of a broken anti-roll bar mount. The Ferrari's engine couldn't last the pace and, when Surtees retired, Hill and Ginther coasted home.

At Mexico City, both BRMs were plagued with gearbox mounting problems, and Ginther headed Hill in third and fourth places with Clark and Brabham first and second. At the final round in South Africa, Hill was third, a lap down on Clark and Gurney. The Championship was undoubtedly Clark's, with Hill second and Ginther third.

The glory days weren't confined to Monaco or Watkins Glen. One of Hill's finest moments was winning the 1963 Tourist Trophy at Goodwood in the exquisite Ferrari 250 GTO entered by Maranello Concessionaires, against such potent machinery as Innes Ireland's Aston Martin DB4GT.

There were still some good placings in 1964, starting with a Monaco win. The BRMs of Hill and Gurney again filled the first two places, from the Lotuses of Pete Arundel and Clark. Ferrari and Lotus were becoming increasingly competitive, and Hill had a string of high-ish places – fourth at Zandvoort, where fuel vaporisation led the mechanics to throw cold water over the fuel pump and Hill himself. He was fifth at Spa, having led for some of the race, finally spluttering to a halt with empty fuel tanks. At Rouen he fought back from 13th after a spin, to finish second, and at Brands Hatch the duel for the lead with Clark was resolved in the Scot's favour with only a second separating them at the finish. Hill was runner up to Surtees at the Nürburgring.

In spite of retirements at Zeltweg, Austria, and Monza, where he fried his clutch on the grid, Hill had a slender lead in the Championship, with 32 points to Clark's 30 and Surtees' 28. Only Clark's fuel injection problems at Watkins Glen lost the title for him, and Hill led Surtees home by half a minute. But by finishing second to Gurney at Mexico City, 'Big John' scooped the Championship for himself.

As well as being seen 'wheel-wagging' in the works Lotus Cortinas in touring car racing, Hill also had successes in sports car events in 1964. Sharing the drives with Bonnier, he won the Rheims 12-hours and the Paris 1000kms at Montlhery, as well as the Tourist Trophy.

In F1, however, the BRM was not being developed at the same rate as Lotus and Ferrari, and with new recruit Jackie Stewart in the team, Graham managed only third in South Africa. As well as Stewart's F1 debut, the Goodyear tyre company entered the Dunlop-dominated fray.

A triumph of willpower

Hill was beginning to make Monaco his own, and was leading the 1965 race comfortably when he encountered Bob Anderson's sick Brabham blocking the chicane. Hill took avoiding action and rushed down the escape road, only to stall and have to push the car back to the track to restart it. It only cost him four places, and, with characteristic resolve, he hounded Stewart, Surtees and Lorenzo Bandini to retake the lead, where he finished, quite exhausted.

At Spa, Hill came fifth, ahead of Ginther, now driving the new V12 Honda. He came fifth again at the undulating Clermont-Ferrand circuit, and second to Clark at Silverstone, reducing a 35-second deficit to five seconds as Clark's Lotus faltered with massive oil consumption. Lack of a rev-counter hindered Hill's progress at Zandvoort, where he came fourth. Theoretically, he could still overhaul Clark for the title as they came to the Nürburgring, but Clark drove a copybook race to win the race – from Hill, Gurney, Rindt and Brabham – and also the 1965 title.

Meanwhile, there were still three races to go. Hill followed Stewart home at Monza and won from pole position at Watkins Glen ahead of Gurney, Brabham and Bandini. At Mexico City, Ginther scored his first and only GP win in the Honda, shod with Goodyear tyres; a first for them too. Hill's engine blew in the race, but he had amassed sufficient points to come second to Clark in the Championship, ahead of Stewart.

The return of 3.0-litre engines in 1966 spelled the end of Coventry Climax's 1500cc V8 domination. For Monaco some teams used 'Tasman' engines – the 2.0-litre versions of F1 units used in the popular winter series in the Antipodes. Hill had already won both the Australian and New Zealand GPs which did not count towards the Championship, but which were not without significance, as a pointer of form. Thus Stewart and Hill's BRM P261s were 2.0-litre V8s, as were the Lotus 33s, and this proved the right choice for the windy street circuit. Stewart won from Bandini and Hill, with Bob Bondurant fourth in another BRM.

Hill gave up any chance of a place in the sodden Spa race to rescue Stewart from his wrecked BRM before it caught fire. At Brands Hatch, the BRM and Lotus were unable to compete with the Repco-Brabhams of Brabham and Hulme. Hill was third however, then second to Brabham at Zandvoort, and fourth at the Nürburgring. By Monza, BRM had their incredible H-16 engine up and running in the P83, which was glorious in its complexity and aural effects, even if it did only last one lap for Hill. The unit was generally regarded as a mechanic's nightmare, being overcomplicated and too heavy.

There were no more points for Hill, and in a sense it was not a good year, but back in May he had notched up one particular win of considerable importance: he had won the prestigious Indianapolis 500 in a Lola T90-Ford. So for 1967 he joined Lotus. He took second place at Monaco in a 2.0-litre Lotus-BRM, but it was a race marred by the fiery death of poor Lorenzo Bandini.

The new Lotus 49s, with their Cosworth-Ford engines forming part of the chassis, debuted at Zandvoort. Hill started well from pole, only to retire with camshaft problems. Clark proved they could hold together, winning handsomely. Thereafter Hill's fortunes were thwarted by a chain of mechanical failures and unfortunate accidents and spins,

Hill in a car from his own team of Lola T370s, at the 1974 Swedish Grand Prix.

tempered by the occasional pole position and high position in the running order, until he took fourth at Mosport, Toronto. He came second behind Jim Clark at Watkins Glen, having led the race. So confident were the pair that they actually tossed a coin to decide which of them would win the race. Hill won the toss, but not the race.

A hellish time

Team Lotus began 1968 well, with Clark and Hill dominating the South African GP at Kyalami. Then, on one of the blackest days in motor racing history, the likeable Scot was killed in an unimportant Formula 2 race at Hockenheim. Hill, although devastated, was immediately elevated to team leader from what had been a more or less equal partnership with Clark. Hill's indomitable spirit pulled the team through those dark days and his achievements gave Chapman the spur he needed to carry on racing.

At Jarama, for the first Spanish Grand Prix since 1954, Hill won a race which saw frequent changes on the leader board. The front men included Pedro Rodriguez in the V12 BRM, Jean-Pierre Beltoise in the Matra-Ford, and Chris Amon in the Ferrari.

Hill won the Monaco GP as all behind him fell by the wayside. It was his last success until Germany, when a close race with Stewart at a typically dismal Nürburgring gained him second place. His 100th Grand Prix, at Monza, ended when a wheel came off. Fourth place at St Jovite in Canada was followed by second place at Watkins Glen. The race for the title was well and truly on. Hill had 39 points, Stewart 36, Hulme 33. Mexico proved decisive. Hill overcame all, to win from McLaren, who was campaigning his own cars along with Hulme.

Team Lotus cars and transporters were resplendent in the red and gold livery of Player's Gold Leaf cigarette brand, and were without doubt the instigators of overt big-time sponsorship in European motor racing.

It was the beginning of the rise of serious commercialism within the sport, and signalled the beginning of the end of any amateurism.

Fatal flaws

If sponsorship was new, aerofoils were the technical gimmick for 1969, and Hill's Lotus 49 should have been equally successful. The high, strut-mounted wings were fragile, and at Barcelona's Montjuich Park circuit, the inevitable happened. Hill and new team-mate Rindt had the biggest wings anyone had ever seen, and they ran first and third – Rindt ahead, with Amon the meat in the sandwich, until Hill's wing buckled and he smashed into the unyielding Armco barrier which lined the circuit. There were no run-off areas, and no escape. The Lotus pit tried to warn Rindt of the possibility of similar failure, as did Hill, but too late, Rindt's aerofoil collapsed at virtually the same place as Hills, and he spun into the wreckage of Hill's car. It seemed that too much downforce had put excessive strain on the uprights supporting the wings, and a lesson was learned a very hard way.

The FIA's response was to ban wings of the type which failed on the Lotus – which could be feathered by the drivers along the straights, and tilted to exert greater downforce in the corners. At Monaco, Hill's Lotus 49 had a much neater spoiler arrangement over the engine, in response to the FIA dictum. After heading Ickx, Beltoise and Courage in close company, Hill extended his lead to win comfortably.

Hill and Rindt were quickest at Zandvoort, and most cars now carried a compromise wing over their gearboxes, although nothing like as dramatic as the original type. Jo Siffert was a new force on the scene, driving Rob Walker's Lotus 49, and he followed Stewart home after the works Lotuses hit problems. Mechanical failures compromised most of Hill's efforts for the rest of the year, although he picked up fourth place at the Nürburgring. On lap 91 of the American GP at Watkins Glen, disaster struck. His Lotus flipped due to a deflating tyre and Hill suffered the consequences of not having his belts done up. He had stopped seconds earlier to push his car back onto the circuit; when it somersaulted, he was thrown out, breaking both legs very badly.

He turned up at Kyalami six months afterwards, still ostensibly recuperating from the accident. He was hobbling badly, but insisted on practising in the Rob Walker 49, drove it in the race, and, much to everyone else's amazement, came sixth. A fourth in the Spanish round at Jarama followed, with fifth at Monaco.

Two great heroes of British sport – Graham Hill and Jackie Stewart – relax before a race.

His performances were all the more remarkable because he had not regained full control of his leg muscles, making braking a real problem. Many of his followers hoped the 40-year old would retire gracefully.

A new test

In 1971 Jack Brabham offered Hill a drive in the 'lobster claw' Brabham BT34 (with radiators either side of the front aerofoil) and he won the Daily Express International Trophy at Silverstone from Pedro Rodriguez. The traditional F2 race at Thruxton on Easter Monday was also Hill's, and he came fifth in August at the beautiful Osterreichring.

In the declining years of his career, Hill's greatest achievement was winning Le Mans, paired with Henri Pescarolo in the dominant Matra team. No-one has beaten Hill's three-way triumph of F1 World Champion, Indianapolis 500, and Le Mans 24-hours winner. Yet still he wouldn't give up. There had been no success at Brabham in 1972, so in 1973 he bought his own car, a Shadow. This marque was as undistinguished in Hill's hands as it proved to be in the works' drivers'. So he made a deal with Lola boss Eric Broadley to create his own GP car. With sponsorship from Embassy cigarettes, the Hill-Lola appeared in 1974, and Hill headed his own two-car team with sponsor-finder extraordinaire Guy Edwards as second driver.

By now awarded the OBE, Graham finally stepped down in 1975 to concentrate on running his own team. There was even a new Hill car, the GH1, designed by Andy Smallman, and the services of the talented Tony Brise, former F3 and Formula Atlantic star, were engaged. Tragedy struck the team on 29 November 1975 as they returned from a test session at Paul Ricard in the south of France, when Hill's light plane crashed into trees on a golf course on its descent to Elstree airfield. It was an unfortunate case of pilot error – bad visibility had apparently caused Hill to miscalculate his altitude.

The sport which had seen the demise of so many, paid its tributes to its greatest ambassador, lost to it by a simple mistake.

DAN GURNEY (1931–)

The lanky Californian won just four Grands Prix during the 1960s, along with a host of other races, but he was so close on many other occasions that had that elusive strand of fortune gone his way he could have been the man. He was the only driver Jimmy Clark considered a threat – the two were best of friends off the track.

Performances in the USA during the mid-1950s in Corvette, Porsche Speedster and 4.9-litre Ferrari brought an invitation to run at Le Mans in a Ferrari Testa Rossa. He impressed everyone, and it earned him a works drive alongside Phil Hill and Tony Brooks for 1959.

With BRM during 1960, successes were few, but, sharing a Birdcage Maserati with Moss, he won the Nürburgring 1000kms. In 1961 he drove for Porsche in Formula 1, and he finished equal third with Moss in the World Championship. He gave Porsche its single Grand Prix victory at Rheims in 1962.

With Brabham from 1963 to 1965, he and Jack were always in the top five, and Dan was fourth in the World Championship in 1965. In 1966 he built his own Eagle F1 cars, powered by the Weslake V12 engine. This unit was less than reliable, and the Eagle's finest hour was

STIRLING MOSS (1929–)

Stirling was a boyhood hero to everyone of a certain age. Whichever car he raced, he was usually out in the lead. In a way it hardly mattered that he failed to win the title. The closest he came was in 1958, when he won four races to the Champion Mike Hawthorn's one, and missed out on the Championship by a single point. But there were plenty of other times when his overall greatness was evident – driving the Mercedes W196 and the Mille Miglia and Targa Florio winning 300SLR, at the Nürburgring 1000kms and TT winning Aston Martins and Ferrari 250GT. The list of cars and victories is endless. His exploits in his privately-owned Maserati 250F, and the Vanwall of 1957 showed that he had the ability to beat Fangio, yet he was runner-up to the Argentinian twice. Moss could win with seemingly uncompetitive cars: the Lotus 18 at Monaco in 1960 and 1961 handled well but lagged behind in straight line speed.

After a bad accident at Goodwood in 1962, Moss retired from top class motor racing, but to this day is active in other categories of the sport. He remains critical of the World Championship scoring system, and is particularly censorious of drivers who win by virtue of driving for the points rather than going for the win.

the Belgian Grand Prix in 1967, when Gurney set the record at 148.8mph. He also shared the winning Mk IV Ford at the 1967 Le Mans 24-hours with A.J. Foyt.

He also competed at Indianapolis, coming second in 1968 and 1969, with other Eagles equally competitive in USAC and Formula A (the American F5000). Dan won several NASCAR and USAC events and drove for McLaren in CanAm, winning occasionally. On retiring in 1971, he concentrated on building Eagle cars for Indianapolis and Formula A, which continued to be successful throughout the 1970s.

JACKY ICKX (1945–)

If Jacky had had the right car at the right time, he would have been champion in F1. The potential was always there but he seemed to switch teams just when the one he was with was on the verge of stability or a winning car was in the pipeline. Instead, his chief accolade is that he was the finest sports car driver – twice World Champion – and won the Le Mans 24-hours six times.

Jacky's early career featured exploits in a BMW 700 GT, and Lotus Cortinas for Ford Belgium, Alan Mann and Lotus, with which he won the Spa 24-hour touring car race two years running in 1965 and 1966. He drove an F3 Matra and F2 Matra-BRM for Ken Tyrrell in 1965 and 1966, and did a full season in F2 in 1967. He also drove the Gulf Mirage, an evolved Ford GT40, to four victories in World Sportscar Championship events.

With Ferrari for F1 in 1968, Jacky won the French GP and came fourth in the World Championship. There were more wins in the Gulf-Ford GT40, notably the BOAC 500.

He finished second to Stewart in the 1969 World series, driving for Brabham, and won a close-fought Le Mans in the Gulf-Ford.

He was runner up to Rindt in 1970, having driven the Brabham to three GP wins. Back with Ferrari in 1971, his wet-weather expertise came to the fore as he won in the rain at Zandvoort, but the team's major successes lay in sports car racing. In 1972 he took six long-distance victories in Ferrari's steam-roller effort with the 312P.

His Formula 1 career extended to Lotus from 1974, to Williams, Ensign and Ligier in 1979, with little attainment. However, Jacky's Le Mans successes are worth chronicling. He won in the Mirage with Derek Bell in 1975, again in a Porsche 936 with Gijs van Lennep in 1976, in a 936 with Jürgen Barth and Hurley Haywood in 1977. He was second with Barth and Bob Wollek in 1978, second in 1980 with Reinhold Jöst in a 936. He was first again in 1981 with Bell in another Porsche 936, and again the following year to make it a record six wins, sharing the closed 956 with Bell. They were second in 1983.

After retiring from top class competition, Jacky's career branched out into events as varied as the Paris Dakar rally-raid with Porsche and Citroën. He acted as clerk of the course at Monaco, and as overseer of Mazdaspeed's Group C Le Mans-winning team in 1991.

Jim Clark

(1936–1969) World Champion 1963, 1965

The mild-mannered farmer from Duns, Berwickshire, in the Scottish Borders, was linked with Lotus for his entire Formula 1 career. He and Colin Chapman formed a partnership which dominated the motor racing scene throughout much of the mid-1960s.

A farmer's son, Jim was born in Kilmany, Fifeshire on 14 March 1936. Soon after his 17th birthday, he won a driving test at Winfield and began rallying the family Sunbeam Talbot 90. A friend, Ian Scott-Watson, was impressed with his talents, and let him drive his DKW Sonderklasse two-stroke saloon, graduating to his Porsche 356 1600 Super. Clark raced and hill-climbed it extensively between 1957 and 1959, coming fifth at Spa-Francorchamps in 1958.

He joined the local Border Reivers team, and during 1958 won 12 races in the team's D-type Jaguar. He also hill-climbed his own Triumph TR2 and raced the Border Reivers' Lotus Elite with success between 1958 and 1962. During 1959 he had much success with the ex-Halford/Scott-Brown Lister Jaguar. At the end of that year, a single-seater drive presented itself – in a Gemini Formula Junior at the festive Brands Hatch Boxing Day meeting. On the strength of his performance he was invited to join Reg Parnell's new Aston Martin F1 team. When this foundered, Clark joined Chapman at the beginning of 1960.

The plan was that he would learn the ropes in Formula Junior, but Chapman also gave him a chance in F1. The new 18 was not pretty by

Lotus standards, but it was a versatile car, and could run with Coventry-Climax motors in F1, F2 or BMC engines in Formula Junior. Team Lotus' junior team contested the latter, which enjoyed a status somewhere between F3 and Formula Ford – there are numerous starter formulae to choose from today, but Formula Junior was first step on the single-seater ladder then. Clark and team-mate Trevor Taylor were equally competitive, and shared the Championship at year's end.

Clark was given his first run in a Grand Prix at Zandvoort. He was brought in to deputise for John Surtees, and was running a praiseworthy fifth when gearbox problems sidelined him. Chapman was sufficiently impressed to get him to do the Spa race the following weekend. This was the race of great tragedy, in which Lotus number one driver Alan Stacey and the promising Chris Bristow died, and Mike Taylor had a bad accident in the ex-Innes Ireland car. Stirling Moss was injured in a practice crash. Three of those cars were Lotus 18s, yet it was a car which handled better than most. Clark came fifth, as he did in the French GP at Rheims, behind four Cooper-Climaxes.

Also in 1960, Clark shared the Border Reivers' Aston Martin DBR1 with Roy Salvadori in the Le Mans 24-Hours, and they finished third. The following year, he drove the John Ogier team's Aston Martin DB4 Zagato, and was fourth in the TT at Goodwood.

Jim Clark (above) in contemplative mood and (left) celebrating victory in the 1966 American Grand Prix.

A new weapon

As the new 1500cc F1 formula came in, Ferrari's latest weapon, the shark-nosed 155, appeared at the first round of the 1961 season at Monaco. Nevertheless, Moss sat on pole, with Ginther's Ferrari and Clark's works Lotus alongside him. The Ferrari's straight-line speed told at Zandvoort. Clark passed Phil Hill in the corners but was retaken by the American down the straights. Clark set a new lap record, coming third behind Hill and von Trips. The same picture emerged at Rheims-Geux. The Lotus was third, a minute behind the duelling Porsche of Gurney and Ferrari of Baghetti. It looked like Ferrari's year, and at Monza the title could have gone to Phil Hill or Wolfgang von Trips.

As Clark took on the Ferraris of Hill and Ricardo Rodriguez on the first lap, he was caught up by von Trips and Ginther in similar cars. He held off the German count for half a lap but the Ferrari came by at the Vialone. As you do in slipstreaming, Clark tucked in behind von Trips to get a tow from the faster machine. As they entered the Parabolica, Clark had enough momentum to edge the nimbler Lotus alongside. But von Trips evidently hadn't seen him, and moved over to get a better line. The wheels touched and the Ferrari went backwards up the bank into the spectator fencing, killing eleven people before hurtling back onto the track. Von Trips was thrown out and died instantly. Clark had merely spun, but his Lotus was impounded and

'Why is it I can never win at Monaco... yet I win at Spa four times on a circuit I hate?'

Jim Clark in a masterful flag-to-flag display in typically grim Spa weather.

he was sought by the police as Italian civil law is peculiarly strict in matters of fatal accidents. He and Chapman were perhaps fortunate to leave the country before they could be arrested.

A dynamic duo

The season was soured for Clark, even though it had been a 'racing accident'. He finished seventh in the USA, a race won by Ireland to give Lotus its first GP victory. Three wins in the South African Springbok series in December 1961 restored his morale. By the beginning of 1962 the British V8s were ready to go. But Britain lost two of its aces when Moss was injured at Goodwood and Tony Brooks retired. Their shoes were filled by Graham Hill and Jim Clark, who between them won 29 out of the following 39 Grands Prix.

It was first blood to Hill, who pipped Clark's Lotus 24 at Silverstone to win the Daily Express International Trophy. At Zandvoort, Chapman introduced the Lotus 25, the first monocoque racing car – consisting of two stressed pontoons linked by an undertray, with front and rear bulkheads, and a stressed panel housing the instruments. All that remained of the space-frame concept was additional cross bracing at the front. The rubber fuel bags were housed in the pontoons, and the whole was clad in glass-fibre panels. It was the first racing car to have the driver in a fully recumbent position. There was a five-speed ZF gearbox and the power unit was the Coventry Climax FWMV-V8.

Clark retired in Holland. At Monaco the Lotus-BRM battle ended with Clark losing two gears. Practice at Spa went badly for him: the Climax engine developed camshaft problems. From 12th on the grid, he sped up to third behind Trevor Taylor and Willy Mairesse. He swept by them, setting a new lap record on his way to a debut victory. Taylor and Mairesse tangled when the number two Lotus jumped out of gear. The Belgian was injured in his blazing Ferrari; Taylor was lucky to escape when the telegraph pole he hit fell on the Lotus.

Retirement followed at Rouen-les-Essarts when Clark's Lotus hit suspension problems. But at Aintree for the British Grand Prix, Clark led from start to finish, with only John Surtees' Lola-Climax putting up anything like a challenge.

On the grid at the Nürburgring, Jimmy forgot to switch on the Lotus' fuel pump, and lost 13 seconds sorting himself out. There followed a meteoric rush through the departed field, taking him eventually up to fourth, behind the battling Gurney, Surtees, and eventual winner Hill.

Gearbox and electrical problems caused a retirement at Monza, although Jim had been quickest in practice. He was still third in the Championship with the possibility of overhauling Graham Hill, provided he won in the USA and South Africa. The pair swapped places a couple of times while lapping back markers, but Clark got away and was never headed, despite a failed clutch. In South Africa, Clark pulled out a massive lead, only to lose everything on lap 62 when a bolt worked loose on the distributor drive-housing. Hill, who had been keeping a watching brief, took the win, and was champion. He scored 42 to Clark's 30, with McLaren third on 27.

Porsche and Lola pulled out at the end of 1962, so Gurney went to Brabham and Surtees to Ferrari, while Phil Hill and Baghetti left autocratic Ferrari to go to Carlo Chiti's ATS team. First round of the 1963 season was at Monaco, and, after a poor start, Jim Clark found a way round the BRMs of Ginther and Hill and pulled out a 17-second lead. On lap 76 his gearbox jammed, and the BRMs claimed the day.

As Clark dominated the Belgian Grand Prix, the weather conditions became so bad that Chapman and Tony Rudd of BRM tried to get the organisers to stop the race. They declined, and several drivers crashed. Clark headed home just six survivors at the slowest average speed at Spa for ten years. That was still 114.1mph.

Back then, Clark's face wasn't so well known, and as he was spectating on the infield at Zandvoort during a practice session, he was arrested by two Dutch policemen for not having a pass. In an uncharacteristic outburst, Clark then hit one of the policemen during the ensuing scuffle and it took some swift negotiations by Chapman to secure his release.

The Lotus Climax was the car to beat at Zandvoort, and Clark lapped the entire field, clocking the first 100mph lap round the sand dunes. Although there was stern fighting going on behind him through the wheat fields of Rheims, Clark was never challenged there either. Hill had been push started, so was never in the hunt, and Ginther's BRM lost its water when a stone holed its radiator.

It took Jimmy four laps of Silverstone to dispatch early leaders Brabham and Gurney, and after 60 out of the total 82 laps he led his pursuers Surtees and Hill by some 50 seconds. As Clark took the chequered flag, so Hill spluttered to a halt with an empty fuel tank.

There were several bad accidents at the Nürburgring, including ones involving Bandini's BRM, Ireland's Lotus-BRM, Mairesse's Ferrari, McLaren's Cooper, and Amon's Lola. Clark diced with Surtees, but the Lotus' engine went down on one cylinder, and the motor cycling champion scored his first GP win.

Monza's legendary banked section, a giant flat-out oval, resembled a patchwork quilt, as it was built out of concrete, laid a portion at a time. The surface was poor and, after practice crashes, the GPDA had the organisers limited the race to the road circuit. The lead was contested by Surtees, Hill, Clark and Gurney, with extremely close slipstreaming the order of the day. As the Ferrari's engine blew up, Clark lost the tow, and was nearly overhauled by Gurney and Hill. Then the BRM's clutch failed, leaving Clark and Gurney to fight it out – lapping the whole field bar Ginther in the process. When the Brabham's fuel pump expired, Clark had guaranteed himself the Championship.

Startling achievements

Fortunes are fickle in Formula 1. The Lotus wouldn't start for the warm-up at Watkins Glen, and Clark was a lap down when he got underway. In spite of this, he drove from last to third place, setting fastest lap on the way. In the rarefied atmosphere of the Mexico Autodrome, 7000 feet up, with a volcano as a backdrop and an Indian cemetery in the centre, Clark left the field behind in another demonstration of skill and control. Only Brabham and Ginther were unlapped, and again Clark set fastest lap. He had also equalled Fangio's record of six wins in a season. Would he make it seven? Only Dan Gurney in a Brabham looked like upsetting the Lotus driver at East London, South Africa, and he finished over a minute behind Clark in a drama-free race. They had lapped everyone else.

The final Championship standings were Clark on 54 points, and Hill and Ginther tying on 29 points, with the best six results counting.

In 1962 and 1963, Clark also drove the Lotus 23 rear-engined sports car in events such as the Nürburgring 1000kms, moving on to the Lotus 30 and 40, big-banger Group 7 CanAm-type sports cars powered by 4.7- and 5.3-litre American Ford V8s. These cars had dodgy handling to say the least, and proved to be no match for the Lola and McLaren equivalents. They were only built between 1964 and 1965. In 1964 Jim won twice in a Lotus Elan R26.

The 1964 Grand Prix opener was Monaco on 10 May; 100 times around almost two miles-worth of the Principality's streets. Jimmy led from pole position, as befitted the new champion, and held the lead in spite of a brush with some straw bales – which stood in for Armco then – which displacedhis front anti-roll bar. He pitted on lap 36 to have it removed, and rejoined in third place. On lap 93, while running between the BRMs of Hill and Ginther, his oil pressure dropped dramatically, and by lap 96 he was walking back to the pits. It was, however, enough to give Jim Clark fourth place in the final results.

A fine study of the maestro at work, at Aintree in 1962 in the Lotus 24.

There wasn't much to say about Zandvoort. Clark looked almost blasé as he blasted off the line to a flag-to-flag victory. Surtees, Gurney and Hill had their own private battle behind him, with Arundell in the second works Lotus eventually taking third from Hill.

A last-gasp victory

The Dutch result gave Arundell the spur to excel at Spa and he rushed through to lead from the second row. Gurney, Surtees and Clark were soon past him, however, and when the Ferrari's engine let go, Gurney's Brabham led. Back markers allowed Hill an advantage over Clark and McLaren. On the final tour, Hill, McLaren and Gurney all ran out of fuel. Clark inherited the win, and promptly ran out himself.

Clark's race at Rouen was over on lap 31 thanks to a holed piston. At that point he had a 15-second lead. Brands Hatch's inaugural hosting of the Grand Prix was full of drama, beginning with a start-line fracas involving the clutchless Amon, Jo Siffert and Frank Gardner. Trevor Taylor went off at the high speed Hawthorn bend, but the real attention centred on the Clark-Hill duel for the lead, which ended in the Scot's favour. These two had another tussle at the Nürburgring, together with Surtees and Gurney. Clark led on lap one, but Gurney and Surtees broke away, and on lap seven the Lotus dropped a valve.

Austria's first shot at holding a World Championship Grand Prix was on the Zeltweg airfield, not far from where they eventually built the magnificent Osterreichring. The setting might have been Sound-of-Music quality, but the concrete surface had huge gaps in it and the timekeeping was carried out in a London Transport double-decker bus. So it was hardly a prestigious venue. By half distance, the Championship contenders were eliminated by breakages. Clark's Lotus snapped a driveshaft on lap 41.

A broken piston halted Clark's progress at Monza and, although he led for a time at Watkins Glen, the Lotus succumbed to injection problems. At Mexico City, Clark needed to win to retain the title, and Hill and Surtees were the challengers. Clark led, Hill was punted off by Bandini, Gurney and Surtees kept their distance. Then the Lotus lost all its oil, and Surtees, with second place, took the title.

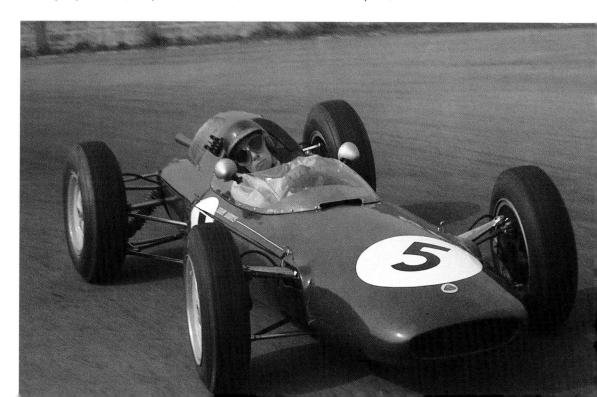

If he had made it look easy in 1963, it certainly didn't look any harder in 1965, as Jimmy dashed off six victories to win back the crown. Even when Clark led a race from start to finish it was never dull, because he would always produce a virtuoso performance. In addition, there were always battles and mechanical disasters going on further back in the running order; they just didn't seem to affect Jimmy.

A happy new year

Starting with a Hogmanay celebration in South Africa on New Year's Day, Jim Clark led throughout. It was also Stewart's debut – which Clark had done much to promote – and Jackie finished an excellent sixth.

Clark won the non-championship *News of the World* trophy at Goodwood in March. In May Lotus ignored Monaco because it clashed with Indianapolis. There were several reasons for going for it. Chapman had his eye on the big prize, and Gurney had convinced him that the nimble F1 cars could show the American dinosaurs the way home. It was in fact their third attempt, and Brabham had paved the way in 1961. In the 1963 Indy, Clark, who loathed the Indy scene, came second, and won a USAC race at Milwaukee to demonstrate that he and Lotus could do it. He was out of contention when a tyre threw a tread in 1964, but it all came to fruition in 1965, and Clark won some £75,000 prize money – plus bonuses like free meat for a year from an Indiana butcher! Although he didn't care for the place, the team returned in subsequent years, Clark being runner-up to Graham Hill in 1966.

Meanwhile, back at Spa in 1965, Clark showed his mastery to win with the new 32-valve Climax engine in his Lotus 25, with Jackie Stewart second for BRM and Ginther gaining a point for the new Honda in sixth. The Flying Scotsmen repeated their Belgian success up in the Auvergne, coming first and second from Surtees at the new Clermont-Ferrand venue.

It was four British Grand Prix wins in a row for Clark, although Hill saw to it that it wasn't a Lotus whitewash. At the end of a thrilling chase, Hill was just 3.2 seconds adrift. Although the Honda showed its potential yet again at Zandvoort, it was Clark's race, from Stewart and Gurney this time. Jimmy's run of victories ended after the German Grand Prix. He had led handsomely from start to finish, setting fastest lap, and had assured himself of the title for the second time. It was still only August. On the remaining rounds, he was dogged with a broken fuel pump, a holed piston, and engine failure.

With the new 3.0-litre rules ushering in new engines for 1966 and Coventry Climax bowing out, Lotus had to start again from scratch. As a temporary expedient they used the long-stroke 2.0-litre version used for the Tasman Series, while waiting for BRM's H-16 unit. The Cosworth-Ford V8 was under development, but wouldn't be ready for another year. It was thus a very lean season for Lotus and for Clark, with just a fourth at Brands Hatch and a third at Zandvoort. Then, at Watkins Glen, Clark inherited the lead to bring the Lotus-BRM home for the H-16 engine's one and only GP triumph.

It was a varied year in other ways, though. Already a star in touring car racing with the 'three-wheeling' Lotus Cortinas, Clark took part in the 1966 RAC Rally. He learned the tricks of the trade from rally champion Roger Clark, and had expert co-driving from Brian Melia. After a whirlwind start he got it wrong on the Loch Achray special stage and the side of the Lotus Cortina was well mangled. Apart from the Lotus Cortinas, Jim won at Brands in 1963 in a 4.7-litre Ford Galaxie, and in 1967 he drove a Ford Fairlane in a NASCAR stock car race in the USA.

Lotus was desperate for a new engine, and at the first two races of the 1967 Grand Prix season Clark and his new team-mate Graham Hill persevered with outmoded engines – Clark a Climax, Hill a BRM unit. At Zandvoort everything changed, with the debut of the new Lotus 49 and its V8 Cosworth-Ford DFV motor. The car looked and performed brilliantly, and this particular engine was so good that its derivatives are still around today, powering F3000 cars.

Although neither Lotus driver had done any testing with the 49, they dominated practice and the race. Hill, starting from pole position, led for 11 laps, only to retire with camshaft problems. Clark led for the rest of the race, putting the Lotus 49 on the same footing as the Maserati 250F and Mercedes W196 in winning 'straight out of the box'.

Britain's best

At Spa-Francorchamps, Clark took an early lead. He then lost two minutes when he pitted for new plugs. It was too much to recoup at this high speed venue, and he ended up sixth. On the 'Mickey Mouse' Bugatti circuit at Le Mans, Clark, then Hill, led initially, only for both Lotuses to retire with gearbox problems. The pair were fastest in practice at Silverstone, and again led almost from the start. Hill's engine failed but Clark had no such problem, and romped away to win the British Grand Prix for the fifth time.

The Nürburgring makes serious demands on suspension systems, with the cars getting airborne at two or three places, and demanding total commitment to drive blind brows flat out. Clark's front suspension couldn't take the pace, and after five laps in the lead – and at a third of the race distance – he retired.

Jimmy's 25th and last victory was the 1968 South African GP at Kyalami.

After close racing with Hulme and McLaren at Mosport Park, Clark's Lotus 49 ignition was drenched by heavy rain as he led on lap 69 out of 90. Back in Europe for the Italian Grand Prix, Clark drove one of his most fantastic races. Having led from the start, he pitted for tyres on lap 13, and lost a whole lap on the others. But by lap 46 he was up to sixth and as his rivals fell by the wayside he moved into the lead on lap 61. He had been going just a bit too hard, and with just half a lap to go, he ran out of fuel, coasting home in third place.

The final hurdle

There were no mistakes at the final round at Watkins Glen. The Lotus stars flipped a coin to see which of them should win, so confident were they after practice. The idea was that of Ford UK's Walter Hayes, who didn't want to risk the Cosworth-Ford powered Lotuses knocking each other off in front of his American peers. Although Hill won the toss, his clutch packed up on lap 41, and Clark, who'd been happy enough to stick to the bet, inherited the lead. Two laps from the finish, his right rear suspension collapsed, but he survived to beat Hill by six seconds.

At Mexico the Championship still wasn't decided, and Clark was fortunate to get away to one of his now typical start-to-finish wins. The starter hadn't raised the flag exactly, just waved it around a bit, and Clark faltered, only to be rammed by Gurney. The Eagle's radiator was holed, but the Lotus was undamaged, and went on to win. The Repco-Brabhams of Brabham and Hulme followed Clark home, however, giving Hulme the title and Brabham runner up spot over Clark.

At the 1968 Championship opener at Kyalami on 1 January, the Lotus cars were still in BRG and yellow strip, and Jim took the lead on lap two and held it to the end, overtaking Fangio's career record of 24 World Championship Grand Prix wins.

Team Lotus astonished race fans at the Tasman Series in Australia and New Zealand by appearing at the winter series early in 1968 in Gold Leaf cigarette livery. Gone was Lotus' version of the traditional British Racing Green with its yellow flashes. Instead the bodywork was in garish red, gold and white, and heavily sign-written with the cigarette name. Jim took five wins from eight races.

Jim's diary was pretty full, with practice and business appointments at Zandvoort and London. Along with Hill, he was also due to test one of the Lotus 56 four-wheel drive Indy gas-turbine cars. There was also a Formula 2 race at Barcelona, counting towards the French national series, which Jimmy and Graham entered, driving the neat Gold Leaf F2 Lotus 48-FVAs. Jim had driven the car the previous year with one or two wins but mostly retirements. In Spain, Matras were dominant, the Lotuses off the pace, and Clark was rammed by Ickx's Ferrari.

The first round in the European F2 series was scheduled to take place at Hockenheim the following weekend, and there was no time to get the car back to Hethel to rebuild it. The Hockenheim race clashed with the BOAC 500, a round of the World Sportscar Championship, and both Clark and Hill had been offered a drive there in the new Alan Mann-built Ford P68 F3L prototype – which they had to decline because of conflicting tyre contracts. The Ford was debuted by McLaren/Spence. Clark disliked the Hockenheim circuit, in much the same way as he hated Spa – long straights were not his thing. He had never raced at the drab German track before, but the long straights and twisty section around the pits and stands were a difficult combination for which to set up a car properly, added to which it was raining. So his Lotus 48 was fitted with new tyres – Firestone wets.

Beltoise's Matra soon led from Ahrens' narrow-tyred Brabham, Amon's Ferrari and Bell's Brabham. By lap five Clark was running a lonely sixth, followed by Widdows and Schlesser. As the track disappeared out past the stands on to a long straight in thick forest, the Lotus twitched, Clark corrected, then as the track began to curve again for a long right-hander, Clark was seen by a lone flag marshal to be wrestling with it from lock to lock, but it careered off sideways into a stand of young trees. There was no barrier, of course, and no run-off area. The engine and gearbox were torn off in the impact, and a tree took the cockpit section amidships. Jim was killed instantly.

There was naturally some delay in staging the second heat. Understandably, Hill withdrew from it. Chief mechanic Jim Endruweit dealt with the tragedy, calling Chapman, who was on a skiing holiday – F2 was not of prime interest to him. Chapman rushed through the night to the scene. He was utterly shattered, as his professional relationship with Jimmy was a particularly close one.

A fatal flaw

According to Clark's mechanic Dave 'Beaky' Sims, Clark had had a puncture in the right rear tyre. That was also given as the official reason for his accident. It's very likely that he picked up a piece of debris from a practice accident, and the tyre developed a slow leak, which was why he was observed correcting a slide in a left-hand bend. He may have assumed that there was oil on the track, and then, as the car accelerated down the straight, the centrifugal force masked the tyre's deflation. When the driver set the car up for the right-hand curve the sidewalls were sucked in and all the remaining air rushed out, making an accident inevitable. The wrestling witnessed by the marshal was Clark grappling with vicious right-hand oversteer on a damp track. The rev-counter in his bent tub testified he had the power on right up to the moment of impact – at 120mph – trying to make the car behave.

It was a needless accident in a race nobody much cared about at a second-division circuit. The only benefit to come from the post-race investigation was that in future wheels were equipped with security bolts to ensure the tyre bead couldn't leave the rim. They subsequently incorporated a couple of chicanes in the long straight at Hockenheim – a favourite trick for slowing down the traffic – and of course the Armco barrier which would have saved him is everywhere now.

Invariably shy and modest, Jim Clark used to scuttle up the A1 in his Elan back to his farm – Edington Mains – after races or visits to Lotus HQ. He had 1242 acres of arable land, three pedigree flocks of sheep, and fattened a herd of Irish cattle. Before becoming champion he once described himself as a farmer who went racing as a hobby. There were girl friends, most notably Sally Stokes, but he never married, declaring that racing and marriage didn't mix. He loved to fly and had his own aircraft, a Piper Twin Commanche, bought from Chapman. The two of them discussed the possibility of going into aircraft rental business, but Clark maintained that he wanted to be a motor racing photographer after he retired from racing.

An indicator as to how good Clark was is given by his biographer Graham Gauld, who describes an analysis in 1966 by Firestone of wear-rates on the tyres of different drivers. For example, Brabham and Hill wore out their back tyres faster than the fronts, and Gurney wore out his front ones first. Clark's tyres bore even wear front and rear, which indicates that his sense of balancing the car and braking technique were extraordinary; no-one else came close.

John Surtees
(1934–) World Champion 1964

John Surtees was born near Westerham in Kent on 11 February 1934, with motor bikes in his blood. Even as a young teenager he was riding passenger in his garage-owning father Jack's racing combination. His upbringing was a combination of working hard and playing hard, and he maintained that regime in his motor racing career. After leaving school, he became an apprentice at the Vincent motorcycle company. These thundering machines – especially the 1000cc Black Shadow – earned an awesome reputation among the Rockers of the 1950s and early 1960s, achieving almost a cult status.

While at Vincent, Surtees built up a 500cc racing machine known as the Grey Shadow, and in his first year as a solo rider – as opposed to passenger in a 'chair', he won a race at his home circuit, Brands Hatch. There followed a period of familiarisation with club circuits up and down the country, on which he practised race craft and technique, surviving the predictable spills and tumbles.

Surtees soon transferred to the more powerful, better handling Norton, alongside the big star of the day Geoff Duke. As Duke moved on to the four cylinder Gilera, Surtees began to beat him consistently with the works Nortons. Two seasons later, at the end of the 1955 season, Surtees defected to ride for the Italian MV Augusta team. For the next three years he rode MVs to no less than seven different World Championships.

Moving up in the world

At the end of 1959 he turned his attention to car racing. He was given a try-out in an Aston Martin at Goodwood by Reg Parnell. But he turned down the offer of a drive until he had more experience. His racing debut came in a Formula Junior Cooper BMC in March 1960 and he was quickly courted by Colin Chapman. Lotus had yet to break into the big time – although the potential was clear – so Surtees agreed to do one or two races on an occasional basis. At Silverstone for the 1960 British Grand Prix, he drove a Lotus 18 Climax, and had a fairly easy race into second place behind Brabham and ahead of Lotus regular Innes Ireland.

Next round was Oporto, and Surtees tailed initial leader Gurney, followed by Moss and Phil Hill. By lap 19, Moss was out of contention with a misfire, and the agile Lotus had a good lead over Hill's front-engined Dino Ferrari. Then a fuel leak from the front-mounted tank began pouring its contents over Surtees' feet, causing his foot to slip off the brake pedal on lap 36, with the resulting brush with kerb and straw bales holing the radiator. He had set fastest lap, at 112.3mph. Clearly Surtees was taking car racing in his stride. At Riverside, California, however, he spun on lap 4 and collected Clark in the process. He had done enough to make his mark, and meanwhile fell back on his privately owned F2 Cooper.

In 1961 Vanwall reappeared with a rear engined car, based on their experiments with a Lotus 18 spaceframe. It was powered by a 2.6-litre Vanwall engine, destined for the short-lived Intercontinental formula, and was driven by Surtees in the *Daily Express* International at Silverstone. While running second, behind Brabham's Cooper, Surtees spun, recovering to finish fifth. It was Vanwall's last appearance in contemporary racing.

During 1961 and 1962 he drove Coopers and Lolas for Reg Parnell's Yeoman Credit-Bowmaker finance team. At Spa-Francorchamps in 1961 his Cooper was the only British car to finish in the first seven. At Rheims-Geux, Surtees was unlucky to hit a bank. He had been taking avoiding action as Ginther spun. The Nürburgring weather served up its traditional mix of wet and dry, and Surtees drove a cool race to finish fifth.

On 1 April 1962, Surtees debuted the Lola-Climax at the Brussels Grand Prix, and, running with an old four-cylinder engine, he did well to stay with the V8 BRMs of Hill and Marsh, Moss' V8 Lotus and Mairesse's winning V6 Ferrari. John finished fifth in the first heat, but blew up his engine in the second.

In the Goodwood Easter Monday Glover Trophy race, won by Graham Hill's new V8 BRM, Surtees set fastest lap, although he was well down the field following a spin and pit-stops. It was likely that Moss was trying to match Surtees' time when he had the accident which was to terminate his F1 career. In the Silverstone International, Surtees' Lola finished third behind the dramatic battle between Hill's BRM and Clark's Lotus. At Zandvoort, in the first GP of the season, Surtees crashed the Lola, due to a broken wishbone. There was a

Surtees in his Championship year, 1964, sets up his Ferrari for Paddock Bend.

certain anti-Surtees element around at the time and, when he spun off, it was the perfect opportunity to criticise him.

At Monaco, Surtees' Lola was fourth, a lap down on McLaren's winning Cooper and the Ferraris of Phil Hill and Bandini. He was fifth at Spa-Francorchamps and fifth again at Rouen-les-Essarts. But at Aintree, for the British GP, Surtees started from the front row. Only the loss of fourth gear prevented him from sustaining his challenge to Clark. He brought the Lola home a creditable second.

Determined driving

Surtees' fine drive with a Ferrari GTO in the 1962 Tourist Trophy at Goodwood ended when Clark's Aston Martin DB4 Zagato slid across in front of him and the pair ended up in the Madgwick bank. By the Nürburgring, Motor Sport was predicting a win for the Lola: 'with a little more luck'. Surtees drove with 'calm determination' on a soaking wet track to second place. This involved a hectic battle for much of the event between Hill's BRM, Surtees, and Gurney's Porsche, and they eventually finished in that order.

Surtees retired at Monza on lap 43 with a holed piston while harassing Ginther in the second BRM for second place. In practice for the American Grand Prix, he hit a massive tree when a steering arm broke on the Lola. He borrowed the team's other car, which was to have been driven by Roy Salvadori, starting from the back of the grid

accordingly, but was out with an oil leak on lap 19. The last race of the season – on 29 December at Kyalami – found Surtees struggling with the works Coopers, and he retired eventually with a damaged valve.

A select band of F1 stars including Hill, Ireland, Surtees and 'locals' McLaren and Brabham, went to New Zealand for the seasonal winter races – summer down under, of course – and on 5 January Surtees won the New Zealand Grand Prix on the Pukekohe circuit. He was the only international ace whose car held together – the Lola running a 2.7-litre Climax unit. After four events in which he didn't feature, Surtees took second place in the Australian Grand Prix at Warwick Farm, sandwiched between Brabham and McLaren. Sponsors Bowmaker pulled out at that point, so Eric Broadley's Lola équipe retired from Formula 1 prior to the 1963 season, and Surtees took up Enzo Ferrari's repeated offer of a works drive for 1963.

Reaching new heights

Monaco looked all set to be Clark's race, but when the gearbox jammed Graham Hill took over, followed by team-mate Ginther. They had been hounded by Surtees' Ferrari, but John had to pull back when his goggles became spattered with oil. In the final laps he tried hard to pass McLaren for third place, but it was the BRM's day.

Clark dominated at Zandvoort and Surtees lost a probable second place by overdoing it at the hairpin. The Ferrari inherited third place when the BRM's engine blew. With Clark having disappeared into the distance, interest at Silverstone centred on the scrap for third between Surtees and Hill, which moved up a slot when Gurney retired. As Jimmy tried a repeat showing at the Nürburgring, 'Big John' tore off after him, the pair leaving all kinds of mayhem in their wake – caused by other factors – and when the Lotus engine dropped to seven cylinders, the Ferrari was through, and never looked like being caught. It was Surtees' first World Championship Grand Prix win.

Race fans in Italy are fanatical in their devotion to Ferrari, and the red cars can do no wrong. If the car fails, it is more likely, in their eyes, just as it was in Enzo Ferrari's mind, that the driver is to blame. If the car wins or runs at the head of the field, the tifosi go wild and the driver is lionised. Italian national drivers on the Ferrari squad are more easily forgiven, but the further away from Italy their homeland, the less forgiving the crowd. Surtees, on the other hand, had a head start because of his motorcycling career with MV Augusta.

Now at Monza here he was again, driving a red Ferrari and fighting for the lead. The Ferrari engine gave up first, on lap 17. But Surtees had shown what was possible, and retained the goodwill of the tifosi.

Breaking the rules

All was looking good at Watkins Glen, with Surtees having surged ahead of the BRMs to take the lead. But on lap 82 out of 110, the Ferrari holed a piston. In Mexico City, he was lying third when he pitted to have an oversteering problem corrected. The car wouldn't start again, and he was disqualified for being given a push-start – the rules said the cars had to start on the button.

A Ferrari contract also committed its driver to do as many of the World Sportscar Championship rounds as possible, and in 1963 Surtees won two major races, with Ludovico Scarfiotti at the Sebring 12-Hours, and with Willy Mairesse to take the Nürburgring 1000kms. The following year, at the Sebring 12-Hours, Surtees and Bandini finished third in a 330P ahead of a trio of AC Cobras.

At the 1964 Le Mans, the same partnership came third in the 4.0-litre 330P, behind the Guichet/Vaccarella 275P and the Graham Hill/Bonnier second-placed 330P. Both 330Ps had overheated in the night, but they kept ahead of the fourth-placed Gurney/Bondurant AC 'Daytona' Cobra.

In the Rheims 12-Hours, Surtees and Bandini were second in their Ferrari 275LM/P to the similar G. Hill/Bonnier car after a race-long duel. Surtees had less good fortune at the British institution called the Tourist Trophy. Innes Ireland's gyrating Ferrari GTO caused Surtees to spin off himself, and he suffered concussion as his GTO clouted the bank. Nevertheless, these were heady days indeed for Maranello, and in fact the development of the sports prototypes and grand touring cars probably took precedence over the F1 cars, especially in 1963.

On the face of it, the 1964 F1 World Championship looked as if it would go Clark's way again, so dominant had he been the previous year. But after Clark fell back to fourth at Monaco it was Hill's race. Surtees was an early retirement with gearbox failure in the Ferrari V8. By half distance at Zandvoort, Clark's Lotus led Surtees' Ferrari by 29 seconds, increasing to 45 seconds by lap 55, and eventually finishing 53.6 seconds

ahead. These two had lapped everybody else.

Both Ferraris retired at Spa, Surtees' when leading on lap four, and Bandini's on lap 12, both with blown engines. The Ferrari jinx struck Surtees once again on the second lap at Rouen, as he vainly pursued Clark and Hill; the Ferrari's engine failed again. Surtees couldn't keep up with Clark's Lotus 25 or Hill's BRM V8 at Brands Hatch. As they eased off in the closing laps, they still had a 10-second lead over the V8 Ferrari. Bandini did well to bring the V6-engined car in fifth behind Brabham.

At the non-championship Solitude Grand Prix at Stuttgart, Surtees came second to Clark as the two of them swapped places in terrible conditions. It had rained heavily so the track surface was smooth and was coated with the residue of oil and rubber deposited during three days of motor cycle racing and F1 practice. Eight cars were lost on the first lap, and Clark and Surtees lapped the eight who were left.

Surtees' triumph at the Nürburgring was the race which surely demonstrated his true class. He was justifiably jubilant on taking the chequered flag, having seen off Clark, Hill and Gurney over 15 laps of the 14.17 mile serpentine switchback.

Team solidarity

Virtually all the key players were eliminated early on at the Zeltweg airfield circuit, mainly because of the atrocious concrete-section surface. On lap eight, Surtees' rear suspension collapsed, and that was that. Or nearly. He walked back to the pits, collected a jack and some spanners, fixed the suspension, and drove back to his pit, thus completing another lap. By this time though, the leader was on lap 35. Curiously, when team-mate Bandini was on his 66th lap, Surtees did one more lap, to act as cover for Bandini when he was under pressure.

The Englishman's reputation with the Italians was secured when he won at Monza. On lap one the order was Gurney, Surtees, McLaren and Clark. They were followed by a second bunch that was much tighter still, including Bandini, Bonnier, Brabham, Ginther, Ireland, Siffert and Anderson. Next time round the spectator stands erupted with one voice at the sight of Surtees' red car in the lead. It seemed anyone could swap positions at will, and only mechanical failure made cars drop out, one by one. Surtees and Gurney duelled, Ferrari V8 versus Brabham-Climax V8, taking it in turns to lead, slipstream a bit, then swap over. Eventually, Gurney's challenge ended with electrical problems. Surtees was home and dry, over a minute ahead of McLaren. Nowhere else do the fans swarm on to the track when the winner crosses the line as they do at Monza. Despite Surtees' victory, it was the third-placed Bandini whom the tifosi lifted shoulder high. Surtees was nearly trampled underfoot.

For the American Grand Prix, the Ferraris were painted blue and white. This astonishing state of affairs came about because of a row Enzo had with Monza officials, declaring that he would never race on Italian soil again, and handing in his competitions licence. The cars were painted American racing colours and entered by NART – Luigi Chinetti's North American Racing Team.

For once, Clark made a poor start, and Surtees, who'd shared the front row of the grid with him, made the most of it to lead, along with Mike Spence in the other works Lotus. By lap 13 however, Clark had pulled back and, by a brilliant move, got past Surtees to take the lead. To keep their Championship hopes alive, both Surtees and Hill had to make sure Clark didn't win – as a fourth victory would see him retain the title. They needn't have worried. On lap 54, Jimmy retired with fuel injection problems, the malady having dropped him to 11th. Surtees was taken by Hill, and then lost more time with a spin on some oil. Gurney too went by him, but dropped out with falling oil pressure. Hill thus won from Surtees. The title looked set to go to either one of them.

Hill had the cruellest luck at Mexico, before things even got under way. As the flag fell to start the race, his goggles slipped off, and he lost valuable seconds sorting himself out. Surtees' Ferrari – still blue and white rather than red – was misfiring, and he lost nine places on lap one before it cleared. Soon Clark was leading Gurney, with Graham Hill strongly challenged by Bandini in the new flat-12 Ferrari. So much so that a spot of fist-waving ensued, and then Bandini caused both cars to spin. This allowed Surtees through, although Bandini, in the faster car, retook him. Still Clark led and the title looked to be his. Hill was out of the picture now with damaged exhaust pipes, and then Clark's Lotus developed an oil leak. On the last lap all the Climax's oil had gone, and he was credited with fifth. Meanwhile Bandini let Surtees through on team orders, and Big John's second place behind Gurney was enough to give him the crown – by just one point from Graham Hill. Hill's

Surtees went on to become a constructor. Here he is with Brazilian Carlos Pace.

contretemps with Surtees' team-mate had been crucial, as things turned out. Nevertheless, Surtees was Champion, and remains the only person to win the world titles on both two and four wheels.

Thereafter, there were good placings during the 1965 Grand Prix season; second in South Africa, fourth at Monaco, third at Clermont-Ferrand, third at Silverstone. He and Scarfiotti also won the Nürburgring 1000kms. But Surtees had also become involved with Eric Broadley in developing the Lola T70 Le Mans and CanAm sports racer. This category had taken off in North America and involved a European chassis powered by a large American V8 – generally a Chevrolet unit. Later in the year, at Mosport, Surtees had his most serious accident when a

suspension upright broke on the Lola, and he was at death's door for a while. It looked like the end of his career.

The determined Surtees was back at Monza the following spring for the 1000kms, and amazed everybody by partnering Mike Parkes to victory in the Ferrari 4.0-litre P3. Driving a V12 Ferrari F1 car in the Belgian Grand Prix, he also won an appalling Spa-Francorchamps race. Eight cars were lost on the first lap as they hit a rain storm flat out. But Surtees was at loggerheads with team manager Dragoni and matters came to a head in practice for Le Mans when Dragoni drafted in a third driver in the Surtees car. This suggestion that the Englishman was not yet fully fit was too much. Big John quit Ferrari on the spot.

He joined the struggling Cooper équipe, and in a magnificent snub to Ferrari, came second at the Nürburgring in the Cooper-Maserati. Bandini was sixth for Ferrari. At Monza, Surtees was forced out when fuel poured over his front wheels from a split tank, but he was third at Watkins Glen and first at Mexico City.

Eastern mystics

At the same time, he was racing the Lola in the CanAm series, and became 1966 Champion. For 1967, he drove for Honda. The V12 was a fabulous engine, but the chassis was dreadful. Surtees faced an uphill struggle, as there was little liaison with Japan, and the Japanese mechanics were operating in a different culture – very different from the 1980s. It came to fruition in a spine-tingling Monza finish, where Surtees duped Brabham while exiting the Parabolica to beat him to the line.

Best result in 1968 was second place at Rouen-les-Essarts. He left Honda for BRM, along with Jackie Oliver, again on a mission to make a bad car a winner. He managed only a third, at Watkins Glen, with the P153. The regime at Bourne was perhaps too top heavy for Surtees to work effectively, and he decided he might as well build his own cars.

Designer Len Terry produced a scheme for a Formula 5000 single-seater – akin to F3000 today – powered by 5.0-litre Chevrolet engines. It became the Surtees TS5. Driven by Trevor Taylor and David Hobbs, it was an immediate success in Britain and the USA in 1969. Surtees then drove for McLaren in 1970. Derek Bell was sixth in a Surtees at Watkins Glen. Surtees drove for Ferrari again in the World Sportscar Championship in 1970. He was third at Monza with Peter Schetty and second in the Spa 1000kms with Ickx in the 512M.

In 1971, Surtees was fifth at Zandvoort and sixth at Silverstone in his own car, but never looked a likely winner. In 1972, Schenken, de Adamich, Stommelen and Hailwood had good placings driving for Surtees. Mike-the-Bike was second at Monza. The following year, with Fina petrol sponsorship, Pace, Hailwood and Mass had no better luck.

The next major landmark for Surtees was his protégé Mike Hailwood's domination of the 1972 European F2 Championship in a Surtees, sponsored by Matchbox toys. This was probably his greatest achievement as a constructor. But 'Shirtsleeves' always had a concerned look about him even then. By 1978, no great results had been achieved, and he withdrew from Formula 1.

A natural worrier, Surtees always did what he thought right, and was said to be one of the few honest men in motor racing. He was never one of the most extrovert individuals on the F1 scene but there's no questioning his abilities as driver and constructor.

Denny Hulme
(1936–1992) World Champion 1967

Denny Hulme had one of the longest, most varied careers in motor sport, spanning four decades. Like most drivers from 'down under', he was gritty, determined and stood no nonsense from anyone. Despite a certain grouchiness – his nickname was 'The Bear' – he was one of the most popular drivers on the scene.

Born on 18 June 1936 at Nelson, New Zealand, Denis was always known in motor racing as Denny. His father Clive had been awarded a VC for his actions in Crete during World War II. Denny spent a lot of his youth on his grandparents' tobacco farm on South Island, and in the late 1940s the family moved to Te Puke where Clive Hulme started a haulage business. After school, Denny worked as a mechanic in a local garage, and maintained his father's trucks and tractors. He earned money delivering equipment and material to farms, and used the proceeds to buy his first car. This was a brand-new MG TF, and as a member of a car club he took part in a local hill-climb in 1956. Three years on and after a few club races, the MG was replaced by an MGA. More serious was the acquisition of a

Cooper Climax, bought with parental help, which he used to good effect in 1959 and 1960. He impressed the New Zealand International Grand Prix Association sufficiently to place him on its 'Driver to Europe' scheme. This scholarship funded a year's competition in what was regarded as the Mecca of motor sport. Bruce McLaren had won it in 1959 and in 1960 it was the turn of Denny and his friend George Lawton. When he came to Europe there was always some confusion over the pronunciation of his surname; which is 'Hulm', rather than 'Hume'.

Racing his Formula Junior Cooper-BMC every weekend at tracks all over Europe, Hulme gained experience quickly. Sadly, Lawton was killed, and Hulme returned home in 1961, along with his Cooper-Climax, somewhat despondent.

He returned to Britain in 1961 to work at Jack Brabham's Chessington garage, and this funded some more competition in Formula Junior. He drove a works Abarth at Le Mans that year, partnering fellow Kiwi Angus Hyslop to 14th place. Opportunities in 1962 included drives for Ken Tyrrell in Formula Junior. Later in the year he took over Jack Brabham's FJ car from the retiring Gavin Youl. Brabham's team manager was Phil Kerr, and he established an enduring rapport with Hulme.

Another successful partnership had just begun: Denny had married his New Zealand girlfriend Greeta, who was his constant companion in pit and paddock at race meetings. His first full season with the FJ Brabham was 1963, and he won seven out of 14 races entered. He kept on working at Brabham's as time permitted.

By now 'Black Jack' was looking for a second driver in F2, and asked Denny to join him. They were sufficiently well placed in F2 races during 1964 for Brabham to win the European F2 Championship and Hulme to be runner-up. Alan Rees and Jo Siffert also featured in Brabham-Cosworth F2s. Denny got his first drives at non-championship F1 events in the Brabham Formula 1 car in 1964.

Further successes

It was much the same story in Formula 2 in 1965. The canny Brabham had obtained an engine deal with Honda, whose engines at that capacity were superior to the Cosworth units employed by the majority. Brabham and Hulme thus cleaned up again.

Denny's first Grand Prix was at Monaco in 1965. He stood in for Dan Gurney, who was away at Indianapolis, and finished eighth. At Clermont-Ferrand, Denny brought his Brabham-Climax home fourth behind Clark, Stewart and Surtees, and ahead of Graham Hill. He was fifth at Zandvoort among much the same company – with Gurney third in the other Brabham. The German Grand Prix was not so successful. Hulme punctured his fuel tank when his seat worked loose. A good all-rounder, he would also make his mark in sports car racing, and his principal achievement in 1965 was a win in the Tourist Trophy in a Brabham BT8.

With the inception of the 3.0-litre formula in 1966, Gurney left Brabham to build his Eagle-Weslake F1 cars and race the 7.0-litre Mk II Fords in World Sportscar events. So Denny took his place alongside Brabham, who had sourced a supply of Australian-built Repco V8 engines. These proved ideal for the new season, where there was a dearth of new power-plants, and Brabham won the Championship. At Spa, Hulme was one of the unfortunate crashers on the notorious first lap, where they encountered a rain storm, but at Rheims-Geux he finished third behind Brabham and Parkes. The Brabham pair were dominant in practice at Brands Hatch, but confusion over whether to run wet or dry tyres during the race made it a less than foregone conclusion. In the event, Brabham won, while Hulme steamed through the field to take second. Hulme, meanwhile, brought his Brabham-Repco home third after a battle with the Ferraris of Scarfiotti and Parkes at Monza. At Mexico City, Brabham was second to Surtees, with Hulme third, ahead of Ginther's Honda and Gurney's Eagle.

Denny was involved in the Ford steamroller attempt on the World Sportscar Championship, in which they sent teams of 7.0-litre Mk IIs to almost every round, backed up by hordes of private GT40s. The might of Dearborn told, and at Le Mans the Mk II Ford of Hulme and Ken Miles actually crossed the line first in a

The first New Zealand champion, Denny Hulme clinched the title at the 1967 Mexican Grand Prix.

*Hulme's Brabham-Repco V8 led the 1967
Monaco GP from lap 14.*

staged three-car finish; but McLaren/Amon had covered marginally more on distance due to their having been further back on the grid at the start of the event. They were consequently awarded the race.

Although they were ostensibly team-mates, Brabham and Hulme hotly contested the 1967 Championship. At Kyalami, Hulme led from the start, chased by Surtees. On lap 59 Hulme brought his BT20 into the pits for brake fluid, demoting himself to fourth, two laps in arrears. He led in the early laps at Monaco, giving best to Stewart briefly. From lap 14 he led Bandini and McLaren, but the Italian was fatally injured when he clipped the bales at the entrance to the harbour section. Hulme thought there was oil at the entrance to the chicane, which Bandini slid on. His inverted Ferrari burned and marshals were hopelessly ill equipped to deal with it. Hulme's first GP victory was thus rather eclipsed. At the post-race presentation at the Royal box, the ageing Clerk of the Course Louis Chiron asked him his name – when he'd been leading for two hours.

At Zandvoort, Denny was third behind Brabham and Clark, beating a trio of Ferraris. On the Bugatti circuit at Le Mans, the Brabhams were victorious, with Denny's second place secure once Amon's throttle cable had broken. At Silverstone, Hulme came through to second when Hill retired and Brabham fell back to fourth.

Hulme's staying power

Denny may not have had the wherewithal to dart off into the lead like Clark, but he was a stayer, and as the opposition dwindled at the Nürburgring, he moved up to second behind Gurney. When the Californian's drive shaft broke, Hulme was on his way to a certain victory. Brabham and Amon finished neck and neck, 40 seconds behind him, keeping Jack's hopes of retaining the title open. Hulme led for 54 laps

of the Canadian Grand Prix at Mosport but was overtaken by his team-leader Brabham when he pitted for a new visor. As Clark had retired, it was again a Brabham 1-2, this time in the pouring rain.

In a typical Monza slipstreamer, Hulme, Hill and Brabham swapped the lead, but the Kiwi faded from the picture with overheating. The Lotus duo of Clark and Hill made it a precarious 1-2 at Watkins Glen with Hill's clutch packing up but Denny inherited third place when Amon's engine blew. His Brabham freewheeled across the line, completely out of fuel.

As they went to Mexico for the final round, the points scoring system meant that Brabham could keep the title if he won and Hulme finished no higher than fifth. There was tension of another kind in the Brabham camp, as it looked likely the Bear would leave his Aussie mentor and throw his lot in with fellow Kiwi Bruce McLaren, with whom he'd been doing the CanAm series between Grands Prix. At the confused start, Hill sped away, with Amon, Clark and Brabham in pursuit. Hulme was way back and with Surtees he began to make up places. He could ill afford to let Brabham get too far ahead. By lap 30 it was Clark, with no clutch, Amon and Brabham, with Hulme in fourth. Clark made it to the finish with Brabham an untroubled second, and, a lap down, the new Champion, Denny Hulme. Clark was feted, while Denny was somewhat overlooked in the confusion. The prize-giving took place in a bull-ring, among dozens of bull-calves.

Denny went ahead and joined McLaren for 1968. Brabham recruited Jochen Rindt. At Kyalami, Rindt was third and Denny fifth. However at Jarama, Madrid, Hulme came second – minus a gear – to Hill's Lotus after Rodriguez's BRM crashed and Beltoise fell back to fifth. Hulme came fifth at Monaco after his new team-mate had lost control exiting the tunnel. At Spa-Francorchamps, Hulme had led after Amon and Surtees retired, and he battled with Stewart until the drive shaft broke on the McLaren. Brabham inherited the lead on the last lap without realising it, to win his first Grand Prix.

A sad day for Formula 1

Denny was fifth at Rouen-les-Essarts. It was a grim race, following the fatal accident on the third lap involving Jo Schlesser, who crashed the latest Honda at the Nouveau Monde hairpin. The large magnesium content in the chassis burned fiercely when the fuel exploded, and the veteran Frenchman could not be saved.

The Brands Hatch round was won by Jo Siffert in the Rob Walker Lotus 49, followed by the Ferraris of Amon and Ickx, then Hulme's McLaren. Neither McLaren featured in Germany, but at Monza both were involved in a struggle with Siffert and Stewart. All the front runners but Hulme retired with mechanical problems. Ickx then harried the improving Servoz-Gavin, but Hulme had a safe lead, and won at an average speed of 145.4mph.

Dan Gurney borrowed a McLaren for the Canadian GP at St Jovite, and out-qualified his team-mates. Amon, Siffert and Rindt led initially, followed by Hill, Hulme and McLaren. Eventually only Amon was left to head the McLarens, in a Kiwi 1-2-3. But with 18 laps to go his Ferrari transmission failed. Hulme scooped the honours, placing himself equal first with Hill in the chase for the Championship. He spun out of contention in a battle with Hill and Stewart at Watkins Glen and at Mexico City he had a dramatic escape. A damper broke and the McLaren pitched into the barrier after the pits and caught fire. With no more points scored, he ended the season third behind Hill and Stewart.

In 1969, the McLarens were usually running well-up, although not quite on the pace of the race leaders. Denny scored a third at Kyalami, a fourth at Montjuich Park, Barcelona, and Bruce and Denny were fifth and sixth at Monaco. Denny was fourth at Zandvoort, but he didn't score again until Mexico, when Goodyear tyres proved superior to the Firestones of Stewart and Rindt. Hulme led from early on and won.

Further tragedies

At Kyalami in 1970, Denny followed his ex-boss Brabham home to second place, and he was fourth at Monaco. In May, Denny was injured in testing at Indy, and in June Bruce was killed testing a CanAm car. So at Zandvoort Gurney and F5000 Champion Peter Gethin deputised for them. Denny was back in action at Clermont-Ferrand, and came fourth. He was third at Monza and Hockenheim and fourth at Monza. He rounded off a sad season with third place at Mexico City.

In the new M19 McLaren he was sixth at Kyalami having led until four laps from the end when a bolt fell out of the front suspension. There followed a fifth at Barcelona, a fourth at Monaco, then a barren period until Mosport, where he carved his way past four drivers to take fourth place. Denny was still in contention. At Buenos Aires in 1972 he came second to Stewart. At Kyalami he stormed back to take the victory after the M19 showed signs of overheating. It was the McLaren Team's first Grand Prix win for three years. Peter Revson was now also on board, enjoying some good placings. In June Hulme was third at Nivelles-Baulers in Belgium, and fifth at Brands Hatch. At the splendid Osterreichring he was second and Revson was third behind Fittipaldi's JPS Lotus 72, and the pair were third and fourth at Monza. The order was reversed, Revson ahead of Hulme, as they followed winner Stewart home in Canada. Third place at Watkins Glen gave Denny third place in the Championship behind Fittipaldi and Stewart.

Despite having a new car – the M23 – for 1973, Denny only managed one victory, at Anderstorp, Sweden, narrowly beating SuperSwede Ronnie Peterson. He was rather upstaged by team-mate Revson, who won the British and Canadian Grands Prix. For 1974, McLaren had Marlboro sponsorship, and Hulme was joined by Fittipaldi. He showed that a 38-year-old could beat all-comers by winning at Buenos Aires. He was also second in Austria. But it was Fittipaldi's year, and the New Zealander announced his retirement at the end of the season.

There was another aspect to Hulme's career, set largely in North America. The story of Denny's involvement with Bruce McLaren's CanAm set-up goes back to 1967. McLaren was in at the beginning of this hugely popular North American category with his Cooper-Zerex Oldsmobile, which won the Guards Trophy at Brands Hatch in 1964. The second McLaren CanAm car was the M1B, with body styling by artist Michael Turner, and over in the USA and Canada McLaren and Amon duelled with Surtees and Hulme who drove Lola T70s. In 1966, Surtees was CanAm champion but for 1967 Hulme joined McLaren.

Driving the new 5.9-litre M6A, Hulme knocked ten seconds off the Elkhart Lake lap record, and won the race. There followed a string of successes, competing against many of the leading American drivers, like Gurney, Parnelli Jones, Mark Donohue and Jim Hall. McLaren was 1967 CanAm champion, with Hulme second, despite having won more races. The M8A, developed for the 1968 series, used 7.0-litre engines, and with it Hulme and McLaren won four out of six races. The 1969 M8B featured a rear wing, mounted on stalks, and McLarens were victorious in all 11

rounds. Bruce had won six of them. This run of five CanAm titles in a row lasted until the twin-turbo Porsche 917 spyders – driven by Donohue and Follmer – took over from the M20s in 1972.

The McLaren team's domination of the CanAm series was legendary. It became known as the 'Bruce and Denny Show', as the pair won race after race in their thundering orange Group 7 sports racers. Denny preferred this type of competition to Formula 1. The atmosphere was relaxed, compared with the precious, self-conscious environment of the Grand Prix world.CanAm cars were easier to drive, handling well in corners and with masses of power on tap from their 7.0-litre Chevrolet engines. Only when they neared maximum speed at 200mph was there a possibility of instability. At Road Atlanta in 1972, Denny's M20 was flipped into the air by the vortex created by a Porsche 917's rear wing.

There was something of his father's heroism in him. At Indianapolis in 1970, officials made the drivers use a different fuel cap. Unknown to Hulme, the cap on the McLaren M15 that he was testing sprang open, releasing fuel droplets on to the driver. Methanol fuel burns with an invisible flame, and Hulme thought at first the droplets of liquid on his screen were rain. After three laps, it caught fire as he was travelling at 200mph. Fireproof racewear was in its infancy, and Hulme was clad in a Nomex suit but only leather shoes and gloves. The car was still moving as he baled out, having sustained severe burns to his hands.

Hulme won the 1974 Argentinian GP for McLaren from Lauda and Regazzoni.

Just one month after his accident, Hulme raced at the Mosport CanAm opener, making light of the great pain he must have been suffering. Every time he took his gloves off, it removed a new layer of skin. Yet he soldiered on to win the 1970 CanAm title in the M8D.

In June 1992 Denny was awarded an OBE, and returned to Goodwood for the unveiling of a commemorative stone to Bruce McLaren. He participated in the European Historic Touring Car round at Silverstone at the Coy's meeting, driving a BMW 2000 against Alfa GTAs, Ford Falcons and the like. Later in the year while driving in the hugely exciting Bathurst Group A races, he succumbed to a heart attack. It had been great to see him enjoying himself to the end.

uring the 1950s the cars themselves gradually became inherently safer and more controllable as tyre technology progressed. The first trend towards improving the safety aspect for the drivers themselves was the wearing of crash helmets, as opposed to the tight-fitting linen headgear universally used until around 1950.

By the mid-1960s, drivers were beginning to take seatbelts seriously. Prior to that, accidents involving drivers being flung out of their cars happened regularly. Volatile fuels used in racing meant fires were more likely in crashes, so on-board fire extinguishers were introduced in the late 1960s, and marshals were instructed in combating fires. Competence was patchy at first, but taken seriously from about 1980.

Back-up cars

By the early 1970s, racing driver Herbert Linge had a fleet of specially equipped 2.2-litre Porsche 914/6s positioned all round the Nürburgring to rush to the scene of a fire and deal with it. An extension of this facility is the course car, an American concept, which is despatched from the pits to lead the pack round in the event of a crisis on the track, until such time as the obstacle is cleared and racing can resume.

By the end of the 1960s, flame-retardant overalls, underwear, balaclavas, gloves and boots were coming in, both for drivers and for the mechanics. During the 1980s, fire crews in the pits became similarly attired; sometimes it's difficult to know who is the driver and who is carrying out the refuelling.

Bell-Star-type full-face helmets replaced the open-face variety in single-seaters, so the driver began to look like a sort of knight in armour. By the mid-1980s, the driver had a breather tube going into his helmet to supply oxygen for a few vital seconds in the event of him becoming trapped in a blazing wreck.

As the new generation of 3.0-litre cars came in for 1966, so rubber bag fuel tanks started to be incorporated, and as the monocoque

chassis replaced the spaceframe, the survival cell – with its carbon-fibre composite construction – became stronger and stronger. In the early 1970s it was merely a concept, but two decades later it had become a reality. FIA President Max Moseley's stated aim is to 'make it extremely difficult to hurt yourself in a Formula 1 car'. In 1975, a 50mph impact in an F1 car could wreck it, whereas in 1995 the tub would withstand a 150mph impact. Gradually all these changes were enshrined in FIA law, and scrutineering before and after races got tougher and tougher. For example, a helmet has to be within its safety date, or you don't race. And that's before the car gets the once-over.

The moves towards serious safety precautions were started in 1966 by Jackie Stewart and quickly taken up by the Grand Prix Drivers' Association, led by Swede Jo Bonnier. They were seen as crusaders and attacked as such by certain purists. But too many drivers had died or been injured through a lack of protection. In the wake of his frightening Spa accident, Jackie campaigned for Armco barriers to line the circuits, preventing cars leaving the track like his had, and needless accidents like the one which had cost Jim Clark his life.

After Armco lined the vast majority of circuits, those with decent run-off areas needed something to prevent contact with the steel barrier. So in the mid-1970s a glut of netted catch fencing popped up

In 1965, drivers wore cotton overalls, goggles and open-face helmets (above) while spectator protection (left) consisted of one row of straw bales.

Modern-day barriers, tyre walls, emergency services and (right) enhanced driver protection.

outside every corner that was worth the name. When drivers got injured by the fence posts which supported the netting, the circuit owners introduced sand and gravel traps to retard the errant cars. Once in, there was no getting out.

Side tracks

As purpose-built circuits like the new Nürburgring came in with the mid-1980s, so the wider margins and run-off areas alongside the track were incorporated. In the old days, road circuits featured all the typical obstacles at the track side, from kerbs, lamp standards and letter boxes, protected only by straw bales. Go to the Isle of Man motorcycle TT and see how racing used to be set. The transformation was a slow process anywhere outside the regularly used commercial tracks.

Even at the Player's Grand Prix at Dublin's Phoenix Park in 1974, the spectators were restrained by nothing more than a rope, with the additional hazard of the odd stray dog and child. All the familiar hazards of the 1950s remained, from park benches to high kerbs, and at the end of the two-day meeting hardly a car was left undamaged. If you think that's bad, picture the 1971 Mexican Grand Prix, where spectators were actually lying on the track with their instamatics, trying to get dramatic pictures of the cars. In rallying it can only be a matter of time before there is a serious accident involving spectators. In the Portuguese TAP Rally it is even regarded by some elements as macho to touch the cars as they hurtle by.

Spectators have always been vulnerable. The worst accident was the well-documented 1955 Le Mans tragedy, where over 80 spectators died in the stand opposite the pits. All that separated them from Levegh's doomed Mercedes was an earth bank. Things only improved marginally in the wake of that disaster. Similarly, the response to Alfonso de

Portago's crash on the 1957 Mille Miglia, killing himself, co-driver Ed Nelson and ten spectators, was to ban the race. After Farina had accidentally slain eleven spectators in Argentina, nothing was done.

Safety measures to protect drivers also went hand in hand with spectator protection. Today there are excessively high mesh fences –Indy-style – separating the stands and certain enclosures from the action. But how high is high enough? At Imola in 1994, a wheel from the JJ Lehto/Pedro Lamy incident flew into the stand, injuring five. Even Armco is not necessarily enough. Improperly installed, it has been responsible for a number of driver and spectator fatalities, and sometimes cars have simply gone over the top of it, like Stommelen at Montjuich in 1975, or Elio de Angelis, terminally, at Paul Ricard. When Alan McNish's F3000 jumped the Armco at Silverstone, a marshal was killed. Ayrton Senna's death at Imola demonstrates that no safety measures are ever absolutely foolproof.

Jochen Rindt
(1942-1970) World Champion 1970

Jochen Rindt remains the only Formula 1 World Champion to have won the title posthumously. By the Italian Grand Prix at Monza in 1970, he had accumulated sufficient points to gain the Championship, provided none of his rivals – Rodriguez, Regazzoni or Ickx – beat his score in the remainder of the season. They did not. His tally prior to his fatal accident practising for Monza gave him the title.

Rindt's reputation was that of a brilliant racing driver who could wring the last drop of potential out of a car. Although he was known as the King of Formula 2 during the mid- to late 1960s, he didn't win a single Grand Prix for five seasons, until late in 1969. By then, he was regarded by no less an authority than Jackie Stewart as a driver of the same calibre as Nuvolari and Clark. No-one got their car as sideways and hauled it back in shape. Said Stewart: 'Only too often did we imagine he'd overcooked it – but he never did.'

A solid background

In Spain in 1969, the rear wing on Rindt's Lotus 49 collapsed. He crashed into Hill.

Although universally hailed as Austrian, Karl Jochen Rindt was born to wealthy parents in Mainz-am-Rhein, Germany, on 18 April 1942. His father was a spice mill owner, his Austrian mother a lawyer, but they were killed in a bombing raid on Hamburg in 1943. Jochen was raised by his maternal grandparents in Graz, Austria, and held himself to be Austrian rather than German. An insubordinate schoolboy, Rindt was later dispatched to England in 1959, and spent a great deal of time sailing from Chichester. He was also a consummate skier and water-skier. The proximity to Goodwood gave him his first taste of motor racing. Having already learned

to drive – under age – in a VW Beetle, his grandfather bought him a Simca Montlhéry for his 18th birthday. Jochen drove it in local rallies and hill-climbs, but he hungered for something with more performance. His widowed grandmother bought a race-prepared Alfa Romeo Giulietta TI, and Jochen was sponsored by the Graz dealer. He didn't disappoint, beating bigger 3.8 Jaguars at Aspern, Vienna in 1962. Eight more successes with the Alfa followed in races and hill-climbs and the following season he went single-seater racing with a Formula Junior Cooper-Ford T59. Fastest in practice at his first event at Vallelunga, Rome, he won the second at Cesanatico, ahead of Italy's top FJ drivers. His contemporaries in Formula Junior included Hulme, Rees, Attwood, Revson and Schlesser.

He risked all financially in 1964 to get into Formula 2. This involved selling the family spice mill and the FJ Cooper as well as his road car, to buy a new Brabham BT10. He managed to get sponsorship from the far-sighted Ford of Austria and the BP petroleum company. The Brabham was powered by the Ford-Cosworth SCA unit and, aged 22, he took on the motor racing establishment.

First race was at the Nürburgring, a daunting prospect at the best of times in those days, but he came in fourth. At the Whitsun meeting at Mallory Park, he was second to Jim Clark and Graham Hill. At Crystal Palace the following day, Jochen and countryman Kurt Ahrens were lined up in the first heat against the likes of Pete Arundell, David Hobbs and Alan Rees. Having been second in the heat, Rindt was in the final against Graham Hill, Jim Clark and Denny Hulme. He won from Hill, Rees and Arundell. As *Motor Sport* put it, he was 'driving beautifully and hardly putting a wheel wrong throughout the race.'

Breaking into Formula 1

Rob Walker gave Rindt his first chance in a Grand Prix. He invited him to drive his Brabham-BRM BT11 at Zeltweg and Rindt was in third place when his steering broke on lap 58 – just one more mechanical failure brought on by the poor track surface. There was also an offer to drive for Ferrari in sports car events but conflicting fuel contracts ruled that out.

For 1965, Rindt was signed up by Cooper for Formula 1, but his only finish of distinction in the outclassed Cooper-Climax was fourth at the Nürburgring, with a sixth at Watkins Glen. In Formula 2 though, Rindt drove for the Roy Winkelmann team and took first place at Rheims-Geux in the Brabham BT16, followed by third placings at Pau and Vallelunga.

There was the compensation of victory at Le Mans, however, when Rindt and Masten Gregory brought Chinetti's NART Ferrari 250LM through to win, after all the Ford Mk IIs, Cobras and works P2 Ferraris had fallen by the wayside. In fact, Rindt and Gregory forced the pace to a great extent. Their car was in the pits early on with a failed condenser and lost ten laps. Rindt was all for quitting, but Masten persuaded him to give it a go, and Rindt agreed on the understanding they drove it flat-out for the remaining 21 hours. Back then, most cars ran for the entire race with one change of pads and tyres, but the 250LM went through six sets of tyres and brake pads, and was often on two wheels

through the bends. It was in such a state after they'd won that the differential failed as it was entering the paddock.

Driving for Cooper again in 1966, Rindt was initially a front runner at Monaco, then at Spa-Francorchamps he had a 20-lap duel with Surtees' Ferrari 312 in treacherous conditions. Having spun several times – including one at 180mph – he did well to finish second, his Cooper-Maserati T81 by now in handling problems. He was fourth at Rheims-Geux, in a race that was dominated by the Ferraris and Repco-Brabhams. The same scenario held at Brands Hatch, with the Cooper-Maserati, on rain tyres, chasing Brabham. As the track dried, Rindt fell back to finish fifth. He was third at the Nürburgring in the wake of Surtees' similar car in another wet race, and at Monza he was third, a lap down on the Ferraris of Scarfiotti and Parkes and Hulme's Brabham. Second place at Watkins Glen took Rindt to third in the World Championship table, and in a better car he would undoubtedly have had a better chance. His F1 season was only a success in so far as he managed to keep an underpowered and overweight car going as others retired.

In 1966, Formula 2 was Brabham and Hulme's year with the Brabham-Honda and, although Rindt was usually well placed, they won every race except one. This was the Motor Show 200 at Brands Hatch. Rindt won his heat and the final – the last race for the 1.0-litre F2 – driving a Winkelmann-entered Brabham-Cosworth, beating Brabham,

Clark and all. Rindt was also active in touring car racing in 1966. He drove for Alfa Romeo's Autodelta competitions subsidiary, run by ex-Ferrari and ATS engineering supremo Dr Carlo Chiti. The team ran the lightweight Alfa Romeo Giulia GTA coupés, which won the European Touring Car Championship four times. Rindt's contribution was a win at the Sebring 4-Hours and, at the rain-soaked Snetterton 500kms he provided an entertaining dice with the Alan Mann Lotus-Cortinas of Jackie Stewart and Sir John Whitmore.

Jochen hung on with Cooper during the 1967 World Championship season, and the new T86 chassis which appeared in time for the British Grand Prix was a lighter car, but one that was seriously outclassed by the new Lotus 49. Only Pedro Rodriguez seemed to be able to make the Cooper-Maserati work, following on from Surtees' success in the previous year's Mexican Grand Prix, by winning the 1967 opener at Kyalami. Rodriguez was fifth at Monaco, while Rindt was fourth at Spa-Francorchamps. Jochen had nothing to show for his endeavours during the mid-season, but brought the ponderous Cooper-Maserati home fourth at Monza. By this time, relations between him and John Cooper had deteriorated, and for 1968 Jochen elected to join Brabham. He was attracted by the prospect of more consistency, in the light of Brabham's and Hulme's recent World Championship successes.

A brush with disaster

Back in May, Jochen had an extremely lucky escape when his Eagle's accelerator jammed at Indianapolis. Steering the car into the retaining wall at an angle, he bounced along it, the car reducing itself with every impact. When the left rear wheel was torn off, the revs rocketed and the engine exploded. When the blazing car had slowed enough, he baled out. In a borrowed Eagle, he started from the back of the grid, and retired after 121 laps, $10,000 the richer.

In Formula 2, the Championship situation was confused in 1967. The French ran a series where it was the entrant who gained the points, and other organisers ran races only for non-graded (those yet to win a Grand Prix) Formula 1 drivers. However, in F2 as a whole, Rindt was by far the most successful individual. He won nine out of 15 F2 races he entered, to become the 1967 European Champion. Possibly the most significant of these events was the Guards Trophy at Brands Hatch on August Bank Holiday Monday, where his 1600cc Brabham-Cosworth beat Stewart and Schlesser and set a new F2 lap record.

Also in 1967 Rindt drove a works Porsche in a couple of World Sportscar Championship races, sharing a 910 with Gerhard Mitter at Sebring, Daytona and the Monza 1000kms, where they were third. At the BOAC 1000kms he partnered Graham Hill but their Porsche 910's 2.2-litre flat-8 engine failed. At the following year's BOAC event he was critical of the Porsche 907's ability to hold together when driven by someone of his calibre, so they got Scarfiotti to drive instead. Mitter and the Italian came second.

Rindt and Masten Gregory thrashed their Ferrari 250LM to victory at Le Mans in 1965.

Undoubtedly Rindt's greatest coup during 1967 was his marriage in Helsinki in March to Nina, daughter of Finnish F2 driver Kurt Lincoln. They'd met in Budapest in 1963, courted in Paris, and moved from Jochen's Lugano flat to a home near Geneva. By mid-1970 the Rindts were living in the chalet of ex-heavyweight boxer Ingmar Johansson while a new home was built, by which time their daughter Natascha was two. Nina's best friend was Sally Courage, wife of Piers, and they became an inseparable foursome around the race circuits. The Stewarts were also close friends of the Rindts, and the new home was to be close to Jackie and Helen's, built on land bought from Jo Bonnier.

Jochen respected Brabham enormously and the Australian always saw to it that Jochen had the better car. Ron Tauranac's chassis were more compliant than most, enabling the driver to get more out of them. Jochen developed the ability to describe a problem with his car and Jack would sort it out. By now, Jochen also had a very capable manager by the name of Bernie Ecclestone.

At Kyalami for the 1968 opener, Rindt's Brabham-Repco BT24 was third, behind the Lotus 49s of Clark and Hill. Then there was a dearth of placings, sometimes due to trivial factors, like being late for the start at Jarama because they were drinking tea in the pits, and Rindt sitting in what amounted to a bath of petrol for ten laps at Rouen, having damaged his fuel tank running over the wreckage of Schlesser's Honda. For a while it looked as if Jochen had jumped ship too soon, as Scarfiotti, Lucien Bianchi and Vic Elford achieved some reasonable results with Cooper-BRMs at Jarama, Monaco, Spa, and Rouen. Then Scarfiotti, ex-hill-climb champion, was killed in such an event at Rossfeld. Jochen was greatly saddened when Mitter was killed a year later. As a result of the deaths of these colleagues, Rindt cut down on the number of races he did outside his F1 and F2 commitments.

In fact, Jochen's only success with Brabham in 1968 was third place at a wet and foggy Nürburgring behind Stewart and Hill – whom he very nearly caught after the Englishman spun on the last lap.

In F2, with Winkelmann Racing, Jochen won at Thruxton on Easter Monday – which he did on several occasions – Zolder, Crystal Palace,

Hockenheim, Tulln-Langenlebarn, and Enna-Pergusa. He considered the Zolder race to be his finest in F2, having fought back from last place after being spun on the grid by Brian Redman, and tigered his way back to the front. His main rivals in 1968 were Alan Rees, Ickx and Stewart.

In the fallow period between seasons, Jochen staged the 'Jochen Rindt Racing Car Show' in Vienna, opened by Stewart. There appeared the possibility that Winkelmann would commission an F1 car for the 1969 season, funded by BP and Firestone and designed by Robin Herd. The project fell apart when the sponsors changed their minds, and Herd's design became the McLaren M7. Rindt now seriously craved a car with which he could win. Matra was a possibility, and Brabham promised Ford-Cosworth engines, but Chapman offered a bigger purse.

With some reluctance, Rindt chose the Lotus option, because Chapman could produce anything he wanted. But things got off to a bad start. A mistake by a mechanic caused a bad accident in the Tasman series, and when Rindt got to Kyalami and found Chapman had hired Andretti as well as Hill, he was most annoyed. Brabham then put his Ford-engined car on pole, to rub salt in the wound.

By the Spanish Grand Prix, Jochen had just signed the Lotus contract, naming him as equal number one driver with Hill. Starting from pole position, Jochen shot into the lead in his Lotus 49. Wings were the order of the day and Lotus' were the biggest – on the principal that the car was by now two years old and needed all the help it could get. On lap nine, one of Hill's wing-supports broke, and he crashed heavily, leaving debris everywhere. He and the Lotus pit tried to alert Rindt to the possible danger to himself, but it was too late. On lap 20, Rindt's also buckled as the car crested the same rise. The car rode the guard rail, struck the remains of Hill's car and careered along the track upside down. Hill managed to free Rindt. The Austrian suffered a broken nose and jaw. After leaving hospital, he campaigned for a ban on wings, which the FIA endorsed prior to Monaco.

The four-wheel drive Lotus 63 was unveiled at Zandvoort, but Jochen refused to drive it, saying that an untried car shouldn't be raced, or tested, during official practice. He drove the 49 instead, dicing with Stewart until its front suspension failed. In the heat at big-dipper Clermont-Ferrand, he was sick every two laps, and was horrified to find before the race that steering column cracks had been found on both Hill's and his own car. In the event he retired, genuinely ill.

Jochen was of the opinion that Chapman worked the mechanics too hard. At Silverstone they ran four cars, a pair of 63s for Miles and Bonnier, and 49s for Hill and Rindt. Jochen lost the race when he ran out of fuel six laps before the end. Hill, and Siffert in the Rob Walker 49, also ran out. Ecclestone and Rindt started to hatch a plan for 1970 involving another project designed by Robin Herd. This actually came to fruition as MARCH, but without Jochen and Bernie.

At Monza, Jochen finished second to Jackie, and he was third at Mosport, pipped by Brabham on superior Goodyears. Finally at Mosport, Rindt emerged the convincing winner from a battle with Stewart. That elusive first victory was tinged with sadness after Graham Hill was badly injured in a high-speed accident.

That was it as far as F1 was concerned, but in F2 Rindt enjoyed more successes in the semi-works Lotus 59B still run by Winkelmann Racing. He won at Thruxton, Pau, Zolder and Tulln-Langenlebarn. Team manager Alan Rees was involved in the MARCH team project, with which Rindt again tried to involve himself. Amon ended up in the March seat. There were offers from Matra, Ferrari, and Brabham for the 1970

season, but more money and the prospect of driving the new Lotus 72 would swing Jochen Chapman's way.

A last-gasp win

When Brabham won at Kyalami, then set fastest lap at Jarama, Rindt's choice once again looked doubtful. At Monaco he reverted to the old Lotus 49 and, as a thrilling race drew to a close, Jochen found himself only 1.5 seconds behind Brabham, who was leading. At the very last corner – the Gasworks Hairpin then – Brabham braked too late and ploughed into the straw bales, handing the victory to Rindt.

From pole position at Zandvoort, Jochen pulled out an immediate lead, and never looked like being challenged. Jochen's season was beginning to look good, although the death of Piers Courage dampened down the celebrations. At Clermont-Ferrand, early leaders Ickx and Beltoise fell by the wayside, and Jochen won there too. At Brands Hatch, Ickx's Ferrari failed again, leaving Jochen and Jack to fight for the lead. When the Lotus driver missed a gear, Brabham was through, only to run out of fuel with just Clearways to go. An astonished Rindt passed him as he freewheeled towards the line.

Hockenheim was the venue for the German Grand Prix, and it proved to be a battleground for Ickx and Rindt, with numerous changes of leader. The final switch put Rindt on top of the podium, from Ickx, Hulme and Fittipaldi, the Brazilian driving in his second Grand Prix. More than 100,000 Austrian fans went to the Osterreichring to see Jochen in action, but they were to be disappointed. His engine failed on lap 21. By this time Rindt had also had four wins and two seconds in F2 races, driving a Lotus 69 managed by Ecclestone.

Then came Monza. In practice Jochen remembered that the previous year he had achieved greater top speed down the straights with no wing – and thus less wind resistance – on the 72 and tried it once again. In theory he could achieve 205mph like that with the right gearing. John Miles in the other 72 tried his car without the rear wing, and promptly demanded his mechanics refit it, as the car's handling was most odd without it. But Rindt, feeling confident, went out a second time to try it in final qualifying. Hulme was following him down to the Parabolica, and saw the Lotus twitch left under braking, and the car pitched into the guard rail at 100mph. The chisel nose dug under the rail, breaking it off, while Jochen, who hated wearing crutch straps with his harness, submarined under his dashboard. He stood no chance.

The most popular theory is that a brake shaft to one of the inboard front discs sheared, and the car was too aerodynamically unstable to be fully controllable under those circumstances. As far as the 1970 World Championship was concerned, Jochen had done enough to win it posthumously. The final tally was Rindt, 45 points, Ickx, 40 points, and Regazzoni, 33 points.

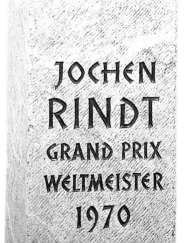

JOCHEN RINDT GRAND PRIX WELTMEISTER 1970

In the 1950s and most of the 1960s, racing cars were painted in their country's national racing colour. Thus you had British Racing Green, Italian Corso Rosso, French blue, Belgian yellow, German silver or white, American white with a blue stripe. In 1968, all that changed. Suddenly we had red-white-and-gold Lotuses and white-and-brown-striped BRMs in Formula 1. The sponsors had arrived, bringing with them the open cheque books

which, throughout the 1970s, brought about major technological changes, exalted driver retainers and transfer fees which had never previously been seen in the sport. Egos blossomed and, just as quickly, were dashed.

The pressures these changes wrought took racing into another league. In the early part of the 1970s it was still reasonably relaxed. The major players carried on as they had during the 1960s but they could now rely on being able to afford engine rebuilds as required, while hiring the best drivers. All that was required in return was turning the car into a mobile billboard. Everyone and everything connected to the teams now wore the sponsors logo bold as brass. Drivers gave press conferences and referred to the cars not as Lotuses but as John Player Specials or Marlboro-BRMs.

As the decade progressed, sponsorship mushroomed. More funds meant bigger and better facilities, the teams and the governing bodies became wealthier and the cars evolved more quickly. In the 1970s Grand Prix stars were still driving in other formulae.

Since then, however, there has gradually been more and more contractual pressure on the top F1 stars to limit their activities to Grands Prix alone.

The firm that got the most out of sponsorship was Ford, who bankrolled the Cosworth Ford DFV, the most widely used engine of the period. And when Renault appeared with the turbocharged unit in 1977, F1 was launched into the modern pressure zone – one of extraordinary proportions.

The Seventies

Commercial Pressures

Jackie Stewart

(1939–) World Champion 1969, 1971, 1973

Some Grand Prix drivers became household names because of their talents, and through having survived long enough for their names to stick – Juan Manuel Fangio and Stirling Moss, for instance. Perhaps only Graham Hill became one by force of personality. It was Jackie Stewart, however, who deliberately started the serious driver-as-personality cult and, having established himself as Champion, took full advantage of the position. Whereas Grand Prix stars of the 1950s would have been hard pressed to make £10,000 a year, by the end of Stewart's career, £200,000 was possible. Salaries used to be made up of prize money and bonuses, of retainers from fuel and tyre companies for the few at the top. Jackie Stewart transformed the orbit of the racing driver from cockpit and paddock to boardroom, TV studio, advertising agency, commentary box and lecture theatre. He lifted the World Champion's status from sportsman to celebrity, rubbing shoulders with film and pop stars, royalty, chat-show hosts and senior politicians.

Young Jackie with an early sporting catch.

Who can blame him? It was the culmination of a trend that grew through the optimism and materialistic culture of the 1960s. Motor sport probably wouldn't be anything like as popular today if Stewart hadn't been the focus for media attention back in the early 1970s. To his eternal credit, though, he used his influence to bring about the most sweeping changes in circuit safety, from compulsory wearing of seat belts to the installation of Armco crash barriers around all circuits. He campaigned for fire engines, for resurfacing and tree-felling near track-sides; he experimented with different crash helmets, and drove with a spanner taped to his steering wheel for emergencies.

His campaign actually began three years before his first World title – at Spa-Francorchamps in 1966, when he was pulled, soaked in petrol, from the wreck of his BRM, which was ready to erupt into a fireball at any second. For this, he and fellow campaigner Jo Bonnier of the GPDA (Grand Prix Drivers' Association) were reviled by certain purists, who saw the removal of unnecessary dangers as detrimental to the sport.

John Young Stewart was born in Dumbarton on 11 June 1939. His father Robert had a garage and had raced motorcycles as an amateur. Jackie's elder brother Jimmy – eight years his senior – introduced him to motor sport, as he drove for the legendary Ecurie Ecosse team in C-type Jaguars. A crash at Le Mans in a works Aston Martin ended Jimmy's promising career. Young Jackie, then 15, was undeterred. He left Dumbarton Academy and went to work at his father's Dumbuck garage, first as a petrol pump attendant, then as a mechanic. Robert and Jimmy made him a partner.

Jackie knew that it was unlikely that he would get into motor racing with parental consent, bearing in mind his brother's narrow escape. Instead, Jackie became a crack shot and in 1959 joined the British clay pigeon shooting team. He was good enough to have been considered for the British Olympic team, and it's likely he would have been given a place for the 1964 games. But by then he was out on the circuits.

'I reckoned that as a driver I was being paid for my skill. I wasn't being paid to risk my life'

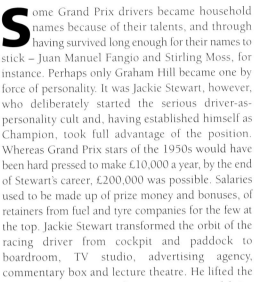

Stewart won the Vanwall Trophy at Snetterton in 1965 in a Lotus 32.

One of the customers whose cars the Stewarts prepared, Glaswegian Barry Filer, offered Jackie a drive at a club race at Charterhall, a now defunct Scottish circuit. Jackie declined, not wishing to upset his mother. But Jackie was unable to resist the challenge of speed for long. His mother found out eventually when the local paper mentioned his racing in the context of a report on his marriage to Helen McGregor.

The golden touch

Jackie's first taste of circuit driving was when he went to Oulton Park to have a go in Filer's Porsche 356 Super 90. In 1961, he raced Filer's Marcos GT, the extraordinary wooden-chassis, fibreglass-bodied offspring of Jem Marsh and Frank Costin. In four local events at Charterhall it proved successful in Stewart's hands, and Filer let him drive his Aston Martin DB4GT, which was state-of-the-art technology. At this stage he was unsure which way his future lay. A series of test drives in 1962 at Oulton Park in the Stewart family's E-type and Filer's Aston and AC Ace-Bristol looked promising. In the Jaguar, Jackie was as quick as Roy Salvadori had been in 1961. There would be no going back. The 12-bores were confined to leisure use for the time being.

On Easter Saturday 1962, Stewart won a couple of events at Rufforth, near Leeds, in the E-type, and this led to Ecurie Ecosse boss David Murray giving him a winning drive in the Tojeiro-Buick EE Mk 2 at Charterhall. He also won a club race at Goodwood in the team's Cooper Monaco T49, and was a member of the winning Jaguar team in the five-hour relay at Oulton Park. He had well and truly arrived on the club scene at least, and took the Ron Flockhart and Chris Bristow memorial trophies.

For the first few months of 1964, Jackie drove Ecurie Ecosse's old stock – a Tojeiro Ford and the Cooper-Monaco, and Charles Bridges' Lotus Cortina. A casual recommendation from Goodwood's Robin McKay saw Stewart at the wheel of one of Ken Tyrrell's Formula 3 Cooper-BMC T72s, alongside ace Mini Cooper dicer John Rhodes. In a test drive, Stewart had gone quicker than Bruce McLaren, who had already graduated to Formula 1. Jackie's performance at a rain drenched Snetterton, when he won a ten-lapper by 44 seconds, led to the

immediate offer of an F1 drive in a Cooper. Again, he turned it down, preferring to build up some time in F3. He ended the season with the Express and Star F3 title under his belt, having won all but two races in the series. He also raced John Coombs' E-type, and was faster than the regular drivers in Ian Walker's Lotus Elan R26. By mid-season he was a reserve driver for the Maranello Concessionaires' Ferrari GTO Le Mans entry.

Always on the lookout for up-and-coming talent, Colin Chapman gave Jackie a try in a works Lotus 33 at the unofficial qualifying session for the British Grand Prix. Jackie held back from accepting the Lotus boss's offer, but did take him up on outings in the works Lotus Cortinas and the F2 Lotus 32. First time out in this he was second at Clermont-Ferrand, and won the Marlboro 12-hours in a Lotus Cortina.

Stewart's Formula 1 debut was in December 1964 at the Rand GP in South Africa, deputising for the injured Jim Clark. Although two half-shafts broke at the start of the first heat, Jackie finished second in the second heat. He rejected offers to drive for Lotus and Cooper in 1965, opting to go to BRM as number two to Graham Hill.

Playing himself in with a sensible drive, he finished sixth at Kyalami in 1965. At the non-championship Daily Express Trophy at Silverstone in May, Stewart scored his first F1 victory. There were many other fine drives during the course of the year, particularly at Spa-Francorchamps, Clermont-Ferrand and Zandvoort, where he was second, and Monaco where he was third. Jackie had long since shaken off the apprentice role by Monza, and took the honours at the Italian GP after an enthralling battle with his team-mate Graham Hill in the 1.5-litre BRM P261. With his win, three second places, a third, a fifth and a sixth, he was third in the World Championship.

World-class drivers drove all kinds of machinery in those days. They thought nothing of hopping from an F1 car into a sports car for another event, and maybe a saloon after that for the 'tin-top' thrash. Nowadays they just specialise in single seaters if they aspire to get to the top. In 1964, Stewart had started in no less than 53 races, covering touring cars, sports cars, F2, and F1.

In 1965 he entered fewer events, but with more variety. As well as]the World Championship series, he drove Ken Tyrrell's F2 Cooper-BRM T75 – which was largely unsuccessful – and took third in John Surtees' Lola T70 Chevrolet in the long-distance Guards Trophy race at Brands Hatch. Perhaps more remarkably, he was placed tenth at Le Mans in the extraordinary Rover-BRM gas turbine car – a piece of technology subsequently left largely unexplored.

In the low-season Tasman series, Jackie drove the 2.1-litre BRM P261, and emerged Tasman champion. Despite the new 3.0-litre Formula 1 regulations for 1966, the 2.1-litre was thought to be a more appropriate power unit to contest Monaco, and Jackie took the honours there.

Jackie then drove the John Mecom-entered Lola T90 Ford V8 at Indianapolis, until with just 20 laps to go the engine gave up.

A narrow escape

It was in the next event on the F1 calendar that Stewart's career – and his life – came closest to ending. Spa-Francorchamps is susceptible to swift changes in the weather, and in pouring rain Stewart's was just one of many cars which spun off. His BRM went down into a concrete drainage conduit and overturned. Fortunately, Graham Hill and Bob Bondurant were also having problems of their own at the same place, and Hill was about to drive off again when he noticed Stewart's car in the ditch below. Hill and Bondurant scrambled down, and managed to extract the petrol-soaked Scot. There was a risk of an explosion, and Stewart was lucky to get away with a mere broken shoulder, a cracked rib and bruising.

Just a couple of months later, he was back on the scene with a fourth place at Zandvoort and fifth at the Nürburgring. The BRMs were in a fallow patch by then, still trying to sort out the complex H-16 unit powering the P83. Jackie still drove for Ken Tyrrell in the F2 Matra, but these were early days for the French marque. One highlight in an otherwise unsuccessful season was a shared win in the Rothmans 12-Hour sports car race at Surfers' Paradise, Australia, in a Ferrari 250LM.

In 1967 he had his one and only works Ferrari drive: it was in the gorgeous 4.0-litre P4 sports car, along with Chris Amon, at the BOAC 500 at Brands Hatch. Stewart finished second to Phil Hill/Mike Spence in the winged Chaparral, and was relaxed enough to wave to his fans in the closing stages of the race.

As for the F1 season, it was pretty well devoid of any success. He finished second at Spa in the H16 BRM behind Dan Gurney's Eagle-Weslake V12, and, back in the BRM V8, was third at the French GP on the Le Mans 'Bugatti' circuit. That was about it. In Formula 2 however, things were better and he won at Karlskoga, Enna-Pergusa, Oulton Park and Albi, driving the Matra MS5 and MS7.

For 1968, Stewart parted company with BRM and signed with Tyrrell. The Ripley, Surrey-based timber merchant had secured a supply of Ford-Cosworth DFV engines to power the Matra MS10 chassis and, although the car was not brilliant, Stewart managed to win at Zandvoort in pouring rain, at the Nürburgring in fog, and at Watkins Glen, New York state. A wrist injury sustained in an F2 race earlier in the year prevented him from racing at Monaco and in Spain and, at Indy, as at Zandvoort, he had to wear a plastic sleeve. As the F1 series went to Mexico for the last round, Stewart was in with a chance of the Championship. His engine let him down, however, and Graham Hill secured the crown.

At this point Jackie and Helen, together with young sons Paul and Mark, exiled themselves to Switzerland, which was convenient for commuting to the European races as well as financially expedient.

In 1969, Stewart's driving talents matured, and it seemed he had it all in the bag. Ken Tyrrell's Matra International Team had the resources

of Elf Petroleum, allied to the Matra MS10 and would soon have the Matra MS80, powered by the Cosworth DFV engine. The MS80 was broader in the beam, accommodating the bag fuel tanks in its flanks.

Jackie won at Kyalami from Graham Hill and Denny Hulme, and took victory at Barcelona from McLaren and Beltoise in the other Matra-Ford. At Barcelona's hilly Montjuich Park, Stewart inherited what had seemed like certain victory for the luckless Chris Amon when the engine of the latter's Ferrari seized. More significantly, Jackie's crusading for barriers was vindicated when the Lotuses of Hill and Rindt crashed heavily as their aerofoils collapsed. They were almost certainly saved from disaster by the Armco.

Stewart set fastest lap at Monaco, leading from Amon for a while. Then the Matra of Beltoise broke a driveshaft, and two laps later so did Stewart's. Ninety laps around the Dutch sand dunes at Zandvoort saw Stewart come through a race of attrition from Siffert's Lotus, Amon's Ferrari, Hulme's McLaren, and Ickx's Brabham.

In spite of only having 13 cars to watch at Clermont-Ferrand, the French enthusiasts were ecstatic to see Stewart's blue Matra pounding away at the opposition, and only Beltoise and Ickx could stay with him. The Frenchman couldn't find a way past the Belgian – much to the disgust of the partisan crowd – until the last lap, to make it a Matra 1-2.

Stewart escaped from a nasty practice crash at Silverstone, but was given Beltoise's car for the race. It quickly developed into a duel with

Stewart powers his F3 Cooper-BMC through Monaco's Casino Square in 1964.

Rindt, only for the Austrian to run out of fuel seven laps from the finish. It began to look as if Stewart was going to run away with the season. Then things changed at the Nürburgring. Ickx made a poor start, but was soon on Stewart's tail. The lead changed three times, then the Matra began to have gear selector problems. Stewart had to let the Belgian go.

Slipstreaming to success

At Monza it looked as if it could turn out to be anyone's race. Having done his homework in practice and sorted out the appropriate gears for the slipstreaming epic – such a significant strategy that a tow could be obtained from a car as far as 250 metres ahead – Stewart soon caught and passed Rindt, only to strike a hare. The animal was dead, so there was no point in the driver reducing pace. Stewart was at the head of an eight-strong posse that was going in search of a win, which included Rindt, Courage, Siffert, Hulme, McLaren, Beltoise and Hill. Hill took the lead briefly. Then as two Englishmen, a Kiwi and a Swiss dropped out, it was down to Frenchman, Austrian, Kiwi and Scot. At the Parabolica, the last bend on the last lap, it looked like Beltoise's race. But Rindt, McLaren and Stewart got the tow out of the bend just right, and the Scot pipped the Austrian by inches.

It was sufficient to give Stewart the Championship, and, as the drivers moved on to Canada, subsequent results were academic. Ickx and Stewart staged a repeat of their German tussle, but Ickx made a move which nudged Stewart into a spin, and retirement. The other North American race found Stewart retired by lap 36 with an oil leak, and although he led the final round at Mexico City for five early laps, his Goodyears weren't a match for the Firestones, and he ended up fourth. He had, nevertheless, accrued the highest number of points that anyone had ever scored – 63 – taken on the best five scores from the first six races, and the best four scores from the last five races. Ickx was second on 37, with McLaren third on 26.

At the 1965 Le Mans 24-hours, Stewart and Hill shared the quiet Rover-BRM.

New faces in Formula 1

As the Championship entered its 21st year, a crop of new contenders was set to challenge the old brigade. The likes of Clay Reggazoni, Ronnie Peterson, Emerson Fittipaldi, Francois Cevert and Reine Wisell were waiting in the wings. Sadly, some stars lost their lives. McLaren died at Goodwood testing his latest CanAm car, Courage was killed at Zandvoort when his Frank Williams-run de Tomaso crashed and burned, and Rindt never lived to know for sure that he was Champion.

Jackie's new Tyrrell team-mate for 1970 was Johnny Servoz-Gavin, and the pair raced new March-Fords, while Beltoise and Pescarolo drove new Matra-Simcas. Having led at Kyalami, Stewart was demoted to third by Brabham and Hulme. He took his revenge at Jarama with an easy victory over McLaren. Jackie led initially at Monaco and Clermont-Ferrand but these races were won by Rindt in the old Lotus 49, and Rodriguez in the BRM P153.

Stewart emerged third at Zandvoort from a three-way contest with Ickx and Rindt, the Austrian in the new Lotus 72 claiming the win.

After triumphs in the subsequent French, British and German Grands Prix, Rindt had the title well-and-truly sewn up. But in his quest for more straight-line speed at Monza he compromised the Lotus' aerodynamics. The inherently unstable car broke a brake shaft as Rindt slowed for the vast Parabolica corner, and swerved sharply and fatally into the barriers. The race was obviously going to be a gloomy affair, for Stewart as much as anyone, for he and Rindt had been firm friends.

The Italian GP developed into a fight between the Ferraris of Ickx and Reggazoni and the cars of Stewart, Oliver, Rodriguez, Stommelen, Hulme and Beltoise. Reggazoni eventually pulled away from the pack to win from Stewart and put Ferrari back on the map as a winning force.

For the Canadian round at St Jovite, Ken Tyrrell launched his new Derek Gardner-designed car, which Stewart took into an instant lead. He seemed uncatchable, but on lap 32 a stub axle broke. At Watkins Glen for the American GP the story was the same. He had lapped everyone except Ickx and Rodriguez by half distance but a faulty oil line ended his race. The winner was 23-year-old Emerson Fittipaldi, picking up the pieces at Lotus in the aftermath of Rindt's death. At the final

of its greatest contemporary exponent – and Siffert was without a partner. Almost as a tribute, Siffert placed his BRM on the front row for the Silverstone event, but Stewart trounced all the 12-cylinder cars to win from Peterson's March. Nürburgring had been treated to a safety facelift, with barriers installed, and the Tyrrell twins won convincingly, with Cevert setting fastest lap on the way.

The BRMs came good at the Osterreichring for Siffert, and at Monza for Peter Gethin, the latter winning what remains the fastest ever Grand Prix with an average speed of 150.7mph. Four cars crossed the line with a mere one-tenth of a second between them: Gethin, Peterson, Cevert and Hailwood also made it the closest four-car finish ever.

The Canadian GP at Mosport was stopped 16 laps early because of torrential rain, and Stewart was declared the winner after he'd duelled successfully with Peterson on the streaming wet track. It was Cevert's turn to win at Watkins Glen, after Stewart's mis-handling car lost

him the lead. The delighted Frenchman won the $50,000 prize money – big bucks even in those days.

Cevert was thus elevated to third place in the Championship, behind Peterson on 33 points, and Stewart, the winner on 62 points.

In 1972, for the first time since 1960, Argentina staged a Grand Prix, and local hero Carlos Reutemann, competing in his first GP, delighted his followers to claim pole position. No-one could catch Stewart in the race, however, and only Hulme got close.

The Scot retired when leading at Kyalami and Jarama, and managed only fourth at a rain-sodden Monaco. It was the start of the modern era, in which manufacturers demurred to sponsors, and the cars were named after the sponsor. 'He who pays the piper calls the tune,' as George Hadfield, one of John Player's executives put it. Thus we suddenly have Yardley-McLaren, John Player Special (alias Lotus 72D), STP-March, and Elf-Tyrrell vying for the title.

The Belgian GP was held at another all-new circuit at Nivelles-Baulers, but Stewart was ill with an ulcer and missed it. Cevert was

round on the Ricardo Rodriguez circuit at Mexico City, Stewart was the Ferraris' only challenger. But his bid failed when he ran into a stray dog.

The 12-cylinder cars didn't live up to their potential in 1971, notably Ferrari with Ickx, Reggazoni and Andretti on the strength. BRM were on the pace only occasionally, due to the brilliance of Rodriguez and Siffert, and Amon was always unlucky in the Matra MS120B. Andretti took the honours at the Kyalami opener, and Reggazoni won the non-title Race of Champions at Brands Hatch. Stewart was second in both events. But at Monaco, due to unseasonal rain storms, Andretti failed even to qualify. Stewart in Tyrrell 002 was a full second faster than Ickx in practice, and he led the way home from Ronnie Peterson.

The French Grand Prix moved venues to the new purpose-built Paul Ricard circuit in the Provence hills near Marseilles. It ranks as one of the faster circuits, and Stewart dominated, while his team-mate Cevert shook off Rodriguez to make it a Tyrrell 1-2.

A week before the British GP, Rodriguez was killed driving a Ferrari 512M at Norisring in Germany. The sports car racing word was robbed

No-one did more to enhance the status of the Grand Prix driver than Jackie Stewart.

The Brazilian GP at Sao Paulo also went to Fittipaldi's JPS, with Stewart in second place, 14 seconds behind. Stewart started the South African GP from the seventh row, having crashed into the catch fencing at 170mph in practice when a brake line burst. As he took precedence in the team hierarchy, Jackie commandeered Cevert's car, and the Frenchman had nothing to drive in practice. He therefore had to start from the back of the grid. In the race, Mike Hailwood gained the George Medal for his bravery in dragging Reggazoni from the burning wreckage of his Ferrari. In the confusion, Jackie moved to first place by lap seven to win from Peter Revson's M19C McLaren and Fittipaldi's JPS-72D.

The drivers revolt

Stewart won Silverstone's annual Spring *Daily Express* Trophy, but a broken brake disc ended his run at Barcelona while pressuring Peterson for the lead. The 1973 Belgian GP moved to Zolder, as the Flemings and the Walloon factions strove to find a circuit capable of replacing the old Spa-Francorchamps track, by now deemed too dangerous for F1 cars. Aided by Marlboro funding, Zolder was hurriedly re-tarmac'd, but too late in the day, as the surface broke up. The GPDA argued with the organisers that it was unstable – both Shadows had crashed in unofficial practice – and eventually agreement was reached that the drivers would get paid even if the race had to be stopped. By maintaining a line where the surface was best, Stewart won after harrying Fittipaldi, and Cevert was second, having led handsomely for much of the race, only to fall back with brake fade.

Stewart recovered from a bad start at Monaco to hunt down Peterson's JPS. On lap eight he was through as the Swede's engine spluttered, and the Brazilian drove as hard as he could to catch the flying Scot, setting fastest lap on the way. The laurels were for Stewart however, with Peterson fourth and Cevert fifth, demonstrating that the Elf-Tyrrells and the JPS-Lotuses were the cars of the day. The final irony was that Stewart and Fittipaldi collided in the tunnel on the slowing down lap when the Brazilian drove up to congratulate the Scot. At Monaco, Stewart had equalled Jim Clark's record of 25 GP wins, and closed to within four points of Fittipaldi for the title.

Fifth in the high-speed train which was made up by the front runners at Anderstorp for Sweden's first World Championship Grand Prix, Jackie's chances were foiled by brake problems. At the Paul Ricard circuit, Stewart stole into fourth position after pitting for a puncture, and took himself into the lead for the title.

There were three Yardley McLarens at Silverstone, for Revson, Hulme, and Scheckter. Two were on the front row with Peterson, but Scheckter's, storming through from the third row, caused the biggest of multiple pile-ups as they passed the pits at the end of lap one. Nine cars were involved. On lap seven of the re-started race, Stewart made his bid to pass Peterson at Stowe corner. Instead he went hay-making, his Tyrrell ploughing, almost invisible, through the tall grasses of the infield. Astonished photographer Charlie Knight had to run for his life, snapping all the while like a true pro. Although Stewart emerged from the undergrowth, his air-intake was blocked and he fell back to tenth.

Enormous amounts of money had been spent at Zandvoort to bring the circuit up to the latest safety standards, but this didn't extend to adequate training for fire marshals. In a repeat of the Piers Courage tragedy, the talented Roger Williamson lost his life when his March-Ford 731 caught fire; only David Purley stopped to try and extricate

second to Fittipaldi, but at Clermont-Ferrand Jackie was back. He and Hulme enjoyed a spirited chase after Amon and, when stones caused both Amon and Hulme to slow with punctures, he was through to win. Another consequence of the stones being flicked up was that Helmut Marko in a BRM was blinded in one eye as a stone pierced his visor. Peter Collins had been luckier at the Nürburgring back in 1957 when Fangio's Maserati flicked a missile and broke Collins' goggles.

Jackie and Emerson traded places several times at Brands Hatch in pursuit of Jacky Ickx's Ferrari. An oil leak put paid to the Belgian's hopes, and the Brazilian won the Players' sponsored event.

Stewart banged wheels with Reggazoni at the Nürburgring, and crashed into retirement, and at the Osterreichring he lost a good lead because of handling problems with the new Tyrrell 005. His clutch failed on the starting line at Monza, but at misty Mosport he forged into the lead on lap four to win by at least a minute with all kinds of mayhem taking place behind him. Stewart claimed pole at Watkins Glen, and asserted himself throughout the race, with Cevert emerging in second place in the other Tyrrell. It wasn't enough for the 1972 World title, which Fittipaldi won with 61 points. But Jackie had 45 points to give him second spot from Denny Hulme on 39.

'Wee Jackie' was noted for his clear thinking and tactical analysis of situations in and out of racing cars, and as the 1973 season approached he had decided that he was soon going to quit while he was ahead.

At the season's opener in Buenos Aires, Stewart led from Cevert until slowed by a puncture, putting him third behind Cevert and Fittipaldi.

Williamson from the blazing car. A nearby fire engine wasn't moved to the scene, and Purley ended up snatching an extinguisher from a reluctant marshal. All, tragically, to no avail. The race went on despite strong condemnation from drivers, especially Hulme, and the result went to Stewart and Cevert from James Hunt in the Hesketh March.

New, stringent fire-safety rules were hastily brought in and the Nürburgring responded with a Porsche 911 fire-car. On a 14.19-mile circuit, this was something of a token gesture, but the new rule where everyone was required to form up behind a pace car in an emergency was most welcome. In a crushing display of supremacy, Stewart and Cevert in their Tyrrells led the race from the start and won convincingly.

An unhelpful individual

In Austria the initial leader was Arturo Merzario, the diminutive Italian driving the new Ferrari 312 B3S. For several drivers, this appeared to be a wider car than before, since it proved very difficult to get by. This was not the case, of course; some drivers are noted 'blockers' or don't look in their mirrors enough. As Fittipaldi retired, the eventual winner was Ronnie Peterson, with Stewart nine seconds in arrears.

At Monza, Fittipaldi still had a faint hope of catching Jackie for the title, as he was still only 15 points behind. But whereas Peterson had sportingly pulled over to let Fittipaldi lead in Austria, he had no such philanthropic ideas in Italy, and led a storming race from start to finish. Fittipaldi was sufficiently annoyed to make his mind up to leave Lotus at the end of the year. Meanwhile, Jackie was the hero of the hour. Suffering from flu, he pitted with a puncture on lap eight, rejoining in 20th place. By lap 49, he was up to fourth, and that's how it finished; Peterson from Fittipaldi, and Revson third, and fourth place was enough to seal the Championship for a third time for Stewart.

Fortunately, it wasn't decided in Canada, as this race was a shambles. On lap 23, a great many of the cars came into the pits for tyre changes, and the lap scorers in these pre-computerised days couldn't keep track of who had pitted and who hadn't, and who was running in what position as they rejoined the race. Then Scheckter and Cevert had a coming together, which prompted the Frenchman to threaten the physical well-being of the South African. The Tyrrell was blocking the track, so out came the pace car. It selected New Zealander Howden Ganley's Iso-Marlboro as the lead car. But, in all probability,

Beltoise or Fittipaldi were leading at the time, and the pace car should have held station ahead of one of them. Once the pace car had gone in, the Brazilian eventually passed Ganley, and, at the end of the race, the Lotus pit thought that their man had won the race. But Revson was the one who took the chequered flag. Stewart finished up fifth in a very confusing race, and a conversion to more sophisticated Le Mans-type electronic lap timing was called for.

As Stewart prepared to enter his 100th – and probably final – Grand Prix race, at Watkins Glen, disaster struck. His personable team-mate Cevert crashed while taking the Esses flat out, and died as his Tyrrell slid upside down along the Armco. The celebratory mood evaporated instantly, and Tyrrell withdrew his cars. It was a devastating end to Stewart's year, and can only have hardened his resolve to stop racing. His final points tally for the year was 71, from Fittipaldi on 55, and Peterson, winner in the USA, on 52.

A more enjoyable aspect of the 1973 season was the guest appearance of several of the Grand Prix stars in the works Ford team contesting the European Touring Car series, with Stewart, Fittipaldi, and Scheckter driving the 2.9-litre Capris in hard-fought duels with the works BMWs and privateer Camaros. Stewart had also driven a Chaparral and Lola in the CanAm series.

Much against the wishes of his parents, Paul Stewart went racing, and his natural talents took him as far as Formula 3. He set up his own team running F3000 cars – the 1990s equivalent of F2 – and, aided and abetted by father Jackie, by the end of 1995 Paul Stewart Racing looked set to break into Formula 1. Jackie, meanwhile, has continued to be a successful businessman, endorsing Ford products, and is still a crack shot. He is frequently to be seen in the F1 paddock at Grands Prix, and if Paul gets involved, then Scotland's canny champion will presumably be around for a long time to come.

Stewart enters the Nürburgring's banked Karussel loop in 1971.

Emerson Fittipaldi

(1946–) World Champion 1972, 1974

E merson's is the archetypal storybook whizz to the top. From his arrival on the European scene in a Formula Ford in 1969, it took just 18 months for him to become team leader at Lotus. He was never a stranger to motor racing. His father Wilson was a journalist who for many years had reported on race meetings. Born in Sao Paolo, Brazil, on 12 December 1946, Emerson started racing bicycles as young as five, moving on to 50cc motorcycles as a young teenager, graduating to karts alongside elder brother Wilson. Aged 18, Emerson won the Sao Paolo Kart Championship, and was promptly brought into a local team running Renault Dauphine Gordinis. He also drove an Alpine Renault A110. This rear-engined GT car brought him the Brazilian Novices title in 1966, and he and his brother built a Formula Vee (Volkswagen engined) single seater, called the FittiVee, with which Emerson took the Brazilian FV Championship in 1967. At the same time, they also raced an Alfa Romeo Giulietta SZ, by then rather long in the tooth but relatively exotic. He had shared a racing 2-stroke DKW GT with a friend, and piloted a Corvette-engined speedboat.

Struggling for success

Brazil was not exposed to the same intensity of motor sport as Europe, and racing cars were hard to source, so a great deal of self reliance was required by budding contenders. The Fittipaldi brothers opened a car accessory shop, they built and sold karts, and had a VW tuning business. They fitted a Porsche 911 engine in an extended 356 chassis and made their own coupé body for it, in which Emerson was runner-up to Carlos Pace in the national GT Championship in 1967.

To advance his career, and find out just how good he was compared with the Europeans, Emerson had to come to Britain. He arrived in March 1969 with his friend Richard Divila, armed with a Formula Ford Merlyn Mk 2A, and they camped out in their clapped-out Cortina in the paddocks at Mallory Park and Silverstone. Successes with the Merlyn led to him being signed up by Jim Russell, who operated a racing drivers' school at Snetterton, to drive his Lotus 59 F3 car. Remarkably, Emerson ended the 1969 season as Lombank Formula 3 Champion, having won eight races. Part of the secret of his success was that he ran the car on narrower tyres than other drivers; it was thus faster down the straights.

Emerson was known to Colin Chapman because part of his deal with Jim Russell involved supplying engines for Emerson's 59. Colin offered him a seat for 1970 in a Gold Leaf Lotus 69 F2 car, alongside Jochen Rindt. There were no major successes, but a second place at Imola and a couple of thirds at Barcelona and Rouen brought third place in the European F2 Championship. Chapman was already certain that Emerson would be Champion, and as other teams – notably Frank Williams – became interested, Colin offered him a place in the Formula 1 team; it was by this time doubtful that John Miles would continue in F1, so he was on fairly safe ground. Emerson was handed the old 49 to use while Rindt and Miles drove the newer 72.

At this point, Emerson's girlfriend Maria Helena came over to Britain, and they were married on the spur of the moment at Norwich Registry Office.

Emerson's Grand Prix debut was the 1970 British Grand Prix, and he brought the 49 home in eighth place, despite having no fourth gear and a broken exhaust. In his second GP, at Hockenheim, he was fourth, but he was classified 15th at the Osterreichring. Driving the 72 in anger for the first time – without the rear wing – he had an accident during the qualifying session for the Italian Grand Prix. When Rindt was killed the following day, the Lotus team pulled out.

Two weeks before the American Grand Prix, Chapman told Emerson that he would be team leader, as Miles was to be a development engineer on the production car side. His new team-mate would be Reine Wisell and their brief was to stop the Ferraris winning.

With 20 laps to go, Emerson was 12 seconds behind Rodriguez, and 12 ahead of Ickx. Or so Chapman thought. He hadn't realised the Belgian was actually a lap behind Emerson, so the Brazilian did everything he could to maintain a gap. When Rodriguez ran out

'I saw Colin jump over the barrier and throw his hat in the air – that was the happiest moment in my career.'

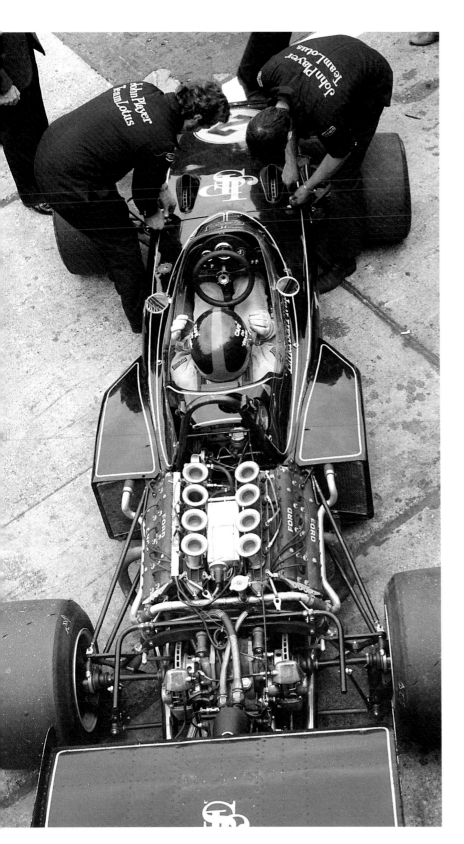

Emerson at Brands Hatch as mechanics secure the Lotus 72's body panels.

of fuel, Emerson had a clear run to the finish. Chapman gave his usual salute to his winning car, leaping onto the track and hurling his cap skywards. In winning, Emerson not only covered himself in glory but secured the title for Jochen. Wisell had come third, so Gold Leaf Team Lotus was back on course again. Meanwhile, over in Paris at Montlhéry, Wilson Fittipaldi was having his first international race in a Formula 3 event, which he also won.

Back in the groove for the 1971 World Championship, Emerson led for three laps at Kyalami, but his race quickly faded. At Monaco, Emerson was fifth. A road accident kept him out of the Dutch GP, but he was back to take third place behind the Tyrrells at Paul Ricard. At Silverstone the Lotus was third behind Stewart and Peterson and, although he posted a retirement at the revamped Nürburgring, Emerson was second to Siffert's Yardley BRM at the Osterreichring. Eighth at Monza was followed by seventh at Mosport and a lowly 19th at Watkins Glen. With 16 points, he was sixth in the points table.

Emerson's golden year

If 1971 had been one of the bleakest in terms of victories in Lotus history, 1972 would put matters to rights. Gone was the flashy red, white and gold, to be replaced by the swish new black and gold livery of John Player Special cigarettes. Emerson's team-mate was now F3 Champ Dave Walker. At Buenos Aires, Emerson was third fastest in practice, but retired in the race with a damaged radius rod. Walker stopped on the first lap. At Kyalami, Emerson came second to Hulme, but it was at the non-championship *Daily Mail* Race of Champions at Brands Hatch where he really made his intentions clear. Fastest in practice, he dominated the race, although, in fairness, there were no Tyrrells present. Back home in Brazil, he took pole position but the 72's suspension broke in the race. Emerson took on the Marlboro BRMs for Silverstone's International Trophy, and narrowly beat Beltoise and Hailwood's Surtees.

At Jarama on May Day, Emerson was third quickest in practice, and won from the Ferraris of Ickx and Regazzoni, although he'd had a fright when the on-board fire extinguisher went off. Monaco suffered one of the wettest race days on record, and the spray factor through the streets of the principality made life exceptionally difficult. Starting from pole, Emerson finished third, having to hold his visor open with one hand to prevent it steaming up.

Back in Britain, Emerson was second in the Oulton Park Gold Cup in a combined F1 and F5000 line up. Then at Nivelles-Baulers, he was completely unchallenged in practice and in the race, taking the honours as he pleased. Stewart was absent with an ulcer. Emerson won another minor race at Vallelunga with the John Player Lotus.

Clermont-Ferrand had 55 corners of every description on its 8km circuit. Emerson, racing there for the first time, did well to come second. The British Grand Prix was sponsored by Players, and there was much accompanying razzmatazz. Emerson won after a 20-lap battle with Ickx. Wilson Fittipaldi was driving for Brabham by this time, and may have gone out of his way to lend his brother a hand on occasion. Nevertheless, Emerson claimed it was his hardest race yet.

A broken gearbox spelled the end of his chances at the Nürburgring, and the leaking oil caught fire, heightening the drama. All went well at the Osterreichring, and Emerson came first after a duel with Hulme. The attraction of £10,000 prize money at the Rothmans 50,000 was too much to resist, and the JPS team went for it. Emerson was clearly the class act in the field, and he won it fair and square, perhaps to the embarrassment of a certain tobacco company. The rivalry between the cigarette sponsors was only partially hyped up.

On the way to Monza, the Lotus transporter was involved in an accident on the autostrada, when a tyre blew. It turned over into a gully and a mechanic was thrown through the windscreen. The racing cars were damaged, and a spare was quickly rushed out for Emerson. Fortunately it held together and he won, confirming himself as 1972 World Champion. He was 26 years old.

The two North American races and the so-called Victory Meeting at Brands Hatch were all a big anti-climax, dogged with retirements.

Team Lotus enjoyed success in 1973, ending the year as Constructors' Champions, but Emerson was nothing like as convincing as his new team-mate Ronnie Peterson. 'SuperSwede' was clearly a faster driver, if not such a good tactician. If the car held together he usually won, but it often broke. Thus Emerson accumulated more points, and finished second to Stewart in the Championship. Highlights included Emerson's meteoric chase of Stewart round the Monaco hairpins, the Lotus 72 riding over kerbs as Emerson tried all he knew to catch the Scot. At the Osterreichring, Ronnie let Emerson by to keep his title

hopes alive, but the Brazilian retired. When hope had gone, Ronnie kept the lead from Emerson at Monza, while Jackie finished fourth. Emerson was furious, and decided to quit Lotus at the end of the season.

A national hero

McLaren had a new big-bucks sponsor in Marlboro, and offered a serious financial incentive for Emerson to change camps. He had achieved hero-status in Brazil, just like footballer Pelé, and this was an attraction for the tobacco company.

There were wins for Emerson at Interlagos, Zolder and Mosport, with second places at Brands Hatch and Monza; fourth at Watkins Glen was sufficient to give him the 1974 Championship. Still with Marlboro McLaren in 1975, Emerson was victorious at Buenos Aires and the rained-off Silverstone event, while second places at Monaco, Monza and Watkins Glen made him runner-up to Niki Lauda.

Together with Richard Divila and his brother Wilson, Emerson then set about constructing his own Grand Prix machine. The car was debuted by Wilson Fittipaldi in Argentina in 1975, where it crashed and caught fire after a suspension breakage. Emerson's sponsors were the giant state-owned Brazilian sugar producers Copersucar, which is what the car was called. Emerson qualified the Copersucar FD/04 fifth on its first outing at Buenos Aires in 1976 but that proved to be a flash-in-the-pan, and Emerson could not even qualify it for some races. In 1980, Fittipaldi took over some of the equipment of the defunct Wolf team, and he was joined by Keke Rosberg as the number two driver. It brought no significant improvement. Emerson should have stuck to racing other peoples' cars,.

After retiring from the Grand Prix scene in 1981, Emerson went to race in the CART Indycar series in the USA, where he became immensely successful, winning the Indianapolis 500. His nephew, Christian Fittipaldi, also forsook F1 in 1995 to join his uncle.

Emerson celebrates with the trophy after winning the 1972 Austrian Grand Prix.

Niki Lauda

(1949–) World Champion 1975, 1977, 1984

In the 1950s and 1960s, many drivers suffered untimely deaths on the track. By the 1970s, safety improvements to the Nürburgring saved Niki Lauda from joining them. Ironically, he had tried to have the German Grand Prix banned earlier on in the year.

When he returned from the brink after his accident in 1976, few believed he would make the grade again. They had seriously underestimated the guts and determination of the Austrian. He was a driven man – despite his dreadful burns, he came back again to win the Championship the following year.

Nicholas von Lauda was born in Vienna on 22 February 1949, the son of a successful paper-processing businessman. Frequently enigmatic, and with a strain of elitism, he once described the family home as a '22-room garret in Vienna'.

Niki was taken to the Nürburgring in 1966 to see the German Grand Prix, and was immediately hooked. He sold his Mini Cooper S road car and bought a similar vehicle from local star Fritz Baumgarten. In order to conceal his racing activities from disapproving parents, the Mini retained its previous colour scheme, and Niki claimed he was simply looking after it for Fritz.

This was partly true. Lauda and Baumgarten teamed up to go hill-climbing in 1968 and circuit racing in 1969. Lauda graduated to Formula Vee with the Austro-Kaimann team and drove for Francis McNamara in Formula 3. He bought a Porsche 908 sports car, and shared the Austrian Bosch Racing Team's Porsche 910 with Otto Stuppacher in the 1969 Osterreichring 1000kms. They finished last.

A determined risk-taker

Lauda was determined to go professional and approached his bank for finance. Banks and finance companies have cropped up as sponsors here and there in the past, and Lauda had the benefit of a wealthy family concern as security. With a £20,000 loan, he rented a March Formula 2 car for the 1971 season. Although Lauda was overshadowed by his more experienced team-mate Ronnie Peterson, he still got some good results. He finished tenth in the final F2 ratings. His Formula 1 debut came at the 1971 Austrian Grand Prix, but an oil pipe broke on his March 711's Cosworth engine on lap 20.

In 1972 he returned to the fray in F2 but despite winning the British John Player Formula 2 title, mechanical failures dogged his efforts to win the European crown. He had staked all on a £100,000 bank loan, 85 per cent repayable over three years. It bought him the second seat at March, and although he raced the whole season, the only reasonably high placing was seventh at Kyalami.

He was now broke, with no visible means of repaying the loans. BRM's Louis Stanley offered him a seat for £80,000, and again the Austrian banks complied. Lauda's best finish in 1973 was a fifth at Zolder, with a string of low placings and retirements. Stanley offered Lauda two more seasons with BRM, at no extra charge. Ferrari had other ideas, having been impressed by Lauda's tenacity at Monaco and Zandvoort, and Lauda was offered a drive for 1974. Although Ickx had just walked out and signed for Lotus, the Ferrari team was on the verge of a minor renaissance at this point, with team manager Luca di Montezemolo and chief engineer Mauro Forghieri at the helm. It was a learning year for Lauda, with many retirements and frustrations, although he came fourth in the Championship; team-mate Regazzoni was second. Contemporaries wondered what all the fuss was about.

They found out in 1975. Lauda came sixth in the year-old Ferrari at Buenos Aires and fifth at Interlagos. Fifth at Kyalami belied the long weeks spent testing the new transverse gearbox 312T. At Barcelona, the Ferraris barged each other at the first corner of the first lap and Lauda was out. Then at Monaco, he led from pole position and that elusive first Grand Prix victory was his. The performance was repeated in Belgium, France, Sweden and the USA, along with second place at Zandvoort and thirds at the Nürburgring and Monza. To clinch the Championship at Monza was some achievement indeed. He had also won the *Daily Express* International Trophy at Silverstone, and obtained nine pole positions.

The following year, 1976, was a cataclysmic one for Lauda. It began well enough with wins in the Brazilian and South African Grands Prix, and later in the season Lauda won in Belgium and Monaco. Prior to the Spanish Grand Prix, Niki had an accident in a tractor, turning it over on himself. A physiotherapist called Willy Dungl appeared on the scene, and he kept Lauda in shape for some time afterwards.

Niki in Argentina in 1972, driving the March 711 with 'tea-tray' front wing.

The Spanish result was confused when James Hunt's victory was at first disallowed, making Lauda the winner. Then Hunt was reinstated as victor, and a series of protests ensued with both McLaren and Ferrari teams trying to outdo one another.

At the British Grand Prix, Regazzoni sparked off a major pile-up on the first lap, causing the race to be restarted. Hunt won the race but, controversially, he was later excluded because his McLaren had not actually been running when the race was originally stopped. Lauda was awarded first place.

Lauda's Nürburgring calamity happened just after Adenau Bridge, where the 312/T2 crashed heavily. Beached in the middle of the track, it was struck by Brett Lunger's Surtees, which pushed it 100 yards down the track where it burst into flames. Harald Ertl and Guy Edwards were next on the scene. In the absence of marshals, they and Lunger tried to extract Lauda from the blazing wreckage. It was Arturo Merzario who got the harness undone, oblivious to the flames.

It seemed that a rear suspension breakage had caused the accident. Lauda was gravely injured. His main rival Hunt won the race. Lauda was even given the last rites in hospital, but after four desperate days he began to pull through. His facial and hand burns were horrific, and he had inhaled burning fuel vapour. Plastic surgery restored much of his former self. In public he has worn a baseball hat ever since.

Five weeks later, he was back in a Ferrari at Monza. To come back after such fearful injuries was an example of absolute courage and bravery. To finish fourth was a most amazing moral and physical achievement. While he was recovering, however, Hunt had stormed ahead in the Championship stakes.

Victories at Kyalami, Hockenheim and Zandvoort in 1977, with second places at Zandvoort and Monza, brought Lauda the World Championship for the second time, ten points clear of Jody Scheckter. But things were not good at Ferrari, and the disintegrating relationship

was hyped up in the Italian press. Gilles Villeneuve was hired to drive in Canada, and Lauda walked out. He had already decided to drive for Ecclestone's Brabham team, and he took his Parmalat sponsorship and mechanic Ermanno Cuoghi with him.

The 1978 Brabham-Alfa was improved by the talents of designer Gordon Murray, and Lauda won the Swedish Grand Prix with the so-called 'fan' car. An engine driven fan sucked the car to the road in the reverse hovercraft principal. After Niki's win at Anderstorp the 'fan' concept was outlawed.

An unhappy victory

Lauda inherited the victory at Monza when Andretti and Villeneuve were penalised for jump-starts, which is always an unsatisfactory way to win. In any event, it was overshadowed by the tragedy surrounding the death of Ronnie Peterson. There were three second places in Argentina, Monaco and Britain, with thirds in Brazil and Holland, so it was not a completely wasted year. However, it had been dominated by the Lotuses of Andretti and Peterson.

The 1979 Brabham's new Alfa Romeo V12 engine was certainly powerful but it lacked reliability. Lauda felt himself to be under threat in the team from new recruit, Brazilian Nelson Piquet, who was faster on occasion. And when the new Cosworth-powered BT49 was introduced at the Canadian Grand Prix in Montreal, Lauda came in after first practice and calmly announced his retirement from the sport. 'I no longer want to drive racing cars round and round in circles,' was his memorable reason for quitting.

Lauda chatting to Fangio at the Japanese Grand Prix in 1976, after his recovery.

'Lauda was given the last rites in hospital after his accident'

to take the lead in the Championship. Prost came back with a win at Zandvoort, with Lauda finishing second.

As alternative drives to McLaren evaporated, he signed for another season. He was still marginally ahead of Prost in the title race as they went to Estoril. Although Prost had qualified with a far better time than Lauda, he had an upset stomach on race day. Lauda caught him up in the race, and upped the turbo boost on his McLaren to eke out more power, although this jeopardised fuel consumption. What he couldn't know was that one turbo was damaged so, by turning the boost up, he wasn't actually using more fuel than normal. In so doing he had maintained second place, and with it clinched the Championship for

Lauda and Hunt share a confidence at the 1977 Belgian GP.

Now a resident of Ibiza, along with Rosberg, Niki and Marlene and their child had moved base from Salzburg in their native Austria, and he began to spend much of his time working at developing his airline business. Then, two years later, Niki asked McLaren's Ron Dennis if he could take a car out for a test drive, just for old-times' sake. The upshot was that he was taken on for a $5million fee.

Formula 1 faces industrial action

At Kyalami, the drivers staged a rebellion. The new 'superlicence', instituted to make it more difficult for inexperienced racers to buy Formula 1 drives, also made it possible for the FIA and the constructors to control drivers' earnings and terms of employment. As a senior statesman in motor racing, Lauda led the revolt, eventually settled in the drivers' favour, but with a $5,000 fine for the disruption levied by FISA, the sporting arm of FIA.

One benefit of the strike was that Lauda was able to exercise a wider role, and helped secure the TAG-Porsche engines which made McLaren so successful. He also contributed to the elevation of McLaren into a super-team, as opposed to merely a winning one. While Niki was preoccupied with developments within the team, his results were not spectacular in 1982 and 1983. John Watson came and went, and Alain Prost arrived for 1984. His presence galvanised Lauda into action, and McLaren almost instantly became the top team. Lauda won at Kyalami, with Prost second and, at Dijon-Prénois, Niki won after a frantic battle with Patrick Tambay.

At this point in the season, Prost was showing better in the races, and a disagreement blew up over fees for the following season. Lauda was offered half what he was getting in 1984, in order that Prost could be paid his just desserts. Lauda approached Gerard Larrousse's team, but the sponsors wouldn't co-operate, while McLaren threatened to hire Keke Rosberg. Lauda won at the Osterreichring, with two gears missing,

the third time. It was clear by now that Prost was merely waiting in the wings, and Lauda sportingly admitted as much. The two drivers would be team-mates for 1985, and at Monaco in 1985, both Lauda, who finished the race 12th and Rosberg, miserable at Williams, cried on each other's shoulders.

A series of mechanical mishaps with Niki's car suggested that McLaren was placing the bulk of its resources with the up-and-coming Prost. Niki had lost all his enthusiasm for racing, and at the Nürburgring he gave in his notice. His resignation at the Osterreichring was acrimonious, in that he was allowed no credit for his contribution to Marlboro McLaren's eminence.

Lauda spent his retirement building up his airline business – Lauda Air – and in 1994 he was brought into the Ferrari team in an advisory capacity. His controversial remarks about drivers Berger and Alesi led to a shake-up, which saw Schumacher join the team for 1996. It would be hard to think of a more dedicated pairing than those two. Perhaps it was Niki's way of getting his own back for successive team managers having sought to promote others at his expense.

Niki exits Zandvoort's huge Tarzan hairpin with the Ferrari 312T2 in 1977.

James Hunt

1947–1993: World Champion 1976

I n the years before his untimely death, James was an acerbic commentator with the team who provided BBC TV's Grand Prix coverage. As in his racing career, he spoke as he found, and spared no-one's blushes. James came to prominence in late 1967, racing a Mini. He quickly attracted a reputation for having accidents and became known as Hunt the Shunt. His casual attitude to the sport was clear from the outset: his Mini failed scrutineering because the driver's seat was nothing more than a deck-chair.

But he was serious enough to punch Dave Morgan – no weakling himself – after a collision between the two in an F3 race at Crystal Palace in 1970. The serious side came out in his TV personality. He continued to blame Patrese for causing the accident at Monza in 1976 which led to Ronnie Peterson's death. James, along with Regazzoni and Depailler, had extracted Ronnie from the stricken Lotus – and he referred to the incident in a number of Grand Prix commentaries. That said, the BBC's Grand Prix coverage improved one-hundred-fold with James' informed and thoroughly entertaining input; he and his fellow commentator Murray Walker complemented one another perfectly.

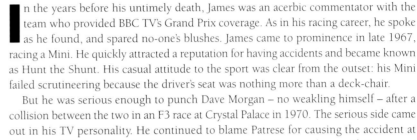

Born in Epsom, Surrey, on 29 August 1947, James' background was thoroughly middle class. He had a stockbroker father and a public school education – Cheam and Wellington – behind him, and a career in the medical profession beckoned. He'd also played at Junior Wimbledon, but preferred racing cars. Had his tennis career blossomed, he would have pre-empted McEnroe's brattishness by ten years, although Hunt always possessed an element of class that the New Yorker lacked. His slobbish arrogance was backed by social grace. He shocked the establishment by arriving for official engagements in T-shirt and jeans, sometimes barefoot. Paradox- ically, his chief interest outside motor racing was breeding budgerigars. Still, Ronnie Peterson's equally unlikely hobby was tropical fish.

The trappings of the 'racing driver as pop star' were evident, and not necessarily forced upon him. His wife Suzy complemented his tousled good looks – although their marriage ended in late 1975, when she was to go off with actor Richard Burton. James was for nine years thereafter associated with Jane Birbeck, and he later married Sarah Lomax. He had two sons, Tom and Freddie.

After the short-lived Mini era, James progressed through Formula Ford with an Alexis and a Merlyn, then funded his time in F3 working as a hospital porter. These were times of financial hardship, such that when his tow car had its petrol siphoned at Pau, James and a colleague set about reclaiming the stolen fluid from other cars. Driving a two-year old Brabham BT21, he demonstrated his class against Peterson's works March at Cadwell Park in 1969, and won the coveted Grovewood Award.

James drove a Lotus 59 in 1970, and won only twice, although he was disqualified twice in run-ins with the authorities while at the front in a couple of other races. The subsequent year produced much the same results. Sacked from the March F3 team in

James relaxes at Monaco with one of his many girlfriends – Jane 'Hottie' Birbeck.

1972, James became involved with the flamboyant Lord Alexander Hesketh and his colourful entourage. He raced one of Lord Alexander's Dastle F3 cars alongside Bubbles Horsley, and James spent the middle part of the season crashing out, more often than not.

Serious fun

After backing James in a couple of outings in an F2 Surtees and a March 712, Hesketh decided to go for the big time in 1973. James finished third in the Race of Champions in a rented Surtees TS9B, and the team went to Monaco with a brand-new March 731 – plus its designer Harvey Postlethwaite. The opulent setting was just right for the ostentatious Hesketh ensemble but nobody imagined they had a hope. Behind the glamour and overtly frivolous exterior, their intentions were completely serious. James finished ninth at Monaco. He followed this with a sixth at Paul Ricard, fourth at Silverstone – a mere 3.4 seconds behind winner Revson. Third place at Zandvoort and second to Peterson at Watkins Glen demonstrated that Hunt was eminently capable of winning. Fleet Street latched on to the fervour surrounding the new ace driver and his patriotic team. Now something of a national celebrity, James won the Tour of Britain, driving Richard Lloyd's Chevrolet Camaro with journalist Robert Fearnall. He was also active in the European Touring Car series with BMW, and even tried CanAm.

Victory in the 1974 *Daily Express* Trophy, where he passed Peterson's struggling Lotus 76 in the pre-chicane Woodcote corner, preceded three third places in the Swedish, Austrian and American Grands Prix.

Hunt's first Grand Prix win was at a wet Zandvoort in 1975, driving Hesketh's own car, the 308B, where he beat Lauda's Ferrari in a finely-judged race. Until then, Alexander Hesketh had bankrolled the whole effort, preferring to choose his company rather than be obliged to sponsors. Not unreasonably, Hesketh could no longer support the effort, and he and James pulled out at the end of the season, having finished fourth in the Drivers' Championship.

James was courted by Brabham supremo Bernie Ecclestone, and there was a fruitless discussion with Colin Chapman. But the successful suitor was Marlboro's marketing boss John Hogan, who realised the potential draw of Hunt's charisma. Accordingly, he went to McLaren for 1976.

Gone was the semi-casual lifestyle of the independent one-driver privateer enterprise. Instead, James landed in the world of huge motor homes and blazer-wearing smoothies; Marlboro-McLaren was even then a very professional set-up. Although the pay wasn't brilliant, it rendered him solvent, and provided a competitive car. On the racing front, the American team boss Teddy Mayer had been Bruce McLaren's manager, and was an old hand, while team manager Alastair Caldwell was already James' friend. It was to be Hunt's World Championship year, but it would be fraught with technical disagreements and protests, and punctuated by Lauda's Nürburgring accident. James and Niki had raced against one another in F2, and had an amiable rapport. But their respective teams didn't, and they became rivals for the Championship. Others were potential contenders: Regazzoni at Ferrari, Scheckter and Depailler at Tyrrell, Reutemann and Pace in Brabham-Alfas, Andretti and Peterson at Lotus, for example.

At Sao Paulo, the first race of 1976, Hunt put the McLaren on pole, alongside Lauda, only to be frustrated by engine problems. At Kyalami, he was second to Lauda, with team-mate Jochen Mass third.

A glorious comeback

But as Lauda racked up the points, Hunt foundered. He won in Spain but the McLaren M23 was disqualified over the width of its rear track, only to be subsequently re-instated. Several races were lost in the meantime because of modifications to the car and James became dispirited. Even Mass was ahead in the points standings, and Lauda had 51 points to Hunt's paltry six. When the McLaren was returned to its original configuration, James won in France and at Brands Hatch, only to have that victory disallowed by a malicious Ferrari protest. A first corner multiple pile-up occasioned by Regazzoni caused the race to be stopped and there was much argument over whether drivers – Hunt and Regga included – should be allowed to start in spare cars, and whether they could take the restart at all if they'd not competed a full lap on the aborted race. James insisted on taking the start no matter what, and after he had won Ferrari complained. Astonishingly, the protest was upheld. Now the points were: Niki 61, James 26.

James won at the Nürburgring, where Niki crashed, and came fourth in Austria, a race, it's alleged, Ferrari tried to have banned. There appeared to be a vendetta against him, as they protested about the McLaren's octane rating at Monza. He spun off in the race, and the Monza tifosi were vicious in their insults as Hunt walked back to the pits from his stranded car. However, fortunes do change. Victories at Zandvoort on his 29th birthday, at the decrepit Mosport circuit and at Watkins Glen took him – and the recovering Lauda – to Fuji for the showdown. By then, there were just three points in it.

The weather was diabolical, and it was madness to go ahead with the race. Hunt said it should be postponed, but he accepted that he would have no choice but to race if it wasn't. The Japanese authorities couldn't back down – these were early days for them. The impenetrable spray from the wide tyres made visibility almost impossible, and the McLaren mechanics had even drilled holes in Hunt's visor to stop it misting up. Lauda very sensibly withdrew after two laps, stating that the Championship just wasn't worth the risk. James raced on, demonstrating considerable fearlessness, but courage turned to anger as a puncture dropped him from first to third place. He had been given

confused pit signals, and it appeared that his drive, bordering on the suicidal, hadn't been absolutely necessary. Still furious at the finish, he needed to be convinced that the title was his.

There were three wins for the Champion in 1977, in Britain, Japan and the USA but by then McLaren had gone into decline and in 1979 he joined industrialist Walter Wolf's team to drive another Postlethwaite creation. It was all starting to get away from him, and he was frequently sick from tension before races. He confessed to fears about his safety, and clearly by then he had had enough. The ground-effect car was not competitive, and there were six retirements from seven races. After Monaco, James announced he was retiring. 'I'm only interested in driving to win,' he said 'This car has no chance of doing that, and for me, the risk is therefore too great. I'm not interested in racing for sixth place.' And with that, he was out.

Hunt's devil-may-care attitude made him a fascinating person to watch in action, and, later, an engaging TV personality. Having been on the pedestal himself he knew exactly how the cars were behaving and the competence or otherwise of the drivers. He was critical of blockers and moneyed back markers, and corrected Murray in the nicest possible way if he'd got something wrong. James was an unsurpassed connoisseur of the sport, and won many new fans. What made him all the more admirable was that he got out when the realisation dawned on him that he'd had enough and didn't want to risk his neck any more.

Latterly, the vagaries of the City and a divorce settlement played havoc with his finances, and his mode of transport was an A35 van. The motor racing world was deeply saddened when he died of a heart attack, aged only 44.

James storming to victory in the Championship in the spray of Fuji.

Sponsorship was a fact of life in the USA long before it entered Formula 1's hallowed portals. For decades, American motor racing had been funded by sponsors whose products often had nothing to do with the motor trade. They saw motor racing as a valuable medium for advertising their products, a glamorous, racy stage for their products, with the potential kudos of being associated with a winning car.

In Formula 1, while factory racing teams were supported by the tyre companies and the oil, fuel and fuel-additive producers, there were no external influences on the sport. The purists resisted, but with the rise

of the driver-turned constructor, such as Brabham or McLaren, outside sponsorship was inevitable. By the early 1970s it was the norm. The presence of the sponsor soon made its mark on the sport. Not only did they they provide budgets to run the cars and pay drivers' fees, they funded the events and influenced decisions about who drove for who.

The first Formula 1 team to wholeheartedly embrace outside sponsorship was Lotus, whose F1 49s and F2 48 were decked out in Gold Leaf cigarette livery in 1968. The same year the Lotus 56 gas-turbine 4WD Indianapolis car was loudly sponsored by STP oil treatment, while its F1 equivalent the 56B was turned out in Gold Leaf colours. In 1969, Rob Walker's 49 – driven by Hill and Siffert – enjoyed Brooke-Bond Oxo's patronage.

The price of the name

Team Lotus went all the way in 1972, and the cars themselves were known as John Player Specials. The PR office expended a great deal of effort tying to persuade hardened journalists that they weren't Lotus 72s any more, usually to no avail! In F2, the Lotus 74 was called the Texaco Star, in deference to its sponsor, and the French fuel company Elf had its name writ large on the Tyrrells. Motul Oil sponsored BRM when Marlboro left, Universal Oil Products sponsored the Shadow F1 and CanAm cars, while Fina backed Team Surtees. The oil and tyre companies' logos have remained a constant presence.

Other major sponsors to appear in Player's wake included Yardley cosmetics, who sponsored first BRM then McLaren. The tobacco industry was beginning to feel the first vibes of the anti-smoking lobby, and saw in the untapped motor racing world a visible means of offsetting taxes as well as gaining a promotional foothold on the marketing front. Thus Marlboro took over at BRM where Yardley left off in 1973, and other teams subsequently attracted other brands, including Gitanes, Rothmans, Embassy, Camel and Mild Seven.

Marlboro began its long-running association with McLaren in 1974, and, with Marlboro backing, the team won the World Championship seven times between 1974 and 1991. Senna's 1993 victory in Adelaide brought the team's total GP tally to 104, making it the most successful in the history of the Championship. Marlboro also sponsors some of the top drivers, and over the years other teams have received its support: Ferrari, Alfa Romeo, Williams' Iso, and Merzario, for example. Both Players and Marlboro have sponsored F3 Championships, which bring on new talent.

When racing in Germany and in Britain, the teams are obliged to mask the names of their tobacco-purveying sponsors because of government dictates on tobacco advertising.

Since the mid-1970s we have seen Olympus and Canon cameras, ICI chemicals, Beta tools, Olivetti office hardware, LEC fridges, Candy washing machines, Saudia airlines, Parmalat dairy products, Martini, Warsteiner beer, Barclays International – enticed by sponsor-getter extraordinaire, Guy Edwards – Pagnossin ceramics, Denim aftershave,

Mansell in 1988, comprehensively covered by logos on his race-suit.

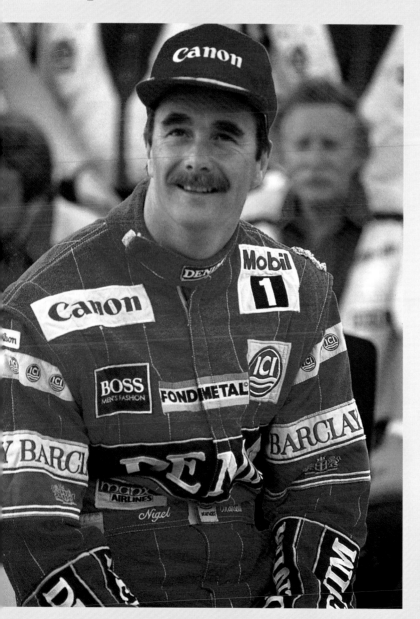

First National City Bank, and Benetton clothes, to name just a few of the major sponsors. As the years have gone by, the diversity has naturally increased, and more than one big name has to be accommodated among the myriad smaller fry on the relatively small surface area of a Formula 1 car. And at the end of the day, the livery also has to look attractive.

Drivers attract sponsors, and, in turn, that makes them more appealing to an under-resourced team. Minor sponsors – or in some cases not so minor – vie with one another for the avaiolable space on the drivers' overalls and helmets.

Formula 1 is big business. Budgets are a thorny subject – not to say a closely guarded secret in many cases. Sums have escalated quite dramatically, with Players putting around £1m into the sport in 1973. Where £5million might have got a team on to the middle of the grid in the mid-1980s, that sum has easily doubled today. The top teams need £20- £25million to budget for a whole Grand Prix season, while the second-rank teams like Jordan and Tyrrell manage to get by with £10million. In 1995, Schumacher was signed to Ferrari for the 1996 season for the princely sum of £12million. Top talent can command such extraordinary fees, whereas at the back of the grid, a driver bearing £250,000 worth of sponsorship might buy himself a season.

Teams may whinge about the costs of F1, it is, after all, meant to be the cutting edge of automotive technology. The paradox is that the sums involved could probably be reduced by getting rid of complex technology – active ride and electric traction control and so on – and thus placing the emphasis more on the drivers. They in turn could argue for higher fees on that basis. There's no turning back the clock and expenditure on development of the cars will never diminish. Either way, there will always be a place for sponsors in motor racing.

Models promote JPS merchandise at Brands Hatch in 1974.

Lavish VIP treatment is available in F1's Paddock Club.

Mario Andretti

(1940–) World Champion 1978

Only now, after a career spanning five decades, is Mario Andretti talking about hanging up his distinctive silver and red helmet. He is the great all-rounder, having driven everything from a Hudson Hornet stock-car in the 1950s, to the Pike's Peak dirt-road hill climb in the 1960s, to a Ferrari 312P in the 1971 World Sportscar Championship, and he is the oldest man to win an Indycar event. In 1995 he drove the second-placed Courage-Porsche C34 at Le Mans with Bob Wollek and Eric Hélary, and even in retirement is contemplating another two or three attempts at the French classic.

He spent seven seasons in Grand Prix racing, and is the only driver to have won the Formula 1 World Championship, the Daytona 500 NASCAR race and the Indianapolis 500. And yet he has always been a modest, home-loving man, preferring to live where he grew up, in Nazareth Pennsylvania. He's content to handle a bit of DIY around the house, loves Italian opera, and his idea of a family treat is a picnic at the cabin in the Pocono mountains. 'If that makes me a stick-in-the-mud, then I'm a happy stick-in-the-mud,' he said. In spite of the pressures of racing and international travel, his marriage to Dee Ann has lasted over 34 years, and they raised three children. Son Michael was Mario's colleague in Indycar racing, and 'swapped' with Nigel Mansell by doing a season with McLaren in F1 when Nigel went off to the USA. Michael couldn't settle because of McLaren's divided commitments to Ayrton Senna and Mika Hakkinen.

More recently, the racing world has seen a more relaxed Mario, but in the early stages of his career he lived life intensely, and he was willing to drive anything he could get his hands on – anywhere he could.

Mario was a farm administrator's son, one of twins who were born on 28 February 1940 in Montona, near Trieste, Italy. Because of the war, the family was evacuated to Lucca, and like many Italian boys, Mario grew up with a passion for motor racing. He and brother Aldo were taken to see the Mille Miglia by a local garage owner for whom they did odd jobs, and before long they were competing with a local businessman's Formula Junior, and doing pretty well with it.

In 1955 the family emigrated to Nazareth, Pennsylvania, and the twins worked at their uncle's garage. In 1959, they competed at the Nazareth speedway – unknown to their parents – with their hotted-up Hudson Hornet and were equally successful. Aldo fractured his skull and retired from the scene, while Mario drove midget racers on dirt ovals, improving the cars he drove in order to win bigger prize money.

Single seater racing in the USA is governed by the USAC (United States Automobile Club) and modified saloons – or stock-cars – are controlled by NASCAR (National Association for Stock Car Auto Racing). Races take place in special stadiums, with the exception of a few road courses, which accounts for the high speeds and close racing of Indycar and the huge V8 stock cars. The accompanying prize money and general razzmatazz has traditionally given this form of racing a higher profile than F1. Mario entered this big time world in 1964 and, guided by veteran mechanic Clint Brawner, he finished the 1965 season as USAC Champion.

'It's all a matter of going to the right team. Go to the wrong team, and it's pure hell'

1978 Dutch Grand Prix

Mario the victor on the podium at Zandvoort, with Peterson (left) and Lauda.

He was third at Indianapolis in a Hawk in 1965, and drove Luigi Chinetti's NART Ferrari at the Bridgehampton round of the World Sportscar series. In 1966 he was USAC Champion again and he started Indianapolis from pole position, before retiring. Sharing a Mk II Ford with Pedro Rodriguez, Mario came fourth in the Daytona 24-hours sports car race and in 1967 he won the Sebring 12-hours with Bruce McLaren in a Mk IV Ford. Driving for Ford at Le Mans, he was unlucky to be injured in the multiple pile-up which took out three Mk IVs in one go. The balance was redressed by his victory in the Daytona 500.

Mario practised in a Lotus 49 at Monza in 1968, but wasn't allowed to race it in the Grand Prix because he'd driven a dirt racer less than 24 hours earlier. However, his Formula 1 break came at Watkins Glen, when he put the Lotus on pole, ahead of all the stars of the day including Stewart, Hill, Gurney and Surtees. Although he failed to finish, it was clear that he was sufficiently talented to make his mark in F1.

Mario's American operation was bought up by STP Oil Treatment in 1969 and he won Indianapolis in his back-up Hawk to consummate the deal. Three further Lotus F1 drives came his way in 1969, at Kyalami, Nürburgring and Watkins Glen, which were totally without success. STP sponsored the embryonic March team in 1970, but Andretti's appearances were few, and his car was wrecked in Austria.

His boyhood hero was Alberto Ascari, so naturally Mario was delighted to sign for Ferrari in 1971. Sensationally, he won the first race at Kyalami, but thereafter conflicting schedules with USAC races drained his input on the F1 front. Results were not good either side of the Atlantic. Additionally, he was committed to the Ferrari World Sportscar Championship programme driving the 512M. At the end of the year, Mario parted company with STP, and joined the Vels-Parnelli USAC team for 1972. Again, results suffered because of conflicting interests, but Mario was part of the Ferrari steamroller in the World Sportscar Championship and he won at Brands Hatch and Watkins Glen sharing a 312P with Jacky Ickx.

The following year Mario concentrated on Formula A in the USA, as the Parnelli team built an F1 car – designed by Maurice Phillipe, who penned the Lotus 72 – to contest the World Championship. At the close of 1974, Mario drove one to seventh place in Canada.

Andretti had a frustrating time in 1975. The Parnelli car was experiencing teething troubles and, although Mario led briefly at Barcelona, his best placing was fourth at Sweden. Here he narrowly beat his chief rival, American CanAm champion Mark Donohue, who was driving Roger Penske's eponymous car. The American stars were rivals of old, but, sadly, Donohue was fatally injured when he collided with an advertising hoarding at the Osterreichring.

At Kyalami in 1976, Mario drove for Lotus, but he and Peterson collided on the first corner. The end was in sight for the now under-funded Parnelli team, and after no successes in the South American and Long Beach rounds, the team folded. After driving for Frank Williams in the *Daily Express* International at Silverstone, Mario returned to Lotus. This time he really got stuck in and, together with designer Tony Southgate, developed the JPS 77 into a race-winner. There is little doubt that Mario's USAC experience was a contributory factor here. Swede Gunnar Nilsson had replaced his disenchanted countryman Peterson in the team, and he and the American scored well in the second half of the season, culminating in Mario's win at Fuji in the rain – the race in which Lauda sensibly declined to drive.

The points scoring system weighed against Andretti in 1977, because although he won at Long Beach and in Spain, France and Italy, he posted ten retirements. These included, in different races, an on-board fire extinguisher going off, his car catching fire, and a run-in with Hunt at Silverstone. Lauda, on the other hand, won three races.

A winning team

For 1978, Lotus had the unbeatable combination of Peterson, Andretti and the ground-effect Lotus 78; the 79 was in the pipeline. Mario had been less than ecstatic about the prospect of another senior F1 driver – quite his equal in terms of talent – joining the team. Nilsson was mortally ill, and Chapman needed to win the Constructors' Championship to support his Lotus Cars' export drive. The deal was that Andretti was to be number one, and, as team leader, he had the best possible number two in Ronnie, who was as good as his word and played the supporting role throughout. Mario won in Buenos Aires, Belgium, France, Germany and Holland, and came second at Long Beach, and fourth in Brazil. The Italian Grand Prix was halted because of the start-line shunt in which Ronnie was fatally injured – although nobody appreciated this at the time – and the mood of the crowd grew hostile as they waited over two hours for the restart. Scheckter had damaged a barrier on the warm-up and there was further debate among the leading drivers as to whether they should race at all. In the end they did, and Mario won after a race-long duel with Villeneuve. Ecstasy turned to acrimony as he and Villeneuve were disqualified for a jumped start, that demoted him to sixth. It was still enough to clinch the Championship. But when Peterson died during the night of an embolism the pleasure turned to grief.

Mario remained at Lotus for 1979, partnered by Carlos Reutemann, but it was a lean period for the American. In fact Reutemann scored more points and the relationship between the two was not brilliant. In desperation Lotus abandoned the new 80 in favour of the 79.

Mario's chief complaint with Lotus was the lack of brakes on the 79 – he had virtually no brakes at all when he won in Belgium in 1978. This was because Chapman insisted on sticking with magnesium callipers, which were light but porous, allowing seepage of brake fluid.

In addition, Chapman was notoriously uncharitable over drivers' fees, and Andretti observed cynically that in 1978 a third of the team's $6m sponsorship fund had gone into buying helicopters.

By 1980, sponsors John Player had withdrawn – temporarily – to be replaced by Martini and the American Essex Petroleum company, and Lotus' livery changed accordingly. Mario stayed at Lotus for 1980, and was joined by the young Italian Elio de Angelis. Success-wise, the cupboard was bare. It got worse. In 1981, he moved to Alfa Romeo, but the engines hardly ever survived race distance. The following year, Mario had occasional outings with Williams, but for him the thrill had gone out of Formula 1 and he stayed in the USA to go USAC and CART racing. There, he was more at home and the winning was easier.

Mario is critical of Grand Prix racing today: 'There is too much arrogance in Formula 1,' he thinks. 'It seems to be in vogue.'

Mario was perhaps the sport's greatest all-rounder, ready to drive in any type of race.

Jody Scheckter

(1950–) World Champion 1979

When you're born in the place where they staged the Grand Prix, and your father has two garages and also builds karts, it's likely you're going to want to be involved with motor sport. That was how it was for Jody Scheckter, born in East London, South Africa on 29 January 1950. Aged 11, he got his first kart.

While serving an apprenticeship in the paternal Renault dealership, Jody tinkered with motor cycles and karts. He soon got his first car, a Renault 8. Paradoxically, in his early days as a club racer he never abided by the rules. This was something of a contradiction with his position as the Grand Prix Drivers' Association's elder statesman in his later years in F1, where he took circuit safety very seriously and insisted on changes.

A ticket to drive

As South Africa's leading racer in 1970, he won a couple of air tickets for himself and wife Pam to London. He found a drive in Formula Ford through the good offices of motor racing luminaries Andy Marriott, Nick Brittan and Stuart Turner, and after some highly agricultural performances, he graduated to F3 with a Merlyn.

At the beginning of 1972 his options ranged from an offer to join John Surtees, a couple of rent-a-drives, and a three-year contract with McLaren. The latter was the obvious one for a colonial boy to go with. McLaren were still into CanAm and USAC racing, so the possibilities were varied. In a Formula 2 race at Crystal Palace, Jody drove the M21 and beat Mike Hailwood in the latter's F2 Championship year. At Mallory and Imola, Scheckter saw off some of the cream of ungraded drivers, including the Fittipaldis, Lauda, Cevert and Reutemann.

He was making his mark, and Chapman invited him to replace the off-form Dave Walker in a JPS 72 at Lotus. Scheckter used this as a bargaining counter to get an F1 drive from McLaren, and he was given the chance in an M19 at Watkins Glen. He finished ninth after a spin in a sudden rain storm.

In 1972, McLaren had different sponsors, Yardley for F1 and Impact in F2. In 1973 however, they could no longer afford to undertake an F2 programme, neither could they run a three car team in F1. But Kyalami was a different matter. The attraction of the 'local boy' in financial terms was enough to subsidise a third car, and Jody was third quickest in practice, sharing the front row with Denny in the new M23 – his first pole position – and Fittipaldi's JPS 72. A third-lap crash involved Charlton, Reutemann, Regazzoni and Hailwood. Oblivious to his own overalls catching fire, the ex-biker Hailwood hauled an unconscious Regazzoni from his blazing BRM, and was later awarded the George Medal. Jody, meanwhile, led the race, but was soon overhauled by the hot-shoes Stewart, Fittipaldi and Peterson. He ended up ninth, complaining that he had been overtaken while the yellow (caution) flags were out.

Jody led the French GP for 41 laps in the M23 before tangling with Emerson as the Brazilian attempted to overtake him. Fittipaldi tore a strip off the bemused South African later on in the pits.

'After some highly agricultural showings, he graduated to F3'

Jody came second at Brands Hatch in 1976,
driving the six-wheeler Tyrell P34.

When he appeared on the scene, Jody wore his hair and sideburns like most young trendies of the early 1970s and bore a strong resemblance to the lead singer of pop hitsters Mungo Jerry. This did not enhance his credibility rating in the paddock. When he slid sideways out of Woodcote and clouted the Silverstone pit wall at the end of the first lap of the 1973 Grand Prix, causing a monumental pile-up, everyone's eyes rolled skywards. Nine cars were sidelined, and the accident would have blighted the career of a lesser man.

Jody was given two more F1 outings in 1973. He tangled with Cevert at Mosport and had a suspension failure at Watkins Glen, the event where Cevert was killed. It wasn't a promising start.

In the great round of driver changes that prefaced the 1974 season, Jody and Patrick Depailler went to Tyrrell. The newly retired maestro Jackie Stewart was on hand to give a little friendly advice, just as Denny had done at McLaren. The season improved, points-wise, and among the lakes and pines at Anderstorp Jody won his first Grand Prix. If Lauda's Ferrari was nearly always pole-sitter, others won the races. At Brands Hatch it was Jody's turn. He ended the season third in the Championship. His best result of 1975 was his win at Kyalami in front of his enthusiastic countrymen. But overall it was a disappointing year.

To the amazement of all, Tyrrell appeared at the 1976 Belgian GP with the Derek Gardner-designed six-wheeler P34, which gave second and third places at Monaco to Scheckter and Depailler. With four tiny F3-sized wheels at the front and a pair of regular F1 wheels at the rear, the P36 proved to be much more effective than the pundits had

expected. The diminutive tyres contributed to a smaller frontal area, and that improved the car's aerodynamics. In 1977, however, the concept was hampered by front tyre problems. In general, Tyrrell achieved reasonable results with the six-wheeler, and Jody finished third overall in the 1976 Championship.

In 1977, Scheckter went to race for Walter Wolf, a wealthy Austrian-born Canadian who had bought up the disbanded Hesketh equipment the previous year. Wolf had also acquired a 60 per cent stake in Frank Williams' organisation and Williams had left. There was little backing except for Wolf's income from oil exploration, and the team was virtually disregarded to begin with.

An excellent year

But all things considered, Scheckter had an excellent year in the new Cosworth-powered WR1-3, winning at the team's debut race in Argentina, and again in Canada and Monaco. A second place in South Africa, and thirds at Long Beach, Spain, Holland and in the USA, gave him second place in the Championship, with 55 points to Lauda's 72. But for some poor results mid-season, he might well have taken the title.

For 1978, Wolf had Peter Warr as team manager. Ex-Lotus, Warr had long been a senior figure in F1, and there was an efficient regime in the pits at least. It was the cars which didn't match up, however, as the old ones were outclassed by the new ground-effect model from Lotus. Despite having new WR5-6 cars of the latest design, Scheckter's best race was to second place in Germany.

Now 29, Jody signed for Ferrari in 1979, alongside Gilles Villeneuve. A new ground-effect car, the 312T4, appeared at Kyalami, the product of wind-tunnel testing at the Pininfarina factory. It was soon established as the most potent car in the Championship. Scheckter and Villeneuve confided in each another about any improvements they discovered in their cars, which is not necessarily how team-mates always deal with one another. How they drove them is another matter, as Gilles, darling of the Ferrari fans, was always harder on the car than Jody.

Gilles was second and Jody third at Kyalami, and thereafter Jody won at Zolder, Monaco and Monza, with second places at Long Beach and Zandvoort, fourth at Hockenheim, the Osterreichring and Montreal, to make him World Champion. Gilles had three wins and three second places to make him runner-up.

Ferrari festivities

The Championship was won at Monza, with Scheckter leading Villeneuve home to a Ferrari 1-2. The scenes in the stands and on the track after the race were uproarious, as the Italian fans ran amok with delight. Said Scheckter: 'What I wanted to do was to win the World Championship, so my objective was to set the car up to make sure of the highest possible position in the race. Gilles meanwhile concentrated on setting fastest laps, which isn't the same thing.' The final races of the season were something of a debacle, with a mere fourth at Montreal and

Jody won at Monaco in 1979 from pole position in the ground-effect Ferrari 312T4.

a retirement at Watkins Glen – the only failure of the year.

Jody was by now living at Monte Carlo, as so many top-class racing drivers and sports personalities do. It's a tax haven, the climate is good, and communications with the rest of Europe aren't bad. Jody's race technique had improved almost on an annual basis, and at Monza his ambition was fulfilled. Winning the world title had settled him, and his new-found persona, relaxed yet serious, enabled him to do a good job as spokesman for the GPDA.

Astonishingly, 1980 was an appalling year for Jody, and for Ferrari, reigning Constructors' Champions. They struggled the entire season and Gilles had no better luck than Jody. The flat-12 312T5s were outclassed, partly because Forghieri and the other engineers were hard at work building a turbocharged car – the 126C – which would be ready the following year, and partly because the Ferraris didn't work so well on the Michelin tyres they were contracted to use, which were designed for the turbo Renault. In one of Ferrari's worst season's ever, Jody's best placing was fifth at Long Beach. He even failed to qualify at Montreal.

That was sufficient motivation for him to decide to call it a day. At the season's end, Scheckter quit, and he has never looked back. After his retirement, Jody lived in Spain, and he was good friends with James Hunt, who was also established there. He did not disappear completely from the picture, and at the Christie's Historic Meeting at Silverstone in 1992, he delighted the classic fans with a demonstration run in Nick Mason's Ferrari 312T3.

The Eighties
Turbos and Ground Effects

During the 1980s, technological development went ahead in leaps and bounds. F1 cars were changed beyond recognition. Some developments were outlawed by the sport's governing body as being too expensive – or effective.

The ground-effect chassis was introduced in 1977 by Lotus on the principal that the underside of the car was like an inverted wing, and through a system of venturi and side-skirts the car was sucked to the track surface. In the wake of the Lotus 88, the team's development engineer Peter Wright developed the active-ride suspension system on aeronautical principals. Broadly speaking, the car responded to changes in the surfaces it was passing over through electronic sensors, and these sensors in turn modulated the suspension accordingly.

The F1 turbo era was ushered in by Renault in 1977. Other teams were slow to follow suit: matching chassis capability with the turbo's sudden, shattering power-delivery took time. It was a fantastically exciting epoch, but it turned out to be a short-lived affair, peaking around 1986.

That season marked a turning point in F1, because turbo technology was so phenomenally expensive that only the wealthiest teams could hope to compete. In 1988, FISA abruptly decided to stem the rising financial tide by announcing a ban on turbo engines. One factor which helped to produce more power was the specialised fuel that was developed by the petrol companies, notably Shell, which produced at least another 10bhp. As fuel restrictions were placed on turbo cars, this factor became more important than ever.

Alan Jones
(1946–) World Champion 1980

Alan Jones' World Championship victory was a long time coming. Perhaps not so surprising for a guy who preferred the off-duty moments to the de-briefing sessions, and only registered his true commitment as the car surged off the grid.

Jones' father Stan was a racer, and was one of the most successful on his home ground during the 1950s. He'd won the Australian Grand Prix in 1959 in a Maserati 250F. Alan, who was born in Melbourne on 2 November 1946, followed his example by going karting, and by 1963 he'd won the national championship. After racing a Mini in club events, Alan borrowed the paternal Cooper Climax for the 1964 season. Progress was suspended for a while because of a recession in the Australian motor trade.

Stan Jones had always dreamed of coming to Europe in the same way Brabham did. Alan eventually made that dream come true by proxy, after a false start in 1967 when he had no luck and returned to Australia. He was back in Britain in 1969 armed with just £50 and a commitment to make a go of it. His entry into the sport was funded by sub-letting large houses to even larger numbers of fellow Australians.

In 1971, Jones was one of a hundred or so budding drivers trying to make their name in Formula 3 and, at the end of a season dominated by Roger Williamson and Dave Walker, Jones was 'highly tipped' for future stardom. Despite some good showings in F3 in 1972, Alan had no wins. But in 1973 he was second in the John Player F3 Championship behind Tony Brise (who would show great promise with Graham Hill, only to die in the plane crash) and fifth in the Lombard F3 series, driving a GRD-Vegantune.

Jones should really have gone into F2 in 1974, but it was a more expensive step than Formula Atlantic, where the cars were basically F2 models running 1600cc engines with carburettors. He was picked by ex-F3 racer Harry Stiller to drive a new March 74B, and won three rounds of the John Player Atlantic series, coming fourth in the Championship.

Jones was taciturn, rather impatient and didn't suffer fools gladly. There was always an air of superiority about the Stiller camp, in spite of Jones' laid-back attitude towards the rule-makers. He gave the impression that he was wasting his time at that level. He had no time for poseurs and hangers on, unless they happened to be female; the actual racing was what life was all about, and he only got wound up once he was installed in the cockpit.

For 1975, Stiller acquired an ex-works F1 Hesketh, and Alan made his debut in the Daily Express International at Silverstone, finishing seventh. After four Grand Prix, his patron sold up and emigrated to the USA. At this point fate intervened, with Rolf Stommelen's place becoming vacant in Graham Hill's Embassy team when the German was injured. Jones drove the Embassy Lola into fifth place at the German Grand Prix but, when Hill and several of his entourage were killed in November that year, Alan was again looking for a drive.

He rejected an offer from BRM, but found mutual satisfaction with John Surtees in 1976. Unfortunately, Surtees was too autocratic and serious for the Australian's more casual outlook, and in any case the American Brett Lunger, who had a stake in the Surtees concern, got preferential treatment. Despite coming fourth in Japan and fifth in Belgium and Britain, Jones decided that he couldn't face another year with Big John.

Meanwhile he had achieved some good results in Formula 5000 with the RAM team's March 75A and tried USAC racing with Teddy Yip's team.

In F1, Jones seemed to be on everyone's list of possibles, but only when Tom Pryce lost his life at Kyalami did Alan get the call. Pryce had the misfortune to collide with a marshal running across the track carrying a fire extinguisher, and both driver and marshal were killed. Jones thus drove for Shadow in 1977, finishing sixth at Monaco, fifth in Belgium, and then first at an unseasonally wet Osterreichring,

The start of the 1981 Las Vegas GP, which Jones led from start to finish.

20 seconds ahead of Lauda's Ferrari. It was a fitting reward for a sterling drive, and marked the first Grand Prix win for both Jones and Shadow. He followed it up with third at Monza and fourth in Canada and Japan.

Jones then made the unlikely choice of joining Frank Williams. The Williams équipe did not then enjoy the same status as it does today, and Frank always seemed to be struggling with uncompetitive Italian machinery. He ran a March 761 for Patrick Neve in 1977, but with Patrick Head as designer, Jones as driver, and Saudia Airlines as sponsor in 1978, Williams was on the up. It is no coincidence that this combination of talents and personalities started the team on the road to success. In 1978, Jones had many retirements with the FW06, but he finished fifth in the French GP and second in the USA. As with Shadow, he had demonstrated the poise and ability to do the job, but the machinery wasn't quite up to it.

He stayed with Williams for 1979, and was joined by Regazzoni, everyone's favourite sparring partner and blocker extraordinaire. They began the season with the old car, and Jones' best placing was third at Long Beach behind the Ferraris of Villeneuve and Scheckter. Jones debuted the new FW07 in Spain, but it was sidelined with gear-linkage problems. In Belgium it was the new sensation, however, and Jones led for 40 laps until an electrical fault brought his race to an end. Such are the teething troubles with new cars. At Monaco he crashed when his tyres went off, leaving second place to Regazzoni. The Swiss also scored Williams' first Grand Prix win with victory at Silverstone after Jones had retired while leading.

For Jones, the season hadn't looked particularly good before then. Then there were three wins on the trot, at Hockenheim, the Österreichring, and Zandvoort, and there was no doubt at all that both Jones' and Williams' cars were world-class players. Jonesey also won at Montreal and but for a bungled tyre change he'd also have won at Watkins Glen. Regazzoni was frequently not far behind. At season's end, Alan had enough points for third place in the World Championship, and had won more Grands Prix than Scheckter, who gained the title.

Before the 1980 season got under way, the FW07B was developed with a stiffer monocoque and the ground-effect under-wings extended. This gave rise to the 'porpoising' phenomenon, so the team reverted to the regular configuration. Jones opened the scoring with victory in Argentina, with Nelson Piquet making his presence felt in second place.

Arnoux's Renault turbo was uncatchable at Sao Paulo and Kyalami, although Alan was third in Sao Paulo and second at Zolder, followed home by new team-mate Carlos Reutemann. Poor Regazzoni had joined the struggling Ensign team, much to everyone's surprise, and crashed badly at Long Beach when the brake pedal snapped, leaving him destined for life in a wheelchair.

The suave Argentinian won at Monaco, while Jones was the victor in Spain, France and Britain. The Spanish result was discounted following FIA President Jean-Marie Baléstre outlawing the race because of driver protests – a decision supported by Ferrari and the French teams. How Williams celebrated when Alan won in France!

Reutemann was second at Hockenheim with Jones third, while the order was reversed in Austria. This was developing into a real sparring contest, and Williams has never really gone in for team orders, where one driver holds back so the one with more chance of the title gets the win. Frank and Patrick place more importance on Williams cars winning rather than the fortunes of individual drivers. Jones was under pressure not only from his team-mate, but also from Nelson Piquet.

Williams' winning ways

The pattern continued, with Jones second to Piquet at Monza, and Reutemann third. After a coming together with Piquet at the first corner, which meant the Brazilian had to use his spare car for the restarted race, Jones then won Montreal with Piquet's title hopes blowing away with his engine. The Brabham team began showing pit signals to Pironi, running second in the Ligier, urging him to greater efforts to displace Jones. Pironi, however, was labouring under a one minute jump-start penalty, and had no real part to play in the proceedings, and the race proved the clincher for Alan.

The Aussie also took the honours in the American Grand Prix at Watkins Glen, with Reutemann trailing him home. Jones' final tally was 67 points to Reutemann's 42, and Williams were Constructors' Champions on 120 points, with Ligier next up with 66. In the low season between World Championships, Alan won the Australian Grand Prix and a touring car race.

The sliding skirts which accompanied the ground-effect principal, creating a tunnel under the car to increase the suction force, were banned in 1981, and Williams' FW07C incorporated the suspension-lowering principle pioneered by Brabham with the BT49C. There were many successful races for Williams, but Nelson Piquet in the Brabham got the drop on them. Jones won the Long Beach opener, with Reutemann second, and the positions were once again reversed at Sao Paulo. Reutemann was second in his home Grand Prix to Piquet, with Jones fourth. The Australian was second at Monaco – a race he was

outspokenly dismissive of, saying that 'the cars have outgrown it, so you end up with a procession rather than a real race there.' Alan rounded off the 1981 season in triumph around the car-park circuit at Las Vegas, and Williams were again Constructors Champions.

However, Alan had become disenchanted with the internecine rivalry between himself and Carlos, and he resigned at the end of the year, returning to his wife Bev and son Christian in Australia. After Las Vegas, Reutemann had offered to 'bury the hatchet' with Jones. Quick as a flash came Alan's reply: 'Yes Carlos, in your back!'

Reutemann was bigger than the sport. In 1991 he became a provincial governor in Argentina with sweeping powers. Jones, on the other hand, was lured back to the circus for one-off appearances, but in 1985 he returned, a trifle overweight, to drive the Beatrice foods-sponsored Carl Haas Lola THL1. Unbeknown to Jones, until he was committed, the team was run by ex-McLaren duo Teddy Mayer and Tyler Alexander, for whom he had little time. The Neil Oatley-designed, Hart-turbo engined car was retired in its three races in 1985. After another dismal season when a Cosworth V6 turbo engine was used, Haas went back to the USA and Jones retired for good. ◼◻

RENAULT RS 10 turbo (1979)

State-owned Régie Renault became involved in motor sport through its Alpine subsidiary and the engine development work of Amédée Gordini. Their assault on the World Sportscar Championship involved turbocharged prototypes, and after the Alpine-Renault of Jaussaud/Pironi won at Le Mans in 1978, they concentrated on F1 under team manager Gérard Larrousse.

Taking advantage of the regulations allowing forced induction engines of 1500cc, Renault had raced the RS01 V6 in 1977. But by 1979, the Michel Tetu-designed RS10 was in the reckoning. It was a ground-effect car, powered by the 1492cc Renault V6 unit, using twin KKK (Kuhnle, Kopp & Kausch) turbochargers – rather than the one large one used previously. At the French Grand Prix at Dijon, Jabouille scored the first turbocharged Grand Prix victory, with Arnoux third. When they were running, they were clearly faster than the normally-aspirated cars, but initially they proved to be unreliable. However, this was the start of the turbo era, which would eventually see massively powerful cars developing up to 1000bhp.

LOTUS 78 (1977-78)

There could be several Lotuses in this chapter, because where Chapman led, the others usually followed. The aluminium monocoque 78 was powered by the ubiquitous 3.0-litre Cosworth DFV engine with Hewland FG400 gearbox and its suspension and aerofoil systems were conventional for the period. However, the 78 was the first 'ground effect' car, the concept of Lotus' development engineer Peter Wright. It proved to be a quantum leap in racing car design.

The car's broad side-pods housed water radiators, which were open at the front for cooling, with hot air passing out through ducts on the top. Behind the radiators were specially-shaped fuel tanks; the undersides curved upwards to the level of the engine mounts. In so doing they formed a relatively wide inverted-wing section, which set up an area of low pressure underneath, and this had the effect of sucking the car to the ground. The pod-ends were closed off, with a bristle skirt extending down to road level.

Chapman was closely involved in the 78's successor, the 79, which carried through the ground-effect principles, but the single fuel cell was carried behind the driver. Mario Andretti won the 1978 title driving the 78 and 79.

Lauda and Alain Prost. Subsequent evolutions of the MP4 featured different bodywork and suspension, but the carbon-fibre tub was by now becoming universally used in single-seater construction.

BENETTON B194 (1994)

The Rory Byrne-designed 1992 Benetton-Cosworth B193B was the first of the 'nose-up' F1 cars, and it proved effective, if not greatly successful, in the hands of Patrese and Schumacher. For 1994, new rules prohibiting traction control and active ride, meant Chief Designer Ross Brawn and Engineering Director Tom Walkinshaw revising the B194's suspension to that of a conventional spring damper system. Schumacher proved himself the master of the new configuration and took the 1994 World Championship.

The B194 was powered by an uprated version of the Cosworth-Ford Zetec-R V8, and it was a first time winner in Brazil. Apart from the controversial 'plank' incident at Spa, where Schumacher was disqualified for allegedly running a shaved under-car skid-block, the Benetton was the car of the year. Had Schumacher not suffered a two race ban as well, the B194 might well have won the Constructors' title.

As it was, the Williams-Renault FW16 V10 proved to be every bit as useful, and with both Hill and Coulthard bringing home high points scores, it won the 1994 Constructors' title for Williams. Its successor, the B195, used the new Renault V10 engine. It also incorporated several new aerodynamic tweaks.

McLAREN MP4/2

In 1981 the McLaren team was revitalised when Ron Dennis, Creighton Brown and designer John Barnard joined. By mid-season 1981, Barnard had a new monocoque ready. It was a radical new concept, constructed entirely from moulded carbon-fibre. The benefits were its strength and stiffness, combined with low weight. It was the first of the 'survival cells' which began to make racing cars much safer.

Barnard would gradually refine the chassis, aiming at weight reduction, improved rigidity, and better suspension. The MP4/1s ran with Cosworth engines, and they were driven by Watson, Lauda and Prost through to 1983, when the 1499cc twin KKK turbo TAG-Porsche PO1 engine was fitted. Barnard developed a new carbon-fibre monocoque – the MP4/2 – which was designed to accommodate the shorter V6 engine and to incorporate the larger fuel tank which was needed to satisfy the car's greater thirst. This was the car which completely dominated the 1984 F1 season, when it was driven by Niki

Nelson Piquet

(1952–) World Champion 1981, 1983, 1987

elson Souto-Maior was born in Rio de Janeiro on 17 August 1952. His father was a politician, so when he was getting started in racing he adopted his mother's maiden name – Piquet – so as not to attract the attention and censure of his wealthy parents, who did not initially approve of their son's dangerous hobby. But they came to his assistance once the die was cast, helping him acquire a kart.

Nelson's father had been a national tennis coach and he was in line to follow suit. He was even sent to high school in California to get a better chance on the world tennis stage. Here he was surrounded by car culture and, on his return to Brazil, he joined forces with his friend Alex Dias Ribeiro to race karts. It was here that the Piquet nom-de-guerre was adopted and in his second season he was national champion.

A natural talent

Piquet's mechanical knowledge was gained in preparation of his Polar Super Vee single seaters, which he raced in the early 1970s. In 1972 he won the Volkswagen-based Brasilia Sports Car series in a Camber-VW, and despite scholastic commitments which kept him occupied for much of 1973, he still managed to win the Brazilian Sports 2000 series in the Camber-VW. Mechanical problems sidelined many of his Brazilian Formula Super Vee outings in 1974 and 1975, but he and Ribeiro appeared briefly on the Formula Atlantic scene in 1974.

There were better results in FV in 1976, and six wins gave him the Brazilian national championship. Accompanied by his wife Maria-Clara, he arrived in Europe to tackle the 1977 F3 scene, armed with a March-Novamotor. With few successes, the March was swapped for a Ralt-Toyota, and three late-season wins pulled him up to third in the Championship. Electing to restrict his efforts to the UK-based BP and Vandervell F3 Championships in 1978, he beat his well-established fellow countryman Chico Serra in the races that mattered, achieving seven wins on the trot.

It had the desired effect. Piquet was noticed, and offered a test drive at Silverstone in an F1 McLaren. As it transpired, Nelson made his first Grand Prix appearance in Mo Nunn's Ensign at Hockenheim. He showed well before retiring. Piquet drove three races in a privately entered McLaren, coming ninth at Monza, then was quickly hired by Bernie Ecclestone to partner Lauda in the Brabham-Alfa.

Although he undoubtedly learned much through being in the same team as Lauda, he was on occasion faster than the Austrian in 1979, although he managed to finish in the points just once – with fourth at Zandvoort. This says more about the reliability of the Italian engines than Piquet's maturing talent. When Niki resigned in Canada, Nelson was instantly elevated to team leader. His team-mate for the following year was Zunino, who was replaced at half season by Rebaque.

Piquet came close to winning the title in 1980. He came second at the Buenos Aires opener in the Brabham-Cosworth BT49, came off in Brazil, but placed fourth at Kyalami. Then at the contrived Long Beach circuit, Nelson scored his first Grand Prix victory. It also gave him the lead in the Championship standings. After crashing in Belgium, he was third at

Monaco, and was second to Jones at Brands Hatch and a close fourth to Jones at Hockenheim. At Zandvoort came Nelson's second win, followed by another at Monza. He lost in Canada and at Watkins Glen he spun off under pressure from the new Champion, Jones.

Nelson had also been taking part in the BMW Procar series in 1980, where identical mid-engined sports-racers were driven at curtain-raisers by the GP stars and celebrities, and he emerged the Champion.

Technical assistance

The BT49C was basically the same car as 1980's but lighter, with more carbon-fibre composite panels and no skirts. Nelson opened his account with second place in the non-championship South African Grand Prix. He was third at Long Beach behind the Williams pair of Reutemann and Jones. His first win was in Argentina, and here the Brabham was equipped with the soft air-springs which lowered the car's suspension under aerodynamic load, allowing it to rise to the regular 6cm ground clearance when travelling slowly or in the pits.

Nelson scored again with a win at Imola, was third in France, first at Hockenheim, third in Austria, second in Holland, sixth at Monza, and fifth in Canada and in the Caesar's Palace hotel car park at Las Vegas – where, unusually, the majority of the corners were anti-clockwise; at most circuits they are clockwise. Coupled with a neck strain suffered in a practice altercation with Reutemann, plus the pounding of the rock-hard ground-effect car's ride, Nelson was exhausted. They had to wait 15 minutes after the race to get him to the podium.

At season's end, Nelson was just one point ahead of Reutemann: 50 points to 49, with Jones on 46. Williams won the Constructors' title, since they had two strong drivers and Brabham just the one. Piquet believed the World Championship crown was only valid from the moment it was won until the beginning of the new season. 'Then it's another year, another Championship,' he said. Once the new line-ups emerge, everything's open once again.

Ecclestone's deal with BMW to run their four-cylinder 1499cc turbocharged engines was done in 1980 but the BT49D didn't actually race until 1982. The BT50 had a longer wheelbase and a curved rear cover over the larger fuel tank. Piquet and new team-mate Patrese retired their BT50s at Kyalami and Piquet's Brazilian victory was disqualified: his BT49D's water-cooled carbon fibre brakes had evaporated some coolant and the car was marginally underweight. Nelson gave the BMW-engined car its first win, in Canada, but with both old and new models being run most of the season, it had to be seen as an evolutionary period.

Brabham designer Gordon Murray produced a new ground-effect car – the BT51 – for the 1983 season, but when these cars were banned, he had to think again. The BT52 proved to be spot-on, and Piquet won in Brazil, Italy, Brands Hatch (European GP), coming second in France, Britain, Monaco, with third place in Austria and a couple of fourths. The title was his for a second time and again it had been a close run thing, with Renault pilot Alain Prost only two points in arrears.

With fuel stops banned for 1984, the BT53 got bigger fuel tanks. But the cars in the ascendant were the McLarens, powered by the

Fans bask in the sun as Nelson takes the honours at the Hungaroring in 1986.

Nelson leads at Long Beach in 1980, on his way to his first GP win.

TAG-Porsche turbo units. The BMW engines might have been churning out 850bhp for Brabham, but reliability was down. Piquet's first win was in Canada, followed by victory in Detroit. A revised rear suspension arrangement helped Piquet score second place at the Osterreichring and a third at the new purpose-built Nürburgring stadium. But he was placed only fifth in the World Championship at the end of the year. His team-mate had been Teo Fabi, who was replaced for 1985 by Francois Hésnault. When he failed to show any promise, Marc Surer then took over as number two.

The BT54's main problem throughout 1985 was the unsuitability of the Pirelli tyres, which proved inferior to the Goodyears in use elsewhere. Piquet took the honours in the French Grand Prix, and second at Monza, but it was not at all a successful year.

Back in August, Nelson had signed for Williams and he, along with Honda, the major sponsor, believed that the twice World Champion would be getting the number one seat, with Mansell in support. That may have been a naïve view, bearing in mind the Englishman's grass-roots popularity. As it turned out, in 1986 Piquet and Mansell were as evenly matched as any pairing in similar cars. But it soon became apparent that there was no love lost between them.

During the early part of the season, Frank Williams was not to be seen at the circuits. He had the grave misfortune to be paralysed in a road accident, and reappeared looking frail in a wheelchair. The Team ran a pair of FW11s for Piquet and Mansell, slightly more compact designs. Nelson won in Rio while Nigel crashed on the first lap while attacking Senna. The opening victory may have caused Piquet to become over-confident, as he appeared to lose his grip on things thereafter. A string of retirements and low placings culminated in a straight fight at Brands Hatch, which Mansell, fortunate to be in the spare car when the race was restarted after a first lap fracas, won, much to the joy of his fans. After that, the fires within Piquet were rekindled, and he took three wins at Hockenheim, the Hungaroring and Monza. Mansell responded with a dominant performance at Estoril, beating Prost, Piquet and Senna in a straight fight. The title went to Prost at Adelaide, where Piquet finished second, and Nigel had a terrifying tyre blow-out at maximum speed.

Meanwhile, Honda had made subtle developments to the twin-turbo G-type engine, and no less than eight new FW11B chassis were built during the winter lay-off. Mansell ran with chassis number 3 throughout the 1987 season, while Piquet took number 4 after writing off number 2 at Imola. Both drivers took the active-suspension chassis when they became available towards the end of the season.

Nelson's attack on the World Championship began with second place at Rio, where he suffered from overheating problems. His luckiest moment of the season was surviving his terrible crash at Imola, while practising for the 1987 San Marino Grand Prix. Goodyear later admitted that tyre failure was the likely cause. Medical experts forbade him to race.

Both Williams retired at Spa-Francorchamps, and then Nelson was second at Monaco to Senna. Following lessons learned in Rio where rubbish had accumulated in the air intakes and had caused overheating, the Williams cars had mesh grids in front of the radiators at Detroit to prevent a recurrence. Here, Piquet was second to Senna once more. He was also second at Paul Ricard, this time to his Williams team-mate, although he had the consolation of setting fastest lap.

Mansell fans will long remember the British Grand Prix, when Piquet looked as if he had the race all sewn up, only to be caught – and passed – by Mansell in one of the most heroic drives of all time. He made

Nelson holds aloft his first GP trophy on the Long Beach podium.

up a 28 second deficit with 28 laps to go, sold Nelson a dummy on braking for Stowe corner with three laps to go, and the race was his.

A careful driver

While Patrick Head looked after Mansell's car, Nelson formed a close working friendship with Williams' engineer Frank Dernie, who had developed the Williams hydraulic-electronic suspension system. Dernie was close enough to Piquet to acknowledge he was an intelligent driver as well as a racer and refuted James Hunt's assertion that Piquet 'lacked motivation'. He was merely more cautious about getting past back-markers, as at Silverstone 1987 when Mansell slashed his lap times.

Nelson came back to win at Hockenheim and the Hungaroring, where he signed for Lotus for 1988. He was second to Mansell at the Osterreichring, won at Monza from Senna, third at Estoril, fourth at Jerez, and second to Mansell in Mexico. With 73 points from his best 11 results, Nelson was Champion, with Mansell second on 61.

After winning his third title in 1987, Piquet was fêted by Honda and the world's motoring press. But the celebrations after Suzuka, where the title was clinched, were decidedly low key, with just Nelson, girlfriend Catherine Valentin and brother Geraldo having a quiet dinner. Not a word from Williams. Instead, Piquet let his hair down – or rather got it full of cream – at a Brabham mechanics' leaving party after Adelaide.

It had always seemed to him that the Williams camp was favouring Mansell at his expense, an opinion which found little sympathy with

Nelson gets a ten-second service at Silverstone in 1983.

Mansell fans, or the out-going Champion Alain Prost. It was a replay of the Jones-Reutemann situation of 1981, and, as a consequence, neither of the Williams drivers were to win the title. Other drivers haven't minded the challenge: Lauda at McLaren alongside Prost, for example. But Nelson saw things in more straightforward terms. 'I'm racing to win the Championship, not to fight with my other driver in the same team,' he said. He wished to develop the car for himself and not for the benefit of his team-mate. In 1988 he moved to Lotus and the bounty of Camel sponsorship.

Lotus themselves had shown much promise in 1987 with Honda V6 turbo engines powering the active-ride 99T. Senna had scored a number of high placings with them, including a win at Monaco. Piquet's partner was the workmanlike Satoru Nakajima, and the season looked good. However Gérard Ducarouge's retrograde pull-rod suspension was not a success and, with questionable wind tunnel results masking other aspects of the 100T's performance, the racing year proved a washout. Nelson's best finishes were third places at the beginning and end of the year, in Brazil and Australia, bracketing a series of fifths and sixths and a fourth in Canada.

Ducarouge left Lotus at this point, to be replaced by Dernie, who quickly prepared the 3.5-litre Judd V8 101 for Nelson and Nakajima.

Early race performances in 1989 were so poor that Nelson became even more dejected than the previous year. There were a couple of fourth places in mid-season in Canada and in Britain, but it was a time of upheaval at Lotus. Team manager Peter Warr left, and Group Lotus chairman Fred Bushell was arraigned in the wake of the De Lorean affair. Neither car qualified for the Belgian Grand Prix, and the season petered out in a couple of fourth places.

For 1990, Nelson joined Benetton, and was at something of a disadvantage in that the team was competing with less-than state-of-the-art Cosworth DFR engines. There were some reasonable placings, but high spot was in Japan, where all the aces dropped out of contention, and Nelson led team-mate and countryman Roberto Moreno home in a Benetton 1-2. Nelson beat Mansell at Adelaide to finish third in the World Championship. Still with Benetton for 1991, Nelson had only one victory, at Montreal, and two third places at Phoenix and Spa. Without a drive for 1992, to some extent as a result of the recession, Nelson's Grand Prix career came to an end.

Keke Rosberg

(1948–) World Champion 1982

Rallying is traditionally what they excel at in the Land of a Thousand Lakes. Keke's father Lars was a rally driver, but, as a vet, he thought his son ought to pursue a similarly responsible career as, for instance, a dentist. Keke's mother, a chemist, had also raced karts. The problem for Finns was that Formula 3 represented the pinnacle of single-seater racing in Finland, and opportunities to shine before the decision makers of F1 were strictly limited.

Keke was born in Stockholm, Sweden on 6 December 1948 but became a naturalised Finn. Young Keijo Rosberg raced anything from motor cycles to karts and in 1965 even competed in a kart race against his father, who promptly retired. He was Finnish Champion five times in an eight-season spell in karts, and in 1973 he was Scandinavian and European Champion. The experience convinced him of the importance of the need for sponsorship. With this in hand, he went motor racing proper. Much against his father's best advice, he bought a Ford Mustang, which wasn't the most suitable vehicle with which to commence a career on the track. Still, all experiences are valuable, and he progressed to Super Vee-1300s. In 1974 he participated in 21 races, recorded seven wins and was placed 14 times. The following year was an equally successful one, and in 1976 Keke moved into F2 driving for Fred Opert. He drove 14 races and finished tenth in the F2 Championship.

In the next couple of seasons he drove in F2, Atlantic and Pacific, and came to the attention of wealthy Theodore team boss Teddy Yip. Several race aces had driven for Yip at one time or another – Schuppan, Jones, Piquet, Cheever and Depailler – and Keke followed in their footsteps for $1000 per race. He continued to take any opportunity to race wherever and whatever – CanAm, for instance, where he was frequently on pole but never in the money – and made his F1 debut in South Africa.

Driving the Ron Tauranac-designed Theodore TR1, Keke won the wet Daily Express International at Silverstone in 1978. Having made his mark, he failed to qualify the Theodore for the next four Grands Prix, so Yip abandoned the TR1 and bought a couple of Wolf WR5s. There were no successes, and Keke had a couple of drives for Gunther Schmidt's ATS team – Schmidt had just bought the March équipe – in the 1978 Canadian and American Grands Prix.

When James Hunt suddenly retired at Monaco in 1979, Rosberg took his place in Walter Wolf's team. He failed to finish in the points, and the Wolf Team was taken over by the Fittipaldi entourage – including Peter Warr as team manager – at the end of the year. Keke and Emerson Fittipaldi raced the Wolfs at the start of 1980, with the Finn coming third in Argentina. By mid-season, the Wolf was redesigned by Harvey Postlethwaite as the F8 Fittipaldi, but the only points finish was Rosberg's fifth at Monza. It made him tenth in the Championship, equal with Watson, Daly, Villeneuve and Jarier. Emerson withdrew at the end of the year, and Harvey went to Ferrari, but Keke soldiered on, joined by Chico Serra. It was a disaster, mainly because there was no major sponsor, and there were no finishes in the points.

Keke was accustomed to the better things in life – like travelling first class – which aren't always achievable when setting out in motor racing. He had a reputation of being 'close' with his money, and while not being averse to owning the odd Mercedes, Ferrari or Learjet, he was of the short-arms-and-long-pockets school in the paddock cafe. That said, it didn't help that he wasn't paid for ten months of the 1981 season.

'What I've learned is that in F1 it's too often a question of who stuffs whom first'

became Williams' number one. Partners were Andretti for one race, then Derek Daly. Rosberg was still thought to be too unruly in some quarters, but he slammed his critics by winning the 'Swiss' Grand Prix at Dijon-Prénois. It was a gritty drive which included a wheel-banging dice with the most notorious blocker, Andrea de Cesaris.

It was his first – and only – Grand Prix win that season, and some would argue that one victory alone does not merit the Championship. But nobody won more than two races all season long, so it was an extremely competitive year, with a mere 19 points spanning first to seventh place in the final standings. As Rosberg said: 'It was the last year you could go to a Grand Prix and not have a clue who was going to win.' Keke's tally was made up of second at Long Beach, then second at Zolder with the new FW08 (originally designed with four rear wheels on two sets of axles), fourth at Detroit – with two gears missing – fifth in France, third in Germany, second in Austria – a scant 5/100ths of a second behind de Angelis – and fifth at Las Vegas, where the 1982 title became his. He scored 44 points, with Pironi and Watson next up with 39.

The icing on the cake

The post-race party was a plane-ride away in San Francisco; it was the 30th birthday celebration of Williams' sponsor Techniques d'Avant Garde (TAG) owner Mansour Ojjeh. Keke and a few of his former F2 colleagues, like Daly and de Angelis, made the trip, and Keke was presented with a cake decorated with a shark's fin in honour of the 'Flying Finn'.

The 1982 season was marred by another show of politics, when several of the FOCA teams boycotted the San Marino GP at Imola. This included Williams, and again Rosberg was furious, as clearly it had undermined his chances of the Championship. Highlight of that event was the acrimonious duel between Villeneuve and Pironi, where the Frenchman overtook the Canadian on the last lap against Ferrari team orders. Both would be out of racing by the end of the year, Villeneuve dead and Pironi's career terminated by a practice accident at Hockenheim.

Thereafter, Williams' fortunes were in a decline. Rosberg was disqualified for receiving a push start at the 1983 Brazilian GP, but won the Race of Champions at Brands Hatch. He was fifth in France ahead of his new team-mate, the amiable Jacques Laffite. First place at Monaco – a circuit he really enjoyed – belonged to him and he was second in Detroit. Rosberg gave the turbocharged Honda-engined FW09 its debut at the South African GP, and came in fifth.

Reliability improved as the 1984 season progressed and, although it was McLaren's year, Keke achieved some reasonably good placings, such as second in Brazil; his only win of the season came at Dallas and thereafter there were no finishes in the points.

A true professional, the irrepressible Rosberg put everything into his racing.

With Jones retiring – from Williams – at the end of 1981, Keke was taken on as number two to Reutemann. But 1982 took off on a bad note with the GPDA strike at Kyalami, which Rosberg condemned, having just arrived in a competitive team. He would have gone straight out and raced no matter what, and saw the strike as being an ego trip for Pironi, who was the prime mover despite Lauda being spokesman. In the event, the race went ahead and Keke was fifth. He and Piquet, first and second, were disqualified in Rio for having underweight cars, although virtually everyone else was using the same water tanks.

When Reutemann departed before Long Beach, the Flying Finn

Keke was not looking forward to having Nigel Mansell on board during the 1985 season, and he was initially rather wary of the Englishman. He had just learned, 18 months after the mid-season low spot, that in 1982 Frank Williams had been touting him around to other teams. Thereafter, Keke's faith in Frank and the Williams team was broken. Only his marriage to Sina and the birth of their son kept his spirits up – as well as the temperate Ibiza climate – and it was an unusual position for an extrovert, self-confident driver to be in. Perhaps that accounted for him being a chain smoker. He felt that Williams had 'never forgiven me for not being Alan Jones'.

Keke, however, was realistic enough to accept that there would be others after him at Williams, and that there was a life after Formula 1. An expert wheeler-dealer, he thoroughly enjoyed setting up his own personal sponsorship arrangements, as demonstarted by the variety of logos displayed on his yellow race-suit.

In spite of the challenge provided by his new team-mate, Keke took the new carbon-composite monocoque FW10 to victory at Detroit and to second in France. He was second to Mansell in South Africa, and he ended up third overall in the Championship behind Alain Prost and Michele Alboreto.

Moving to the McLaren team for the 1986 season, Keke joined the well-established Prost. Two Champions to a team made for a potentially difficult season, but it was actually Keke's best bet. He might even have done better to have gone to McLaren sooner than he did. Driving the McLaren TAG-Porsche V6s, the Prost-Rosberg train finished third and fourth in Spain, the same in Montreal, and finished in first and second positions at Monaco. Rosberg was fourth at the Paul Ricard circuit and at Monza, and he came fifth at Hockenheim. After a memorable drive at Adelaide at the end of the season, he was sixth in Prost's narrowly-won Championship year, having suffered many more mechanical and tyre failures than his colleague. After 114 Grands Prix starts, Keke felt that it was time to finish.

In the wake of his F1 career, Rosberg was Mika Hakkinen's manager and mentor to another fellow Finn, JJ Lehto, who until mid-1994 drove for Benetton. Rosberg was hauled back out of retirement in 1991 by the Peugeot-Talbot Sport team for their assault on the World Sportscar Championship, using the 905.

Most recently, Keke has been active in the 1995 German Supertouring series, driving a highly modified Opel Calibra. True to form, he'll drive anything, anywhere.

Rosberg acknowledges the applause after his win at Dijon-Prénois in 1982.

The pits have always been a key feature of motor racing and have developed along with the circuits and the machines that use them. The original concept of the pits was just that – a convenient place to work on the cars. The pits were organised in one place – by the start and finish line – for convenience of lap scoring and because that was beside the location of fuel stocks. It quickly became necessary to have storage for spares and fuel, and the pits became a sort of base for the entrant and his or her car. Here they could find a bit of shelter, and keep lap charts and carry out timing. There needed to be a base from which to pass on signals to the drivers about their performance, their position as it stood relative to their nearest rival and the duration of the race. On a long circuit such as Le Mans, signalling pits were installed halfway round.

In the 1920s pits were quite rudimentary, but gradually there developed a long, low line of individual rough-and-ready sheds, roofed but open to the elements. Each car was allocated its own pit. By the 1930s, the motor trade saw the pits as a convenient way of advertising their products, and another dimension was added. Flags and banners sprouted forth, and structures became more robust, built in brick or concrete with corrugated iron roofs. This was how most of them stayed until well into the 1960s.

There was a pit counter for sitting on, keeping out of the way of the traffic, or standing on to get a better view of the cars. When a car drove up to its pit, the mechanics jumped over the pit counter to administer whatever was necessary. The pits were still very much a part of the circuit, and cars racing by came very close. At purpose-built circuits, a pit lane was defined, but not until the implementation of wholesale safety revisions in the late 1960s and early 1970s did the pit lane become physically separated from the track.

Expansion of the pits

As the pits facility grew, and teams' requirements burgeoned, the buildings themselves got wider and taller. At Silverstone and Snetterton, members of the public could watch the race from atop the pits, while savouring the delights and dramas of pit and paddock activity. The pit counters were the provinces of wives and girlfriends, to be seen clutching lap tables and stop watches. During the 1960s this band of women developed into a very powerful and influential coterie, with key figures including Sally Stokes, Bette Hill – Damon's mother – Pat McLaren, Helen Stewart, Sally Courage and Nina Rindt. These were the insiders, along with a select band of dedicated journalists and photographers. The beautiful people of the late 1960s were joined in the pits by a new wave of sponsors and their PR advisors, with fleets of promotions girls passing through during lulls in the proceedings.

By the 1970s, the pits at Le Mans had become positively luxurious. Circuits became wealthier and commerce became increasingly important, and the trend towards the pits complexes that we see nowadays was inevitable. Now all circuits hosting World Championship events conform to a standard which gives most teams a pristine garage for each car where the original pit counter used to be. During a race the toolboxes, refuelling rig, fresh tyres, and all the computer hardware are to be found here.

With the advent of the separate pit lane, it wasn't long before the pit counter moved out to the barrier separating pit lane from circuit. There still needed to be a vantage point from which to communicate with the drivers, in spite of the car-to-pits intercom. The pit wall became a concrete bastion, with teams setting up their timekeeping and telemetry equipment behind its parapets. This too sprouted shelters against sun and rain.

Photographers and hangers-on who used to lurk in the pits are now virtually absent. With so much resting on refuelling and tyre changing in the mid-1990s, there's no room for anyone without a serious purpose. The pits are full to overflowing with mechanics and

Spa in 1961. No pit lane or barrier separates the pits from the track.

technicians. They practise ad nauseam between races to polish their act, to get their times down to a bare minimum – so that four wheels can be replaced in around four seconds, three men to a wheel, two men on the fuel line, one at each end on a jack, and one to hold the pole saying 'Brakes On', letting the driver know when the job is done. Someone else will clean his visor, while fire crews stand by. An average fuel and tyre stop can last just ten seconds – depending on the quantity of fuel put in – but the time taken to enter the pits and to exit the pit lane has also to be taken into account.

The power of an F1 car means that high velocities can be achieved very rapidly, so in 1994 a 75mph limit was imposed on pit lane speed, to make it less likely that an unwary mechanic would be run over. Drivers contravening this are obliged to come into the pits and submit to a ten second stop-go penalty.

Above the pits garages at places like Paul Ricard, Monza or Silverstone are lofty corporate entertainment suites, topped by the press office and administration departments. The days when the ordinary enthusiast, doing the rounds of the Paddock, could gain access are long gone.

A McLaren refueller in 1995 (right) and Williams' 16-strong pit crew (below).

Alain Prost

(1955–) World Champion 1985, 1986, 1989, 1993

Born in St Chamond, near Lyons, France, on 24 February, 1955, Alain was a budding football talent at school. He went motor racing instead, and won the Volant Elf-Ricard Trophy in 1975. He became known nationally in 1976 when he won 12 of the 13 rounds in the French Formule Renault Championship, driving a Martini. Still in Formule Renault and also in a Martini, Alain won the European title in 1977, and turned his attentions to Formula 3.

Alain was supported by the French fuel giant, Elf petroleum, and was joint first in the French F3 series in a Martini-Renault in 1978. He won the prestigious Monaco F3 race, opener to the F1 Grand Prix and traditionally the making of a star; by the end of 1979, the European F3 Championship was his.

Alain's appeal as far as sponsors Elf were concerned was that he was clearly a strategist, unlike certain of his French colleagues, such as Jean-Pierre Jarier and Rene Arnoux, who were of the old school, quick on their day but unreliable. Pironi was fast but flighty, and was on course for Ferrari, while Jabouille was older and dedicated to Renault's quest for turbo success. Laffite, another Monaco F3 winner, spent too long relaxed in the wilderness with Ligier – although he and Prost became best friends, sharing ownership of a golf course.

A happy traveller

Aged 24, Prost signed to McLaren, then on something of a slide. Still, it was an entrée into the big time, and it removed him from the claustrophobic pressures of his domestic scene. Alain was sixth in Argentina, and fifth in Brazil driving the M29C – a Williams FW07 lookalike. These were excellent results for someone who'd never been out of Europe before, let alone driven the circuits. For the rest of the season he and Watson used the Gordon Coppuck-designed M30. Prost was sixth at Zandvoort, then crashed in practice for Watkins Glen. He was still 15th in the Championship in only his first year in F1 – tied with Fittipaldi, and ahead of Scheckter and Andretti. McLaren was on the verge of a shake-up, but Alain joined the Renault team for 1981.

The transition was marked. Instead of the on-the-spot intimacy of a small private team, all decision making at state-owned Renault came from on-high. The revised turbocharged RE20B was a difficult car for someone used to driving a normally aspirated car to learn, a task made especially difficult because side skirts had been banned for 1981. In addition, the Cosworth-engined ground-effect cars developed suspension-lowering systems, and the Renaults were suddenly outclassed.

Prost began badly, being involved in an accident at Long Beach. In Brazil, both he and team-mate Arnoux crashed. There was momentary respite in Argentina, where Alain came third and Arnoux fifth, but the turbo engines were still temperamental, and a string of non-finishes followed. Renault introduced the new, lighter RE30 for Zolder, but Prost's clutch failed and Arnoux non-qualified. Out of the blue, success came on home territory at Dijon-Prénois; Alain took the honours and scored his first GP win in a rain-troubled race.

The duck was broken, and Alain finished second at Hockenheim, topped the podium at Zandvoort, having led for all but one lap, and triumphed again at Monza. Second place at Las Vegas took him to fifth place in the Drivers' Championship, and, amazingly, Renault came third in the Constructors' Cup. It was a very close-run thing, with just nine points separating the top five drivers.

'I was absolutely sure I was going to win or have an accident, because I knew he [Senna] wanted to win absolutely'

Alain came second to team-mate Niki Lauda at Zandvoort in 1985.

Renault updated and refined the RE30 with each round of the 1982 Championship. Alain won at Kyalami with his increasingly disgruntled team-mate Arnoux third. Prost picked up the win at Rio. Then came a string of disappointments. At Long Beach, the cars ran with water ballast – like empty barges – because they were thought to be underweight; Alain's brakes failed. A crash at Monaco kept him out of the points until he obtained a desultory sixth at Brands Hatch.

Four Frenchmen filled the first four places at Paul Ricard; Pironi and Tambay in Ferraris were third and fourth while Arnoux contrived a scandal of national proportions by winning. Team etiquette said he should have given the win to Prost in support of the latter's Championship chances. The post-race scenes outside the Renault motorhome in the paddock were adolescent in character and probably accounted for Arnoux's departure to Ferrari at season's end.

Alain won at Dijon-Prénois, while Arnoux was first at Monza. A fourth at Las Vegas gave Prost fourth place in the World Championship, and Renault were third again.

At Renault, the pressures from the boardroom for outright success in the World Championship weighed heavily on competitions director Gérard Larrousse and team manager Jean Sage. Both men had been successful sports car and rally drivers and knew the form. But it seemed they couldn't get the car to work equally well on the quick circuits – where it could excel – and on the slow circuits like Monaco and Detroit. Prost was becoming discontented. Renault were now supplying their demon engines to Lotus, and a year later Ligier would get them too.

Alain undertook most of the team's testing as they tried to improve the RE30 in accordance with the latest 'flat-bottom' regulations. Eddie Cheever was the new driver and, using the new carbon composite RE40, Prost won at Paul Ricard with Cheever third. Alain was second to Tambay's Ferrari at Imola, and third at Monaco. Here the Renaults had full-width under-wings to compensate for the new rules, and while other teams were quick to protest about them, they were equally quick to incorporate the idea once it had been declared legal.

The Renault duo was first and third at the newly revised Spa-Francorchamps and Alain won at Silverstone and at the Osterreichring. He was now leading Piquet in the Championship by 14 points. Prost was runner-up to Piquet at the Brands Hatch European Grand Prix and, although he'd won four GPs to Piquet's three, the Brazilian was the 1983

Champion. Arnoux was third, having won three GPs for Ferrari. He also had a point to make to Renault.

Alain then moved on, to McLaren, who ditched Watson when he asked for too high a fee. Things had changed radically at McLaren since 1980. The old guard had departed, to be replaced by Ron Dennis' smooth, businesslike operation. John Barnard's new, carbon-fibre, TAG-Porsche turbo-powered MP4/2 was available for both Niki Lauda and the rising star, Alain Prost.

The Frenchman won seven races in 1984, two more than his Austrian team-mate, who clinched the Championship at the last GP of the year in Portugal. The McLarens were virtually unbeatable, winning 12 out of 15 events. Prost won at Rio, Imola, the curtailed Monaco – which then counted for half points – Hockenheim, Zandvoort, the Nürburgring and Estoril. Lauda's second place at Estoril gave him the Championship by just half a point. Never has the Championship result been so close.

Matching that kind of success was a tall order, but McLaren came close in 1985. Lauda's car proved less reliable, and the Austrian, on his way to retirement, missed a couple of races after damaging his wrist. A win at Zandvoort and two fourth places meant he was well down in the ratings – 14th in fact. Alain meanwhile got off to a flying start with victory in Rio, before missing out in Estoril and at Imola – where he was first on the road, though disqualified – but winning at Monaco. He was third at l'Isle Notre Dame circuit at Montreal behind the Ferraris of Alboreto and Johansson, and third at Paul Ricard behind Piquet and Rosberg. At Silverstone he won from Alboreto, setting fastest lap at 151.04mph, and was second to the Italian's Ferrari at the Nürburgring, ahead of Laffite's Ligier. Prost led Senna's Lotus home at the Osterreichring, and was beaten into second at Zandvoort by team-mate Lauda. His final win of the year was to be at Monza, although there was a fourth place at the Brands Hatch European GP, plus a couple of restrained thirds at Spa, behind Senna and Mansell, and Kyalami, behind Mansell and Rosberg. As it turned out, the crucial points had been won at Brands Hatch.

At this point, Alboreto was his closest rival, and he needed two points from the Brands race to ensure the Ferrari driver couldn't catch up. A first corner avoidance of Rosberg put Prost back down in 14th place, with Alboreto 11th. As attrition set in, both drivers moved up through the field and, when Alboreto's turbo blew, causing a fire, Prost was cruising. He avoided becoming embroiled in other people's feuds,

and ended the race in fourth place, gaining the four points that he needed to become Champion.

For 1986, Alain was partnered by the ebullient Keke Rosberg, and the MP4/2C now featured a lower driving position, reshaped engine cover and altered rear suspension geometry. The pair were third and fourth in Spain, and, despite running out of fuel on the last lap, Prost won at Imola, with Rosberg fifth. They were first and second at Monaco, giving Alain his third consecutive win in the Principality. Delayed by the first lap accident at Spa-Francorchamps, Alain moved through the pack to finish sixth. They were second and fourth in Montreal, and similarly placed at Paul Ricard. Mansell had won both races and Piquet separated

Alain scored his first Grand Prix victory at Paul Ricard in 1981.

the McLarens. Prost was third at Detroit and Brands Hatch, while Keke headed Alain in fifth place at Hockenheim. Alain was second at Estoril and Mexico City, and the winner at the Osterreichring and in Adelaide. His points tally of 72 gave him the Championship, but Mansell was only two points behind, and Piquet also close enough on 69.

The statistics don't reveal quite how dramatic the Australian race was. Mansell led from the start, giving way to Senna and Piquet. Rosberg followed, and before long the Finn was ahead. Prost was making up ground, and was soon lying third. When Rosberg heard what he thought was his TAG engine giving up, he pulled off, only to discover the strange noise was a rear tyre throwing its tread. Now if Mansell

Prost leads Mansell at Ste Devote during the sodden 1984 Monaco GP.

could stay ahead of Prost, he could still win the title. But as the Williams pit debated whether or not to bring their cars in for fresh rubber, Mansell's left rear Goodyear simply exploded as he was passing a Ligier at nearly 200mph. Miraculously, he was unscathed, and Goodyear urged that Piquet be brought in immediately. Prost was now ahead, but a faulty fuel reading told him he was about to run out of fuel; he backed off accordingly, so much that Piquet was in his mirrors as he crossed the line to win his second Championship in succession.

In mid-season, designer John Barnard left McLaren, unhappy with team politics, and joined Ferrari as technical director. His place was taken at McLaren by his protégé Steve Nichols, who drew a more aerodynamic car, thanks to a smaller fuel cell. Gordon Murray was technical director. With Porsche having tweaked the TAG engine, Alain went out and won at Rio and Spa-Francorchamps. In winning the Belgian GP, Prost equalled Jackie Stewart's record of 27 GP wins, which had stood for 14 years. Stewart didn't mind; he believed Prost was 'in a class of his own'. His team-mate Stefan Johansson was doing a good job too, being third in Brazil and second at Spa. The next two GPs brought Alain a couple of third places, in Detroit behind Senna and Piquet, and at Paul Ricard behind Mansell and Piquet. He was third again at the Hungaroring and sixth in Austria. A win at Estoril and a

second place at Jerez completed Alain's 1987 score card, giving him a total of 46 points and fourth place in the Championship. But for a couple of retirements when in command, at Imola and Hockenheim, when the alternator drive belt snapped, Alain would have been in contention for the title.

Ever since Ron Dennis had seen Senna race in Formula Ford 2000 at support races for the Grand Prix, he had wanted him in the McLaren team. A deal was arrived at through the Honda engine connection: Ayrton was hired for 1988. He vowed to beat his two-times Champion team-mate 'by being fitter, better motivated and more dedicated'.

The turbo engines were down to 2.5 bar boost pressure, and limited to just 150 litres of fuel, implying drastic improvements in fuel efficiency. Pundits wrongly predicted the normally-aspirated cars, with their lower weight limit, had a good chance of winning. The turbo cars had on-board computers showing how much fuel was available at any point in the race, enabling the driver to establish a balance of critical factors, including boost pressure, fuel temperature, air intake temperature, and the appropriate fuel and air mixture. Not only could he increase or diminish boost, and hence power, as necessary, but he now effectively controlled fuel consumption. The Honda-powered Lotuses and McLarens were at a considerable advantage over Ferrari and the BMW Megatron-powered Arrows, who suffered from higher consumption. Later in the year at Detroit they demoralised the opposition by starting with 140 litres on board – that was ten less than the regulations permitted.

At Rio in 1988, Senna got black flagged for swapping cars after the green all-clear flag was shown, while Prost eased ahead of the pack and won as he pleased. Behind him, all was despondency. He was second to Senna at Imola, first at Monaco, and again at Mexico City. In Montreal and Detroit, Senna won from Prost, who complained that with so many excellent circuits in the USA, it was a great shame they had to race around the artificial Detroit track.

At Paul Ricard, Alain beat Ayrton, but after that the Brazilian notched up four wins in succession. Then it was Prost's turn, and he won at Estoril and at Jerez, where he led from start to finish. Ultimately, Alain had no answer to Ayrton's growing powers, particularly his ruthless overtaking of back markers. At the penultimate round at Suzuka, Senna fought back from last on the grid, after bump-starting his stalled McLaren, taking Prost for the lead at half distance, despite a track made greasy by a rain shower. The final shout was with Alain, who won at Adelaide, but the title was Senna's. He had scored 90 points to Prost's 87. Gerhard Berger languished in third place on 41 points, and McLaren took the Constructor's title with an incredible 199 points.

A controversial season begins

For 1989, Prost stayed at McLaren with Senna, and the season would end in rage and fury. There were also significant driver changes elsewhere. Mansell moved to Ferrari, alongside Berger, with Boutsen and Patrese at Williams. Benetton hired Nannini and Herbert, with Piquet and Nakajima staying at Lotus.

At Rio on the Autodromo Nelson Piquet, Mansell scored for Ferrari, while Prost finished a masterful second. Senna was two laps down having challenged Berger a bit too hard on the first lap. Said Berger: 'Once you give way to Senna, he'll never forget it.'

Prost hadn't learned that one yet, although he was angry enough to storm off after coming second to Senna in the San Marino Grand Prix; he was furious at the way Senna had jumped him early on in the race, going against an agreement that neither would hamper the other's Championship chances. In retrospect it seems naïve to imagine that such a pact would remain intact for long. Prost was fined $5000 by FISA for failing to attend the Imola post race interview.

The McLaren Honda V10s howled round the Monaco harbour to finish first and second, with Senna nearly a minute ahead. Monaco may be a tight squeeze for F1 cars these days, but nowhere else in Grand Prix motor racing can match it for atmosphere. However it wasn't all sweetness and light, as Prost was livid that Senna had once again overtaken him early on lap one. 'He has not been honest,' said Prost.

In Mexico, Prost was fifth after tyre troubles slowed him, but he won the American GP at Phoenix to the accompaniment of rumours that he might quit McLaren at the end of the season. Both McLarens failed in Montreal, and at Paul Ricard Prost confirmed he would be retiring because of the friction caused within the team – his team – by Senna. This meeting saw the heart-stopping first corner crash where Gugelmin's airborne March CG891 flew over most of the front runners, losing its side on landing. Amazingly, he was unhurt. Prost went on to win the restarted race, which was more notable for Mansell's charge from the pit

A third consecutive win at Monaco came Alain's way in 1986.

A jubilant McLaren team greets the hero of the hour at the Osterreichring in 1985.

lane, and the exciting F1 debut of Prost's countryman Jean Alesi. At Silverstone, Senna's unpopularity with race fans was apparent when he was jeered on spinning off. The partisan crowd was rooting for Mansell but Prost emerged the winner. At Hockenheim, normal service was resumed, with Senna beating his 'team-mate'. For the first time, some cars were timed at 200mph on that circuit's long straights.

Mansell took the fight to the McLarens at the Hungaroring and beat them fair and square. Prost was fourth behind Boutsen and Senna. But at Spa-Francorchamps in the pouring rain, both McLarens were out in front again, Senna leading Prost by just 1.5 seconds, and Mansell a mere half a second behind.

Back in the Renault days of 1983, Prost was not popular with the tifosi, and even needed bodyguards at Monza. But they're a fickle lot. With Prost committed to Ferrari, he was cheered even as his McLaren took their out-going hero Berger. As Senna's leading car faltered, Prost was hailed as the new hope, as he would be joining il Leone Mansell for 1990. To Ron Dennis' disgust, Prost even gave his trophy to the fans at the foot of the podium, a mark of his anti-McLaren feeling; there were rumours – bitterly refuted by the mechanics – that Senna's car was receiving preferential treatment, as he'd been so much faster in practice.

In Portugal, the aggravation was between Senna and Mansell, and the Englishman received a black flag for reversing in the pits, then took

himself and Senna out when the Brazilian failed to give ground. Prost came in second to Berger. Practising for Jerez, Senna was in trouble for passing black flags at an accident site, flat-out. He won the race, however, and Prost was third.

The inevitable coming-together between Prost and Senna happened on lap 47 at Suzuka. Prost refused to give way to Senna at the chicane and the McLarens locked wheels. Prost got out, perhaps prematurely, while Senna was pushed up an escape road, enabling him to restart. After pitting for a new nose-cone, he carried on racing. Disqualification was inevitable as he'd received outside assistance. The win went to Nannini. Surprisingly, McLaren protested, while FISA President Baléstre declared Prost World Champion. Prost said he was tired of giving way to Senna, and it was only what he'd expected would happen. 'This time I said before the race that if this happens, I will not open the door.'

There was no good reason for Prost to race at rain-drenched Adelaide, and like Japan in 1976, when Lauda declined to race, the organisers should have postponed it. Prost did one lap of a race that inevitably had to be restarted, and retired. He could refute the inevitable criticism by pointing out that it had been his car which Pironi had hit at Hockenheim back in 1982 in similar weather conditions.

So Prost took the number one to Ferrari for 1990, and promptly retired at Phoenix with gear selection problems. Alain won at Sao Paulo – his 40th GP win. Senna was third, and the two studiously ignored one another on the podium.

Fourth at Imola, fifth at Montreal, Alain now had a run of successes, scoring a hat-trick with wins at Mexico with Nigel second, Paul Ricard,

The 'Professor' (below right) was admired for his smooth, fast driving.

and then Silverstone. Senna was third, and it seemed McLaren had been firmly put in their place. Senna bounced back to win at Hockenheim, with Prost's Ferrari F1/90 fourth. The Frenchman couldn't match the Brazilian's winning pace round Spa-Francorchamps and at Monza his Ferrari was second to the McLaren once again.

It was Mansell's turn to beat Senna at Estoril, with Prost third, but at Jerez, Alain beat his team-mate.

Vicious rivalry

That other rift was well and truly opened at Suzuka, when Senna, as he later openly admitted, deliberately took Prost out at the first corner, thus ending Prost's title aspirations, and confirming Senna's own. The title race over, Adelaide was a formality, but a clean dice between Mansell and Piquet – who won – with Prost cruising home third.

For 1991, Senna and Berger's McLaren MP4/6s ran with V12 Honda engines, and Senna scored 10 points for a win at Phoenix, with Prost second in the V12 Ferrari 642. (Points were now 10, 6, 4, 3, 2, down to 1 for sixth.) Senna won at Interlagos, with Prost fourth and new team-mate Alesi sixth.

As the season wore on, it became obvious that the Ferraris were uncompetitive. Behind the scenes, the team was in turmoil. At Paul Ricard and Barcelona, Prost was second to Mansell. He was third at Silverstone and Monza, and fourth at Suzuka. But the week before the final GP at Adelaide, Ferrari unceremoniously fired him.

Alain took a sabbatical for 1992, and spent the year as a commentator for French TV. He signed for Williams for 1993, alongside the team's former test driver Damon Hill. Alain threw down the gauntlet in no uncertain terms with victory at Kyalami. Hill was second at Interlagos, and beat Prost to second at Donington for the European GP. Prost won at Imola from Schumacher, and beat Senna at Barcelona. Fourth at Monaco after an alleged jumped start, Alain was first at Montreal ahead of Schumacher, and headed a Williams 1-2 at Magny-Cours. Alain's Silverstone victory – after Damon retired – was his 50th Grand Prix win. Alain won at Hockenheim, set fastest lap at the Hungaroring and was third at Spa-Francorchamps behind Hill and Schumacher. Second place at Estoril gave him the Championship for the fourth time. He rounded off the year with two second places, to Senna, at Suzuka and Adelaide.

During the year, Alain came to the decision to retire at the end of the season. After 13 years in F1, the politics had really got him down. Always a clean competitor, his style perhaps belonged to an earlier, more courteous era. After a test run, he agreed to act as test driver for McLaren-Mercedes for 1996.

Alain is married to Anne-Marie, with a son, and they live at Yens, near Lake Geneva. The choice of this location had as much to do with political preferences and tax advantages as spectacular scenery. Prost was always an accomplished skier and competent sportsman, and kept up a training programme which maintained his fitness for the cockpit. But it was his strategic planning and use of race tactics that he will be best remembered for. His smooth, economical style was deceptively fast; not for nothing was he known as the Professor.

The Nineties
Restrictive Practices

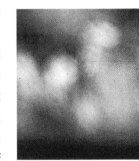

In 1989, the end of turbos and the return of naturally-aspirated 3.5-litre engines in Formula 1 was meant to re-establish parity of performance between teams. It didn't. Anyone without a contract with a major engine supplier – like Honda, Renault, or Ferrari – was destined to be an also-ran.

Another form of restriction was that of physical proportions. Tubs were being designed with the smaller, lighter driver in mind.

The most sweeping changes to the cars came in 1994. Starting with the narrowing of tyre widths, a programme of simplification set in; reactive suspension and anti-lock brakes were outlawed, the fly-by-wire electronic throttle was banned and traction control was kicked into touch. Technical people mourned; after all, some road cars were now better equipped than Grand Prix machines. They believed that F1 should be the pinnacle of automotive technology and felt manacled by FIA.

Still, technicians always found a way of circumventing the rules. For example, the top teams had the ability to produce complex software for the engine management systems which could duplicate the effect of traction control. This could be undetectable and thus impossible to police.

The most extraordinary piece of restrictive practice was the introduction of the plank, the skid-blocks intended to foul the airflow underneath the cars and thus slow them down.

However, the sport of motor racing is always going to be bigger than the legislators, and the next generation will have doubtless leapfrogged any further restrictions.

Ayrton Senna

(1960–1994) World Champion 1988, 1990, 1991

One word describes Ayrton Senna's progress in most races: devastating. The first lap of the European Grand Prix at Donington in 1993 sums up his uncanny ability to scythe through the traffic, and, in this instance, it was the cream of the field – Schumacher, Wendlinger, Hill and Prost. It was wet, yet he had passed all of them by the time he'd completed the lap. He was driving the McLaren with only a 'customer' Ford HB V8 engine, too.

A key weapon in Senna's personal arsenal was his ability to go fast the moment that the race started. Other drivers would take a couple of laps to settle down, but Senna set the pace from the word go.

He was born Ayrton Senna da Silva on 21 March 1960 into a well-off farming family – which also had an interest in the motor trade – and had an elder sister, Viviane, and a younger brother, Leonardo. Aged four, Ayrton's father Milton built him a 1hp kart to trundle round in, and gave him another one to toy with at the age of ten. In 1973, legally able to race it, he drove on the kart circuit at Interlagos. Right from the word go he was a winner, and backed by his father's car components business, he employed the best chassis and engines. In 1977 he was South American karting Champion, and the following year he arrived at the Milanese DAP kart factory to try his luck in Europe.

Ayrton's route to the top was the now accepted way, which barely looks at anything which has closed-in wheels and more than one seat. He was known as Ayrton da Silva, and he teamed up with fellow Brazilian kart-racer Mauricio Gugelmin to travel the circuits. It was clear then that he was focused on his driving to the point of ruthlessness.

However, he didn't quite win the European title. Instead he moved into Formula Ford, driving for Snetterton-based van Dieman. By now he was married – aged 19 – to Liliane, and lived in a rented bungalow in Norwich. He was still called Ayrton da Silva, sometimes affectionately as Harry, and in 1981 he ran in three British FF championships. He won the RAC and Townsend-Thoresen titles, and after a winter working for his father he was back at Snetterton, buying an FF2000 drive with Rushen Green Racing for £10,000.

His career was clearly taking off and to make his name easier for people to remember he was now called Ayrton Senna. He had photographer Keith Sutton send pictures of him to the media and F1 team managers. Sadly, his marriage failed, mainly because he was so focused on his racing. Indeed, he gained a reputation for being somewhat serious and introverted.

When Alex Hawkridge of Toleman offered Ayrton a season in F3 on the understanding he would drive in F1 for Toleman the following year, the Brazilian was reluctant. Senna took the view that in the lower orders it's the individual talent that wins races, while success in F1 is governed by the quality of the equipment. He was only interested in F1 if the car was a potential winner. He tested for Eddie Jordan in F3 in 1982, and emerged European and British FF2000 Champion. He won the end-of-season F3 race at Thruxton driving for

'He made the biggest mistake closing the door; he knows I always go for the gap'

Prost (right) was worn down by Senna's predominant position at McLaren-Honda.

Dick Bennetts, and, despite enticing offers from Toleman and McLaren, he elected to do F3 in Bennetts' Ralt-Toyota in 1983. Despite the best efforts of Martin Brundle, who was his equal for sheer pace, Senna won many races. There were shunts, protests and counter-protests, but he finished undisputed Champion. He also won the inaugural Macau F3 race while jet-lagged and on cold tyres.

In mid-season, Senna was given an F1 test at Donington by Williams, and impressed by his ability to be on the pace quickly despite never having driven anything so quick before. Stepping from 150bhp to 550bhp is a quantum leap indeed. A test for McLaren followed, and he blew the engine on the first lap. This was followed by one for Toleman, and the rest is history.

When Derek Warwick moved to Renault, Toleman hired Senna; as F3 Champion he was hot property, and the established stars were too dear for a small independent team to afford. His Grand Prix debut was in the Toleman-Hart TG183B at Rio in 1984, where he retired, but he came sixth at Kyalami and Zolder. But he would make his name at Monaco. It rained, and Senna excelled, hounding Prost, who was always wary of wet races. Before Senna could take the lead, which had seemed certain, Clerk of the Course Jacky Ickx stopped the race. He overtook Prost on the line, but the previous lap's positions gave the final result.

The remainder of the season was an anti-climax, with many retirements, and third places at Brands Hatch and Estoril. At Zandvoort he signed for Lotus for the following year – 1985 – so Toleman refused to let him drive at Monza. During 1984, Ayrton also had a couple of

one-off races; he won a celebrity event featuring all the stars at the Nürburgring, promoting the new Mercedes 190 saloon, and came eighth partnering Pescarolo and Johansson in Reinhold Jöest's Porsche 956 in the Nürburgring 1000kms.

He then took up his position at Lotus alongside de Angelis in the Renault-engined 97T. Senna's first GP pole position was at Estoril in 1985, and the race was wet. It was his first Grand Prix victory. Towards the end of the year, results improved – the mid-season was dogged with retirements – and he scored second place at the Osterreichring, third in Holland and Italy, first at Spa-Francorchamps, 28 seconds ahead of Mansell, and second at the Brands Hatch European GP. De Angelis was sufficiently fazed by Senna's magnetism within the team to leave for Brabham and Johnny Dumfries replaced him. But it was as much Senna's decision to hire him as team manager Peter Warr's, as the Brazilian didn't wish to see Lotus' energies divided between two number one drivers; Dumfries – the modest Earl of Dumfries and future Lord Bute – was decidedly in the subservient position.

Senna's reputation grew, not only for elegant car-control, but as a dedicated professional. He would spend hours in the garages with the mechanics after practice, and at de-briefings he would identify exactly how the car was behaving, lap by lap at given points on the circuit. He was more deeply analytical than anyone else, in the days before electronic telemetry surpassed the drivers' capabilities. If a race was lost through his mistake on the circuit, he apologised to the mechanics.

The record of 1986 began with second at Rio, while at Jerez he narrowly beat Mansell and was completely exhausted in the process. 'I recover quickly,' he told reporters afterwards. 'Winning is the best medicine to regain strength,' he said. Third at Monaco, second at Spa, fifth at Montreal, first at Detroit, second at Hockenheim and the

Hungaroring, fourth at Estoril, and third in Mexico City, stacked up to make him fourth in the World Championship with 55 points. Dumfries scored just three points.

For 1987, Lotus became allied to Honda for its engine supply, and probably no race engine builder was as committed to success as Honda. However, there were some problems, naturally. At Imola, the Honda turbo's relatively high fuel consumption made Senna drop back to conserve fuel before coming through to second.

Equally significantly, Senna was enthusiastic about the active-suspension car which had resurfaced after Mansell's indifference, and the computerised suspension on the 99T showed great potential. Despite having to rely on the conventional back-up springs to finish third at Hockenheim, Senna proved the worth of active-ride, winning on the street circuits of Monaco and Detroit. One major advantage was that the driver was far less stressed by bumpy track surfaces. Broadly, though, the data it produced was too vast to comprehend.

Although Ayrton still had a mathematical chance of the title until Mexico, the rest of his 1987 results were limited to third at Silverstone, second in Hungary, fifth in Austria, second at Monza, fifth at Jerez, and second at Suzuka. He was third in the title chase on 57 points.

A motor racing mercenary

Like Fangio, Ayrton was not sentimental about whom he drove for; it would be the team most likely to give him the Championship, and for 1988 he moved to McLaren-Honda to join Alain Prost. Like Piquet two years earlier, Senna had established an excellent rapport with Honda's race engineers, and in effect the Brazilians traded places, with Piquet going to Lotus. Back in '82, Senna had been snubbed by Piquet at Zolder, when Ayrton was in FF2000 and Nelson in F1, so he had always been determined to beat him. In terms of team membership it looked as though he had the upper hand.

On home ground in Brazil, Senna's gear linkage broke on the parade lap and, as he threw up his hands on the grid to indicate immobility, he was able to start from the pit lane in the spare car when the race was restarted. However, he was judged to have swapped vehicles after the green all-clear flag had been shown and was disqualified.

At Monaco, Senna led comfortably for 67 laps, then lost concentration and hit the barrier just before the tunnel. Although it was a minor accident, he claimed it was a pivotal point in his career, causing him to reconsider his own abilities, and reawakening his religious faith. In practice he'd gone so fast that it seemed to him he'd moved into another dimension. From then on, his successes were shared with and attributed to the Almighty.

There then began a constant battle with team-mate Prost, with Senna giving way to the Frenchman at Mexico, and beating him at Montreal and Detroit. When Prost retired from a wet Silverstone with a failed clutch, the French press pilloried him, and, little by little, he was worn down by Senna's success. Senna won at Silverstone, Hockenheim, Budapest and Spa in succession, and Prost admitted then that Senna had as good as won the Championship. There was an uncharacteristic blunder at Monza, when, with the race in the bag, Senna collided with

back-marker Schlesser at the chicane. At Suzuka he stalled on the grid and he was saved by the gradient, which allowed him to bump-start the MP4/4. By half-distance, he had overtaken the entire field, including race-leader Prost – and in a rain shower too. It was his eighth victory of the season, one more than Jim Clark's 1963 record. The frugal Prost had dominated the two Iberian races, with Senna a gas-guzzling sixth and fourth, and he beat the Brazilian in the final race at Adelaide. But the 1988 Championship was Senna's, by three points from Prost. McLaren-Honda were Constructors' Champions by a massive 134 points. By the end of the season, Senna was the most admired and the most resented driver in the F1 paddock. While acknowledging his skills, most wished he would retire and give someone else a chance.

Senna was a genius, but his bullying tactics made some question his greatness.

The 1989 season began at Rio, with Patrese, Berger and Senna going for the same bit of track, and the McLaren lost its nose cone. Then Senna set the tone for the inter-team squabbling by winning at Imola. It had been agreed that whichever of the two McLarens arrived at the first corner in the lead would not then be challenged by the other. Senna broke the 'accord' with Prost at Imola and, although Ron Dennis made him apologise, from Monaco on the drivers never spoke to each other for the rest of the season.

At Monza, Senna's practice times were some two seconds better than Prost's, and it looked as though he was enjoying preferential treatment. When Senna retired and Prost won, there were great recriminations about Alain's giving away the trophy to the fans.

The price of victory

It was Mansell's turn to feel Senna's icy blast as the pair collided at Estoril when, by rights, Nigel was black-flagged for his pit-lane offence. While Mansell was fined and banned from the Spanish GP, Senna was himself black-flagged during practice for Jerez, and fined $20,000 for failing to stop. He won the race, however.

Suzuka has gone down as the race where Prost finally closed the door on Senna, ending the Brazilian's Championship hopes and confirming his own. Senna got a push on to a slip road, obtained a new nose cone, and proceeded to overtake Nannini for the race at the very same chicane as the coming-together with Prost. He was disqualified because of the push-start and for taking a short-cut, and the enmity grew deeper. On appeal, FISA fined him $10,000 with a six-month suspended ban. Chicken-feed, perhaps, on an annual retainer of $15 million. The final, rain-drenched, Adelaide round found Prost sheltering in the pits, and Senna stuffed into the back of Brundle's Brabham.

Initially, there was doubt that Senna would be granted his superlicence for 1990. It was mid-February before Senna and McLaren sorted things out with FISA. But there was equanimity within the team. Gerhard Berger was much more relaxed – a joker who would think nothing of jettisoning Senna's case from the helicopter – and Senna found him easier to get on with.

At Phoenix, Senna led, and was passed brilliantly by Alesi in the Tyrrell; inevitably the McLaren regained the place, and Senna won. He was nudged by Nakajima at Sao Paulo, and settled for third, won Monaco from pole, was first at Hockenheim and took Nannini off for second place at the Hungaroring. He beat Prost at Spa, and they shook hands afterwards; the result was repeated at Monza. Senna took his 50th pole position at Jerez in storming style. It was almost an act of revenge on the circuit, achieved in the wake of Donnelly's awful accident.

By Suzuka Senna looked set to be Champion. Prost made the better start, and Senna basically drove into him at the first corner, taking both of them out and sealing the Championship for himself at a stroke. Ferrari was sufficiently incensed to threaten to withdraw from the scene altogether. A year on at Suzuka, Senna publicly admitted it had been deliberate, yet made a blistering attack on FISA and its recently ousted president Baléstre for cheating him out of the 1989 title.

Senna rattled off wins at the first four races of 1991 – Phoenix,

Ayrton makes a poor start to the 1988 Spanish GP; Mansell's Williams blocks him.

Interlagos, Imola and Monaco – then Williams-Renault caught up. The McLaren-Honda was suddenly off the pace, and Senna didn't win again until Hungary. He took Spa-Francorchamps, was second at Monza, Estoril and Suzuka, and first at Adelaide. Now all 16 races counted for the title, and Senna also had a couple of thirds, a fourth and a fifth as he took the Championship.

McLaren came under more pressure from the Williams team during 1992. Having finished third at Kyalami and at Imola, Senna won at Monaco, came second at Hockenheim, first at the Hungaroring, fifth at Spa, won at Monza, and was second at Estoril. But at the end of 1992, it was Honda who shut up shop.

Now powered by the Ford HB V8 engines, the McLaren MP4/8 was still a force to be reckoned with during 1993. Senna was second at Kyalami, first at Interlagos and Donington, second at Barcelona, first at Monaco, fourth at Magny-Cours, fifth at Silverstone, fourth at Hockenheim, fourth at Spa-Francorchamps, and first at Suzuka – scene of the post-race contretemps with Irishman Eddie Irvine, and Adelaide, where the rift with Prost appeared to be over. It gave him second place in the Championship.

Even back in 1992, Senna was offering to drive for Williams for nothing, as manifestly he didn't need the money, just the best car. Prost, back from his sabbatical, vetoed the idea, and Williams ran with Damon Hill. With Prost retired, Senna was the obvious choice for 1994. But he was under pressure from the young lion, Michael Schumacher, and

perhaps was trying a bit too hard in cars which now lacked driver-aids like traction-control and which ran on narrower tyres. Driving the Renault-powered FW16, Senna retired from Interlagos and Aida, Japan, and that brought him to Imola.

A tragic series of accidents punctuated the weekend, from Barrichello's awful crash in the Jordan and Roland Ratzenberger's fatal accident in the Simtek during practice, to the start-line shunt between Lamy and Lehto, which brought about the restart.

As the pace car pulled off, Senna stormed into the lead, followed by Schumacher. As they entered the fast left Tamburello for the second time, Senna's Williams suddenly veered right and almost instantly plunged into a concrete retaining wall. The wrecked car was flung down the track, and Senna was fatally injured, his helmet having been pierced by a front suspension component.

Eighteen months later, the Italian authorities had still not released the car, but it was suggested that a steering column weld which Senna had asked for prior to the race had broken. Telemetry revealed he had reduced the speed to 130mph by the time of impact. Whatever, he had very little chance, although the errant suspension arm was as flukey as the front wheel which killed Mike Spence at Indianapolis in 1968; the Tamburello's concrete wall shielded a drop to a stream, and the corner has now been altered.

Motor sport had lost one of the all-time greats. He had started from a record 65 pole positions – Imola was the last – and scored 41 Grand Prix wins. He was marketing a range of youth-oriented products and did a lot of good behind the scenes, founding a charity for underprivileged Brazilian children. He was given a state funeral in Brazil and his death was mourned grievously there.

Ayrton was a surprise victor at Monaco in 1987 in the active-ride Lotus-Honda 99T.

Nigel Mansell

(1954–) World Champion 1992

Nigel Mansell was the first Grand Prix driver since Stirling Moss to capture the popular support of the British public. Champions like Clark and Stewart were adored by the aficionados, and Hill was admired by a wider audience. But Mansell was a hero of the people.

Born in Upton-on-Severn near Malvern, Worcestershire, on 8 August 1954, Nigel strove hard to make his name in motor racing. Although he took the recognised route to the top, starting with karts in 1968, it was a hard road indeed. Nigel's first car race was a Formula Ford 1600 event at Mallory Park in July 1976, driving a Hawke DL11, and it was a first-time win. In 1977 he won the Brush Fusegear FF Championship in a Javelin and a Crosslé. His career almost came to a premature end when his neck was broken in a Formula Ford accident, but, amazingly, he had recovered in a matter of weeks.

In 1978, Mansell made his biggest commitment to the sport up to that point by packing in his job with Lucas-Girling Aerospace, and re-mortgaging his house, supported by his wife Rosanne, to get into Formula 3. Driving a March-Dolomite for Dave Price, he was runner-up for the prestigious Grovewood Award in 1979, and was given a test drive for Lotus that year at the Paul Ricard circuit. Following a year in F2, Mansell made his debut in Formula 1 with Lotus in a new 81B at the Osterreichring in 1980. He drove it again at Zandvoort, but crashed in practice for Imola.

Mansell's first points placing was at Zolder in 1981, when he was third and team-mate de Angelis fifth. By Monaco, the new 87 was ready, and in Spain Mansell was sixth behind de Angelis. The RAC had indicated that the recently outlawed twin-chassis 88 would be accepted at the British Grand Prix, but it was overruled by FISA. Lotus mechanics had to quickly convert one to 87 spec for Mansell, but he failed to qualify.

Engineering power

For 1982, Lotus had renewed sponsorship from John Player Special. In a largely barren year, Mansell came third in Brazil and fourth at Monaco driving the cockpit-forward, variable-wheelbase Lotus 91. De Angelis scored a surprise victory at the Osterreichring in a 91, marking the 150th GP win for the venerable Cosworth-Ford DFV engine. For 1983, Chapman had lined up a supply of Renault turbo engines, but Mansell was destined to drive a Cosworth-powered car until the British GP at Silverstone when he came fourth in the 93T. With the Ducarouge-engineered 94T Nigel was fifth in Austria and third in the European GP at Brands Hatch.

The 95T appeared to be the best-handling F1 car of the 1984 season, and consistent performances yielded deceptively modest results; Mansell was third at Dijon-Prénois, fourth at Hockenheim, third at Zandvoort and Monza, and sixth at Dallas, where he started from pole position for the first time.

Lotus had given Nigel a good grounding in F1, even though there were no victories, and he remained ever-grateful to Chapman for the opportunity. In 1985 however, he moved to Williams, joining Keke Rosberg. Driving the carbon-composite Honda-powered FW10, Mansell came fifth at Estoril and Imola, sixth at the new Nürburgring and Zandvoort, second to Senna at Spa-Francorchamps, and finally won his first Grand Prix at Brands Hatch, beating Senna. He followed this up with victory at Kyalami, with team-mate Rosberg second, and ended the year sixth in the Championship.

Nigel was joined by Nelson Piquet for 1986, the year Frank Williams was paralysed in a car accident. The Championship chase would be as much between the Williams team-mates as the other leading contenders, Prost and Senna. Piquet won in Rio, and Mansell opened his account with second at Jerez. He was fourth at Monaco, first from Senna at Spa-Francorchamps, first from Prost at Montreal, fifth at Detroit, first at Paul Ricard ahead of Prost, and won at Brands Hatch ahead of his team-mate. At Hockenheim and the Hungaroring, Mansell was third, second to Piquet at Monza, first at Estoril, and fifth at Mexico City after stalling at the start. Prost, Piquet and Mansell went to Adelaide with a chance of the Championship, but a dramatic tyre incident ended his hopes for 1986. Incredibly, he managed to control the FW11 and its exploding Goodyear, and was fortunate indeed not to crash at nearly 200mph. Perhaps by way of consolation, he was voted BBC TV sports personality of the year.

If everything had gone according to form, Mansell would probably have been Champion in 1987. But a crash during practice for the Japanese Grand Prix damaged his back, so he missed both that race and Adelaide.

Nigel's pained expression often showed the pressure he'd suffered in a race.

The season's results stacked up well, with wins at Imola, Paul Ricard, Silverstone – where he made the legendary feint on Piquet down Hanger straight, passing him as they approached Stowe corner with only a lap and a half to go – the Osterreichring, Jerez and Mexico City. Other points placings were sixth in Rio, fifth in Detroit, and third at Monza.

At the Italian GP, Piquet opted for the active-ride FW11B, while Mansell, unimpressed with earlier experience of Lotus' exploratory ventures into reactive suspension, chose to race the standard car. Piquet proved the reactive system worked by winning from Senna's similarly equipped 99T. This serves to illustrate the difference between Piquet and Mansell – the Brazilian liked to set up a technical advantage for himself in private testing, while the Englishman was more straightforward in a racing sense; one stealthy, the other aggressive.

One of Nigel's less endearing moments was when he shook Senna warmly by the throat in the pits at Spa, and had to be restrained by the Lotus mechanics. The incident which led to this confrontation was on the first lap of the re-started race, when Mansell moved his Williams inside Senna's Lotus on a right-hander. The cars collided, Senna retiring in a sand trap, and Mansell soon afterwards with a damaged undertray.

In 1988, the final season of the turbo era saw Mansell and Patrese's Williams FW12s running normally-aspirated 3.5-litre Judd V8s, while Senna and Prost at McLaren had turbocharged Honda power. The Judd engine was a stop-gap until such time as a major manufacturer was contracted. Despite the power deficit, Mansell was only 0.6 seconds slower than Senna in qualifying at Rio. For the most part though, McLarens dominated, and Nigel finished in the points only twice, coming second at Silverstone to Senna, and second to Prost at Jerez. He tied with Nannini for a lowly ninth place in the Championship.

For 1989, Nigel switched to Maranello; Ferrari's 'GTO' F1 factory was based at Guildford, Surrey. He partnered hard-charger Gerhard Berger driving the John Barnard-designed 3.5-litre V12 F1/89. The latest innovation was the semi-automatic gearbox and electronic gear change mounted on the steering wheel, which Nigel didn't adjust to immediately.

A surprise winner

In Rio, Nigel surprised everyone by beating the fancied runners, Williams and McLaren – and became instantly lionised by the Italian fans. At Imola Berger had an appalling accident when his Ferrari went off at the Tamburello at 170mph, sustaining burns to his hands. In spite of being in the flames for over 20 seconds, he discharged himself from hospital the following day for treatment in Austria.

Following Gugelmins' aerobatics at the start of the French GP, Mansell just had time to change cars, and started from the pit lane. His meteoric drive through the entire pack to finish second was marvellous to behold. He fully deserved the tifosi's nickname, il Leone.

Nigel always goes well on home ground, and his second place at Silverstone gave his fans something to cheer about. But it's a fast circuit, which suited the Ferrari's high speed characteristics. He was third at Hockenheim, but scored a fine victory at the Hungaroring, beating Senna fair and square with a devastating passing move at the only place on the circuit where it could be done.

At Spa-Francorchamps in the wet, the Ferrari was probably the best handling car, but it couldn't match the power of the McLarens' Honda V10. Thus Mansell was third, but only two seconds behind the winning Senna, himself a second ahead of Prost. Unfortunately Ferrari's gearbox let Mansell down at Monza, although Berger was second.

Estoril was a farce. Mansell slightly overshot his pit on a tyre stop, and made the error of reversing instead of waiting to be pushed back. He was thus black-flagged for the infringement – hardly a dangerous one, but before he'd seen the flag, he'd collided with Senna who was in the lead. Mansell was fined $50,000 and given a one race ban for failing to heed the black flag.

The melodrama continued before the Spanish GP, with Senna complaining of suicidal driving, and Mansell threatening to retire from F1 if the ban was enforced. It was, and he didn't.

The Ferraris came good at Sao Paulo in 1990, with Prost winning and Mansell fourth; Berger and Senna were the filling in a McLaren sandwich. With Prost the 1989 Champion, the Ferraris carried numbers 1 and 2, thwarting Nigel's plans to market a range of products bearing 27, his old number. Red 5 would have its day though.

Again the electronic gear change was the Ferrari's Achilles' heel, with retirements including Monaco and Silverstone. Nigel was third at Montreal, and in Mexico Prost and Mansell made it a red 1-2 for Ferrari. Mansell's next finish in what had been so far a dreadful season was fourth at Monza. However it all came together again for a win at Estoril, Nigel starting from pole in a wild tail-slide that forced his team-mate to fall back. The result was reversed at Jerez, with Prost taking the victory, and the momentary hitch in their rapport was glossed over. On the whole it was a disappointing partnership, Mansell maintaining that Prost was manipulative within the team. Mansell's farewell present to Ferrari was a storming second place to Piquet at Adelaide.

With Williams for 1991, Nigel retired at Phoenix, then set fastest lap at Interlagos in the Renault V10-engined FW14 but retired. Imola started in a downpour, and Nigel collided with Brundle on the first lap. At Monaco he was second to Senna after besting Prost, and at Montreal the Williams of Mansell and Patrese were dominant; but when Nigel was leading and on his last lap, he lost his gears and was classified fifth.

Global glory

At Mexico, Mansell slashed Patrese's 22-second lead to just over one second by the finish. Mansell beat Prost to the line at Magny-Cours, the first time the Nevers track had hosted the Grand Prix. At Silverstone, Mansell was indisputably the hero of the day, and fans swarmed onto the track as never before on a British circuit.

Mansell scored a comfortable win over team-mate Patrese at Hockenheim, and settled for second to Senna at the Hungaroring when his brake pedal started acting up. After retiring at Spa, Mansell won relatively easily at Monza. Disqualification followed in Portugal. Mansell had just left his pit following a tyre-stop at Estoril, when one of the rear wheels came off, hitting a couple of Tyrrell mechanics, and the Williams team did the only sensible thing and replaced the wheel where the car stood. Mansell rejoined the race, and reeled off a succession of fastest laps, before the black flag was hung out. He'd received assistance outside his own pit, and that was against the rules.

Despite injuring an ankle in a pre-race football match, he won at Montmelo, Barcelona. He spun off in Japan and at Adelaide the Australian GP was held in torrential rain. The race was stopped after 14 laps – the shortest and possibly the wettest GP ever – with Senna winning and Mansell stuffed motionless in front of the pits. It gave him second place, however, and second place in the Championship.

Mansell was now living in Florida, and was mentally and physically psyched-up for the 1992 season. He triumphed at Kyalami in a Williams 1-2, repeating the exercise at Mexico City and Interlagos.

Nigel rounds Surtees bend at Brands Hatch on his way to his first GP victory.

Mansell's fourth consecutive victory came at a damp Barcelona, and the Williams pair were again the class act in the field at Imola. At Monaco Nigel lost a certain win when he pitted with a puncture, which turned out to be a loose wheel nut, before hounding Senna dramatically – but pointlessly – all the way to the flag. Mansell appeared near to collapse at the prize-giving.

By now Mansell had a commanding lead in the title race, and at Magny-Cours, he equalled Jackie Stewart's 27 GP wins to place himself even further ahead. Predictably, the fans went wild again as he won from Patrese at Silverstone. He won again at Hockenheim, then second place at the Hungaroring clinched the Championship.

At Spa, Mansell was second to Schumacher, and, as he retired at Monza, so he announced his imminent retirement from the F1 scene. A career in Indycar racing beckoned, where among his chief rivals would be ex-F1 Champion and twice Indy 500 winner Emerson Fittipaldi. Mansell rounded off 1992 with a win at Estoril, but at Adelaide he had a coming together with Senna which took them both out.

Nigel had an amazing season as a 'Rookie' in the PPG/CART 'Indycar' series driving for Carl Haas and Paul Newman, coming away with the 1993 title. The following year was the exact opposite and he was lured back to F1 to race for Williams on an ad-hoc basis by a large fee from Renault, distraught at losing Senna. By the time he got to race, at Magny-Cours, Hill was in form, Coulthard was on the up and up, and Mansell never looked like being on the pace. He had a great race in Japan, however, battling in the wet with Alesi, and won Adelaide magnificently from Berger in the wake of the Schumacher-Hill debacle. But an attempt to re-join the fray in 1995 faltered when he was unable to get to grips with the disappointing McLaren-Mercedes MP4/10B.

There was a dramatic appearance in 1994 in a Ford Mondeo in a round of the British Touring Car Championship, which ended with Nigel sliding sideways into the Donington tyrewall. Fast they may be, but ex-F1 drivers don't always get to grips with front-drive saloons. Whether or not he continues racing in the years ahead, Nigel will retain an interest in in the motor trade, through his Ferrari and TVR dealership in Hampshire. ◼

RONNIE PETERSON (1944–1978)

The sight of Ronnie taking Silverstone's pre-chicane Woodcote flat-out and on the ragged edge at 150mph is unforgettable. He was clearly the fastest in his day. Yet there was perhaps a lack of mechanical

sympathy. Ronnie drove around any problem that there might have been with the car. If it held together, he usually won. The phlegmatic Peterson could handle even the most evil-handling racing car.

High spots of his career were his season with March in 1971 when he was the runner-up in the World Championship, and the 1973 season at Lotus, when he won four races with the JPS 72. Possibly his finest hour was at Monaco in 1974 when he won with the four-year-old car. Ronnie also drove the Ferrari 312P sports cars during 1972 and the BMW 3.0 CSL touring cars in 1973. After a spell in the wilderness, which included drives with March and in the six-wheeler Tyrrell, he joined Andretti at Lotus for the magnificent run of successes with the Lotus 78 and 79s, which were to earn him second place in the 1978 World Championship.

His injuries in the start line shunt at Monza in 1978 were not life-threatening, but, tragically, there were complications at the Milan hospital. The future looked bright. Ronnie had already signed for McLaren for 1979 when he died.

GILLES VILLENEUVE (1952–1982)

Snowmobiles are perhaps not the most promising introduction to a Formula 1 career, but Villeneuve got started this way, aged 13. He won the Canadian snowmobile championship, and used the $13,000 prize money to buy a Formula Ford. In 1973 he proceeded to win some 70 per cent of his first season's races. That winter he won the World Snowmobile Championship, which encouraged potential backers. With sponsorship from Schweppes, he joined Ecurie Canada to race in Formula Atlantic. But it was a steep learning curve, and he broke a leg practising for a race at Mosport.

In 1976, Villeneuve won nine out of ten Formula Atlantic rounds in his March 76B; the series enjoyed a status somewhere between F2 and F3. Last race of the season was at Trois Rivières, where he beat established stars like Hunt, Depailler and Brambilla.

He was instantly invited to drive a third McLaren at selected Grands Prix in 1977, but just one outing materialised, at Silverstone, where he ran seventh for a while. When Lauda left Ferrari prematurely, Villeneuve got the seat. His second race at Fuji was a disaster, as his cartwheeling Ferrari killed two spectators.

Nevertheless, he teamed with Reutemann for 1978 and the season culminated in victory at his home Grand Prix. By then he was a national hero in Canada. Driving the new 312T4 Ferrari in 1979, he won at Kyalami, Las Vegas and Watkins Glen. A string of second places, including a wheel-banging duel with Arnoux at Dijon, made him runner-up to team-mate Scheckter.

Ferrari suffered a lacklustre year in 1980. But in 1981, driving the Tipo 126CK turbo car, Villeneuve narrowly beat Jones at Monaco, and then won at Jarama. For 1982, Ferrari had the neat, Harvey Postlethwaite-designed 126C2, producing some 580bhp at 11,800rpm. At Imola, having dispatched Arnoux's Renault, the Ferraris of Villeneuve and Pironi led the race. Team orders were that the drivers should maintain places in the closing laps but they were broken by Pironi on the last lap, and Villeneuve vowed that he would never speak to his team-mate again.

A week later, Villeneuve was dead. In trying to beat Pironi's qualifying time during practice at Zolder, he encountered Mass' wayward March, clipped the rear wheel and was launched into the sand trap in a horrific accident. His belts broke and he was thrown out of the car, breaking his neck.

The wheel turns, and Gilles' Indycar Champion son Jacques joins Damon Hill at the Williams Team for 1996.

JEAN ALESI (1964–)

When Jean Alesi burst on the scene at Paul Ricard in 1989 – finishing fourth in the Tyrrell 018 – one could not help thinking that here was a future Champion. For one reason or another Tyrrell had never put together a turbo engine deal, so Alesi was driving a normally aspirated Cosworth DFR-engined car. It was lighter and more agile than the more powerful turbos and the way he flung it around was so reminiscent of Senna, Peterson or Rindt that one instinctively knew that here was someone out of the ordinary.

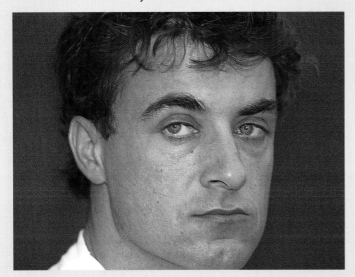

Having raced for Eddie Jordan in F3000 – where results in 1988 were thin indeed, although better in 1989 – Alesi graduated to F1 when Alboreto left Tyrrell. Some stirring drives ensued, like his Paul Ricard debut, and fourth places at Hockenheim and Jerez. Alesi began 1990 with a brilliant second place to Senna at Phoenix and again at Monaco. For 1991, he signed to Ferrari as team-mate to Prost. He managed third places at Hockenheim and Estoril, fourth at Magny Cours and fifth in Hungary. And so it went on. He always qualified well, and if the Ferrari proved reliable, he was in the points. Alesi is a real racer who never derived much comfort from the on-board aids like traction control and active-ride suspension. 'Nothing to do with me,' he shrugged when congratulated on his performance in the 1992 French GP, when he was running as fast on slicks as Mansell was on wets.

But the results that his talent deserved were always to elude him, and the Sicilian-born Frenchman never managed to win a Grand Prix until the Canadian race in 1995. His move to a more reliable car at Benetton in 1996 may redress the balance.

DAMON HILL (1961–)

Londoner Damon was elevated to the Williams number two seat from the role of test driver, and confidently established himself as Professor Prost's understudy in 1993 after Mansell quit the scene.

Damon's competition career began on two wheels in the late 1970s, and although he started racing cars in 1983 with an Argo JM16, he was sufficiently unmoved by the experience to return to bikes in 1984. Subsequently, he raced F3 for the Dick Bennetts and Murray Taylor teams, moving into F3000 with Cobra in 1989, when he was also David Hobbs' co-driver in Richard Lloyd's Porsche 962 at Le Mans.

He drove Eddie Jordan's Lola T91/50 in F3000 during the 1991 season, and was a front-runner in the Middlebridge F3000 Lola, attracting the attention of Frank Williams, who signed him as a test driver at the end of the 1992 season.

Before Williams, Damon had had just two races in an uncompetitive F1 Brabham, and although he'd been competitive in F3 and F3000, lack of funds more than anything else prevented him from being a Championship winner. His unexpected arrival in F1's plum seat, coupled with high expectations because of his father Graham's reputation, led on occasion to unjustified criticism of his failure thus far to win the F1 World Championship. That said, by mid-season 1995 he had the fourth-highest all-time race-starts to race-wins ratio, with 11 out of 41, bettered only by Fangio, Ascari and Stewart.

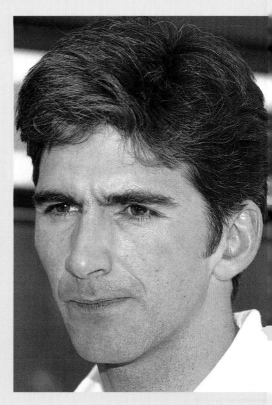

Damon lives in Dublin and is married to Georgie, with two sons, Oliver and Joshua. His easy-going demeanour has gained him millions of fans back home, and his jousting with Schumacher led to an even more partisan following, in a conflict where he is seen very much as the good guy.

Although behaving with great dignity when evidently taken out by Schumacher at Adelaide in 1994, when within a point of the Championship, Damon was sufficiently rattled to wrong-foot himself on a couple of occasions – Silverstone and Monza – in 1995. A real pragmatist, after the Nürburgring race Damon conceded the 1995 Championship to his biggest rival, by which time he was also under pressure from on-form team-mate David Coulthard.

Signed for the Williams team for the 1996 season for a reputed $1milion salary, Damon still stands a good chance of taking the title. But prospective team-mate Jacques Villeneuve may be equally as forceful as Coulthard was in 1995.

Michael Schumacher

(1969–) World Champion 1994, 1995

'Some cars are forgiving. Others,

like the Benetton, are critical.'

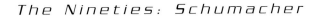

When someone breaks the lap record at Le Mans, he must be pretty good. But when he does it at night, it's another matter altogether. He must be astonishingly good, as, for obvious reasons, lap times normally come down at night. Michael Schumacher did exactly that in a Mercedes C11 in 1991, giving due warning of the potential waiting to be unleashed on the F1 World Championship. Like a shooting star, his is the kind of talent only seen perhaps once in a generation: there have been Fangio, Moss, Clark, Stewart, Rindt, and, after a long gap, Senna.

Schumacher had a head start. His father ran a karting track at Kerpen, near Aachen, in northern Germany, where Michael was born on 3 February 1969. Michael was encouraged to drive karts from the age of four. By the time he reached his late teens he had an astute business manager, and he had already taken up the fitness regime which makes him look so unflustered after a 90-lap Grand Prix.

First rung on the ladder was a place in the works Mercedes Benz team, along with Karl Wendlinger. The pair were groomed for stardom from late 1990, driving the 5.0-litre turbocharged C11 'Silver Arrows' against the cream of the Group C cars of the time: Jaguar XJRs, Peugeot 905Bs, Mazda 767Bs, Nissan R90Cs, and privately entered Porsche 962Cs. Then, in 1992, Mercedes withdrew and both were embroiled in Formula 1. Long distance car racing instils different disciplines, as it requires more physical endurance and the ability to nurse a car for long periods. Schumacher lowered the Le Mans lap record by an amazing five seconds in 1991 and, had it not been for a jammed gearbox, he, Wendlinger and Kreutzpointer would have won instead of coming fifth.

A promising debut

Michael's first Grand Prix was at Spa-Francorchamps in 1991. He qualified Eddie Jordan's 191 car a very promising seventh. Jordan has always been an accomplished talent spotter, and several of his F3 and F3000 drivers have moved on to better things. Despite the fact that the German fried his clutch on the line, Jordan was undoubtedly right about Schumacher. Others thought so too, and Schumacher was poached away from Jordan to Benetton, coming fifth in his first race for them at Monza, running confidently behind the stars of the day, Senna, Mansell, Berger and Prost. He had survived heated exchanges between Jordan and Benetton legal representatives, and much debate in the press. For a short time the ousted Roberto Moreno got an injunction against Schumacher driving 'his' car. The move in itself was, if abrupt, nothing out of the ordinary in F1 circles, but because Benetton was fairly well established and Jordan was not, it demonstrated Schumacher was out for himself and for personal advancement. Not exactly the way Jackie Stewart would have gone about it, though.

He drove the Benetton B191-Cosworth for the rest of the season, but, despite good grid placings, his equipment let him down in the races, and he went off in torrential rain at Adelaide. In the Mercedes C291, he and Wendlinger won the Autopolis 430km in October.

In 1992 Michael came fourth at Kyalami behind Senna's McLaren and the two Williams of Patrese and Mansell. At Interlagos, he was third, lapped, just, by the flying Williams pair, and a second ahead of Alesi in the Ferrari F92A-V12. At a wet Barcelona, Michael started from the front row alongside Mansell, and, in fairly dire conditions, finished second, within five seconds of the Williams driver.

At Monaco he was fourth after a lively duel with Alesi, and at Montreal he was second to Berger after the Williams pair and Senna had retired. At Magny-Cours, Schumacher took out Senna on the first corner, and was himself eliminated by an accident on lap 17. A bad race was inevitable at some point. Nevertheless, he was fourth at Silverstone. Interestingly, he was behind Martin Brundle in the other Benetton, after a struggle for much of the race with Senna.

Third at Hockenheim behind Senna and the victorious Mansell, with a car slightly damaged after a skirmish with the chicane, Schumacher was proving that he was very much here to stay, and was performing brilliantly in the wake of the far superior Williams-Renault V10s and Senna's more powerful Honda V12 McLaren. At the Hungaroring, Michael spun off on lap 63 when his rear wing sheared off as the result of team-mate Brundle inadvertently running into the back of him.

The big breakthrough

Just a year on from his F1 debut, Michael won his first Grand Prix at Spa-Francorchamps, apparently making light work of the treacherous Ardennes driving conditions. He was the first German to win a Grand Prix since Jochen Mass in Spain in 1975, and indeed only the third (von Trips was the other) since the Championship was instituted. Alongside him on the podium were the Williams duo and his mentor Flavio Briatore. It was a great moment, as it marked the dawning of a new era.

Michael rounded off the season with third at Monza behind Brundle and Senna and he finished seventh at Estoril after having been obliged to start from the back in the spare car. His gearbox failed in Japan, but Benettons came second and third – the German ahead of the Englishman – behind Berger's McLaren. They had been in the points in every round.

At the start of the 1993 season, gamesmanship reared its ugly head. Williams had made their entries too late for the season's deadline, and Benetton blocked a unanimous agreement by the other teams to grant Williams a late licence. These trivial matters were eventually overcome, however, but it was a mark of the atmosphere pervading the scene.

For 1993 Benetton used the active-ride Benetton B193A-Ford HB V8, and Michael took it to third place in Brazil behind Damon Hill's Williams

FW15C-Renault V10 and Senna's McLaren MP4/8-Ford V8. His team-mate Ricardo Patrese was somewhat outclassed. The circus came to Tom Wheatcroft's splendid Donington Park circuit in Derbyshire, the first time a Grand Prix had been staged there since pre-war days. The circuit was completely different now, having been resurfaced in 1973/74. This was the Grand Prix of Europe, and Senna quite magnificently out-drove everyone in pouring rain to beat the Williams duo of Hill and Prost. Schumacher spun out on lap 22.

At Imola, Senna was a late arrival having played brinkmanship with Ford over engine equality with Benetton – an exclusive agreement which Ford wouldn't violate. In the event, Prost won from Schumacher, Senna having been let down by hydraulics failure. Prost notched up his 47th victory at Barcelona, from Senna and Schumacher, although Hill had the jump on them all at the start.

Monaco proved an easy run for Senna. Prost stalled in the pits after being brought in for a ten-second stop-go penalty after allegedly jumping the start, and Schumacher's car caught fire, through an oil leak from the hydraulics, while he was leading. In Montreal, Michael came through to second place to split the Williams of Prost and Hill.

The French crowd at Magny-Cours saw Prost win his 49th grand épreuve although Hill was a scant 0.3 of a second behind him after 72 laps, with Schumacher third. As Hill's engine failed at Silverstone, Michael came second to Prost, with Patrese third. As far as the public was

concerned, astronomical entry charges, poor access to F1 cars in the paddock, plus Mansell's absence in the USA, meant meagre spectator numbers, and Hill's retirement from the lead sent many more home early.

Hockenheim is a power circuit, in spite of the twisty inner section in front of the tribunes. The Williams team were surprised to find that the V8 Fords of the Benettons were closer, rather than further behind, in practice. A race which was Hill's by rights, ended with a puncture with ten laps to go, and Prost took the win, from Schumacher. Hill didn't have to wait long for that elusive first GP win. At the Hungaroring on 15 August, Hill drove an excellent race to secure his first victory. Patrese was second from a hard-charging Berger; Schuey had retired with a broken drive belt on lap 26.

Staggering at the start

The traction control devices on the Benettons played up at Spa, and both Schumacher and Patrese staggered away at the start. Normally, the system limits the revs while the driver buries his foot on the accelerator, and as he flicks the clutch the car is hurtled forwards but without risk to its engine and drive shafts and so on. As Michael recovered and repeatedly set fastest lap, Hill responded, and the two eventually finished three seconds apart. Prost, third, had ultimately set fastest lap. There were complaints from Blundell about Berger's 'loutish driving', to which the Austrian replied that it was 'only a game'.

A blown V8 on lap 21 put Michael out of the Italian GP, although he had managed to split the Williams duo. Hill took another win from Alesi and Michael Andretti in a McLaren.

It all came good for Michael at Estoril, and he led the Williams cars home by a narrow margin. As ever, pit-stops for tyres complicated the picture, and Benetton timed their stop to perfection. After his stop, Michael controlled the race from the front.

Ayrton Senna took his 40th victory at Suzuka but what most people remember is his delivery of a punch to newcomer Eddie Irvine after the race, as the insouciant Irishman had dared to unlap himself when he was blocked by Senna in the race. It wasn't so much the on-track manoeuvre which upset Senna, it was Irvine's disrespectful attitude – wound up further by the mischievous Berger. The incident brought back memories of Mansell shaking Senna by the throat at Spa in 1987.

The result in Adelaide seemed to sum up the status quo fairly well, although Benettons didn't feature in the points. It was Senna from Prost and Hill, followed by the Ferraris of Alesi and Berger. It was Senna's last drive for McLaren and his final victory. The Championship was Prost's, though, and he honoured his earlier statement that he would retire at season's end.

A new set of rules for the 1994 season would make the cars more difficult to drive, in so far as the lack of active ride and anti-lock brakes make life easier. While appreciating that F1 needs to represent the pinnacle of car technology and keep pushing back the frontiers, FIA needed to address the increasing speeds and lack of excitement in the sport. Making the cars more difficult to control was one possibility. There would also be refuelling, which implied smaller cars with smaller fuel cells, not to mention the appalling fire hazard ever present in the pit lane.

At the beginning of the 1994 season, FIA President Max Moseley had said: 'If somebody was found to be cheating... then I think Draconian penalties are completely correct.'

The Benetton livery changed for 1994 as well, Camel withdrawing in

Prior to practice at Adelaide in 1994, Michael checks the progress of his rivals on the screen.

Michael and Karl Wendlinger drove together in the Sauber Mercedes C291 in 1991.

favour of Japan Tobacco Inc., with the two-tone blue Mild Seven brand name prominent. Race Engineer was Tom Walkinshaw, erstwhile Touring Car champion and Jaguar TWR supremo. The B194 was powered by the new Ford Zetec-RV8 engine; a unit which may well achieve the same success as the ubiquitous Cosworth-Ford DFV.

An early advantage

The season began well for Schumacher. Against the odds he won the Brazilian GP when the much fancied Senna had taken off into the lead. Slightly superior pit-work told – although much rested on stuck fuel valves and wheel lock-nuts – and Schumacher was back in the race fractionally ahead of the Brazilian. Although he managed to reduce Schumacher's lead, Senna spun, blaming cramp in his shoulder, a legacy possibly of a narrower cockpit. Hill finished second with Alesi third.

The circus journeyed east to Japan's TI Circuit Aida for the Pacific Grand Prix, and Senna put the Williams on pole. It was still potentially the fastest car but, as the flag fell, Senna got too much wheelspin, Schumacher was away, and the charging Hakkinen was too committed to the first corner to avoid Senna as he veered right. Off spun the Finn and the Brazilian, with the luckless Italian Larini slicing off Senna's front wheel. Schumacher was never challenged, and took a relatively easy victory, with Berger second and Barrichello third.

The first race on the European calendar was Imola for the San Marino Grand Prix. Events took place which stunned the motor racing fraternity everywhere, and made headlines the world over. To start with, the genial Roland Ratzenburger was killed in practice when his Simtek's nosecone became detached, losing any kind of downforce at the front of the car. Rubens Barrichello too had a very lucky escape from a serious practice crash. As the actual race started, JJ Lehto's Benetton sat stalled on the grid, and most drivers managed to avoid him. Pedro Lamy's Lotus was less fortunate, clipping the Benetton's left rear wheel, sending this missile high over the catch fencing and into the crowd, injuring four. Events were getting more and more bizarre. Naturally the pace car came out, to lead Senna, Schumacher, Berger, Hill, Frentzen, Hakkinen and the rest in crocodile round the circuit, as marshals cleared the debris.

After five laps the safety car pulled off and the race was on again. As they went into the Tamburello curve on lap six, Senna's Williams turned right instead of left, and at scarcely unreduced speed went headlong into a concrete wall. Senna sat slumped in the cockpit, and it was immediately clear that he was hurt. The race was stopped and everyone waited for the dreaded news. Before any report was received of Senna's death, the race was restarted, although most had no stomach for it. Not so the Italian tifosi, who cheered on Berger in the leading Ferrari and Larini in fourth. Eventually Schumacher won, from Larini and Hakkinen.

More glory

Schumacher's Mercedes team-mate Karl Wendlinger was badly concussed in practice at Monaco, and the Sauber team withdrew as a consequence. After an eventful race Schumacher won from Martin Brundle in a McLaren-Peugeot MP4/9-V10 and Gerhard Berger's Ferrari 412 T1-V12 – three different cars, three engine configurations. Hill, meanwhile, had tangled with Hakkinen soon after the start, unable to raise the sense of despair in the Williams team.

For Spain they called up David Coulthard as replacement for Senna, and although his race was over after 32 laps he had qualified well. Hill inherited the lead from Schumacher when the Benetton got stuck in fifth gear, and, amazingly, the German cruised round for two thirds of the race like that – even managing a pit stop – and came second, with Mark Blundell third in the Tyrrell-Yamaha 022-V10. The Williams team could start to rebuild its act. By a quirky coincidence, Damon's father Graham had won the same event 26 years previously in the wake of Jim Clark's death, to give fresh hope to Team Lotus.

With Jean Alesi and Michael on the front row of the grid in Canada, the scene looked set for some fireworks. But Michael soon built up an unassailable lead, barring mishap, and finished ahead of Hill and Alesi, who was stuck in second gear and only yards ahead of Berger at the finish.

Refuelling tactics told at Magny Cours, when Michael made three stops to most other teams' two. But by running a lighter car with fresher tyres, Schumacher was able to go faster and maintain an advantage. To the accompaniment of much hype, Williams' sponsors Rothmans and engine suppliers Renault had insisted on hiring Mansell to get a 'star' in one of their cars. The former champ had a hard time of it in the less compliant car, and his $1.5m drive ended in anticlimax on lap 46. The familiar 1-2-3 result of Schumacher, Hill, and Berger completed the picture.

The stewards at Silverstone came in for a slating for not sending Schumacher to the back of the grid after he flouted the rules and passed Hill on the warming-up lap. Instead they allowed him to race on, and bungled the message to the Benetton pit about a 10-second stop-go penalty, eventually black-flagging him. Schumacher failed to respond to this, doubtless in communication with Briatore over the on-board two-way radio. Eventually the matter was settled with a $25,000 fine – later upped to $500,000 at appeal – with a two-race suspension for Michael. While this was going on, Damon was busy winning in front of a partisan crowd. This was to be the last race for 'flat bottomed' cars.

The recriminations begin

At Hockenheim, the mud began to fly. Apart from the black flag incident, there were allegations that Benetton's electronic systems – its 'launch control' – used at Imola were in breach of the rules. The Ferraris dominated practice, but 11 cars were involved in a pile up at the start, as de Cesaris shoved Zanardi into the pit wall, and the rest piled into the debris. There were only eight finishers, with Berger heading Olivier Panis and Eric Bernard; Schumacher's engine gave up at 20 laps, while team-mate Jos Verstappen and the pit crew were incredibly lucky to escape with minor burns when a flash fire erupted during the Dutchman's refuelling stop.

This started another row, another investigation, as it was suggested the Benetton refuelling rig had a filter missing in order to get the petrol into the car faster. The FIA found that by removing the filter, a 'foreign body' had jammed the hose nozzle with a consequent sealing defect. According to Benetton and its safety consultants AFTA, there had been a manufacturing problem with the system. Whatever, there seemed no question that the filter had been removed, and the Benettons were being refuelled some 12 per cent faster than other teams managed. None of this seemed to bother Michael at the Hungaroring, who led away from pole and was never seriously challenged, although Damon was second.

It didn't end there. The cars were now directed to carry planks of wood underneath them in order to foul the airflow underneath and thus slow them down. The skid-block measured 224cm long, and 10mm deep across its 30mm width. A decrease of just 1 mm was allowable during the course of the race, in case of going over kerbs, and so on. Schumacher drove an excellent race to beat Hill, Hakkinen and Verstappen – on the road – but in the paddock afterwards chief scrutineer Charlie Whiting got his callipers out and measured up the plank. Instead of 10mm depth, in some areas it was down to 7.4mm. The pinnacle of automotive engineering had come down to wood shavings.

Whether a driver of Schumacher's calibre would have reaped any benefit from a fractionally lowered ride height is questionable. On 7 September, the FIA tribunal in Paris declared that Schumacher's two-race ban would take effect from Monza, and the German was clearly upset.

When he appeared on the F1 scene, Schumacher was like a breath of fresh air, all cheery smiles and grinning waves. That was 1991, when race fans were subjected to Ayrton's grim countenance, Nigel's whinging, and Alain's gloomy side. There weren't many cheerful guys around at the top. Another thing which made him attractive was his outspoken criticism of Senna's forceful tactics in Brazil: 'Not what you'd expect of a World Champion,' he said. Times change.

After the Monza and Portugal suspension, Michael was hard pressed to summon up the beaming countenance of his early days in F1. This had much to do with pressures from sponsors, who may well have prevailed on him to bad-mouth Hill – not a worthy number one driver, he said – and the press, who seized on the rivalry between the two.

Although Benetton had a miserable Monza, with both Verstappen and

Lehto retiring, and seeing Hill and Coulthard completely dominant at Estoril, Schumacher returned from his suspension all fired up and took the honours at Jerez in the European Grand Prix.

An absorbing race

In Japan, Hill beat Schumacher to the line by 3.3 seconds. That was the bare fact. But, confusingly, the drivers were circulating on opposite sides of the track, due to tactical tyre and fuel stops – Hill made just one, Schumacher two. The race had been stopped early on because of heavy rain and crashes in front of the pits. All the time the debate went on to see about a restart, Hill sat on the grid in his car as if in a traffic jam. What made the closing laps so enthralling was the fact that the times for the earlier, truncated part of the race were added on, so, for example, while Alesi and Mansell jousted on the road, and Mansell eventually went by Alesi, the positions were reversed by the aggregate times. Hill's tyres were so bad by the end that his car was virtually sideways out of corners, but he kept it on the road and won fair and square. Any doubts about his talent were dispelled. Schumacher even congratulated him.

The final outrage as far as many were concerned came at the final at Adelaide. Damon was just one point in arrears, so the title could easily be his. He challenged Schumacher for every centimetre of track, and looked capable of winning. No-one else could stay with these two, as Mansell and Berger brought up the rest. On the 36th lap, the German lost the Benetton on a bump going into a left-right complex and struck the retaining wall, bouncing back onto the track. Hill arrived not having seen the incident and went to dive to the right of the stricken Benetton, but Schumacher closed the door. Hill's Williams' front suspension was too badly bent to continue with any hope of a points finish, and he retired. Schumacher had won the title controversially – he claimed he hadn't seen Damon – but it showed that under pressure he was as vulnerable as anyone. At 26 he was the youngest World Champion ever.

The 1995 season started in Rio de Janeiro with what appeared to be a clear cut victory for Schumacher with Coulthard second. Their fuels were analysed after the race, and found to be irregular. So they were disqualified pending an appeal, which subsequently reinstated them. At the post race weigh-in, Michael was found to have lost 6.5 kilos in weight from the pre-race weigh-in three days earlier – when he was 77 kilos; this in itself had been a surprising gain from the 69 kilos of 1994. While surprised himself, he blamed the discrepancy on different helmets and his blood-thinning regime, under which he drinks copious amounts of liquid the week before a race to 'thin' his blood so he doesn't need a water bottle in the car during the race.

Meanwhile, Michael and his party had a lucky escape while diving at sea, between the two South American races. Their boat drifted away when they were in the water. Super-fit Michael swam for an hour to get help.

At Buenos Aires for the first Argentinian GP since 1981, Hill won from Alesi and Schumacher, and Damon won at Imola from the Ferrari duo of Berger and Alesi. In Spain it was Schumacher's turn to win, with team-mate Johnny Herbert second. The amiable Essex man had always been critical of his second-class treatment in the Benetton team, claiming Schumacher kept technical information on the cars to himself, so he was always at a disadvantage. Herbert's wins at Silverstone and Monza proved he certainly didn't lack potential. Hill, meanwhile, lost throttle and gear control when running a safe second and dropped to fourth.

Benetton's one-stop fuel strategy paid off at Monaco, as Hill made two and couldn't recover the ground on Schumacher, although he took second place after Alesi tangled with Brundle. Having dominated practice in Canada, Michael dropped to fifth place with gearbox problems, and the race was won by a jubilant Alesi – his long-overdue first Grand Prix victory. Magny Cours went to Schumacher from Hill, with Brundle just failing to pass Coulthard for third.

Bitter rivalry

For the second half of the 1995 season Schumacher was involved in what built into a grudge match with Damon Hill. The pendulum of controversy now swung the other way. The Williams looked to be the better car at Silverstone, and Hill might well have been able to jink past Schumacher. But, as the German braked late, Hill tried an impossible undertaking move into the corner and took them both out. Some said it was revenge for Adelaide. But why bother when he could have bided his time for a proper chance?

In Germany, Hill appeared to throw away the lead on the first lap by braking too late for a corner and spinning off. Schumacher was able to give his exuberant fans a copybook demonstration of driving.

In Hungary Schumacher retired, while Hill won. The most entertaining race of the first half of the season – by far – was the 1995 Belgian Grand Prix at Spa. Schumacher and Hill had been caught out by rain during practice, and both started from relatively lowly grid positions: Damon eighth and Schuey 16th. After Herbert and Alesi had briefly fought it out at the front, Coulthard led, only for a gearbox to let him down. By the 16th lap the German was in first place. Hill had pitted for wet tyres, probably a smart move considering the vagaries of the Ardennes weather. Schumacher hadn't, and Hill caught him up very quickly. But try as he might, Hill couldn't find a way past. There was a certain amount of wheel banging, and Damon was well and truly on the marbles at some corners. Schumacher drove brilliantly to maintain what he saw as the racing line – under pressure – and on slick tyres. Realising that he had maybe been premature in stopping for wets, Damon made a swift change to slicks again, only to be wrong footed as the rain intensified. The course car came out, and with everyone obliged to tow the line behind it, most drivers dived into the pits for wets.

As Schumacher pulled away, Damon was given a ten-second penalty for exceeding the 75mph pit lane speed limit and, in his bid to haul in Schumacher, he spun. After the race he was to be seen congratulating the German. But implicit in his greeting was the condemnation of the German's

driving tactics, and a protest was lodged. Schumacher was given a one-race ban, suspended for four races. In view of the ruling body's dictum that a following car only had to get its nose alongside the rear wheel of the car ahead to have right of passage around a bend, it was perhaps a fair verdict. But considering that racing has always been about scrapping – Fangio and Hawthorn and Collins at the Nürburgring in 1957, for example – it seems pretty steep.

The grudge match continued at Monza, with Hill ruffled by team-mate Coulthard's pole position while the Englishman started from the second row among the Ferraris. Nevertheless he caught up well with Schumacher, running behind Berger and Coulthard. When the Scot's front wheel bearing failed, spinning him into the gravel trap, the race was really on. But as the pair came up to lap the hesitant Inoue, Hill braked too late and pounded into the back of Schumacher. Clearly Hill was at fault, and he was given a one race ban, suspended for one race.

Alesi's bid to outrun everyone by using a one-stop tyre strategy at the Nürburgring almost paid off. He showed his true brilliance by opening out a race-winning gap as the Benetton and Williams drivers traded wets for drys. Hill made the mistake of trying to pass Alesi at the chicane, and damaged his nosecone, a move Schumacher completed successfully when he finally caught the Ferrari with the race all but run and the Frenchman's tyres by now long past their best.

Michael clinched the 1995 title at Aida, the Pacific Grand Prix, in a masterful display of skill and a successful three-stop strategy, which allowed him to leap-frog the Williams and Ferrari runners. Instead of worrying about practice times he spent the periods out on worn tyres, establishing how the tricky Benetton handled in racing trim. He was now the youngest-ever double-World Champion.

Michael's fee at Ferrari in 1996 would, according to Martin Brundle, be about the same as the combined salaries of all the other drivers put together. Such is the price of excellence. With Schumacher partnered by Eddie Irvine at Maranello, and the Ferrari duo Alesi and Berger running for Benetton, there are bound to be changes in the faces on the podium. But maybe just the order in which they appear.

Schumacher gets away from Mansell at the start at Adelaide in 1994.

1950–1995: The top three drivers in each year

1950

Farina	30 points
Fangio	27 points
Fagioli	24 points

1951

Fangio	31
Ascari	25
González	24

1952

Ascari	36
Farina	24
Taruffi	22

1953

Ascari	34.5
Fangio	28
Farina	26

1954

Fangio	40
González	25.75
Hawthorn	24.8

(fractions were because of
shared fastest laps)

1955

Fangio	40
Moss	23
Castellotti	12

1956

Fangio	30
Moss	27
Collins	25

1957

Fangio	40
Moss	25
Musso	16

1958

Hawthorn	42
Moss	41
Brooks	24

1959

Brabham	31
Brooks	27
Moss	25.5

1960

Brabham	43
McLaren	34
Moss	19

1961

Hill P	34
von Trips	33
Moss	21
Gurney	21

1962

Hill G	42
Clark	30
McLaren	27

1963

Clark	54
Hill G	29
Ginther	29

1964

Surtees	40
Hill G	39
Clark	32

1965

Clark	54
Hill G	40
Stewart	33

1966

Brabham	42
Surtees	28
Rindt	22

1967

Hulme	51
Brabham	46
Clark	41

1968

Hill G	48
Stewart	36
Hulme	33

1969

Stewart	63
Ickx	37
McLaren	26

1970

Rindt	45
Ickx	40
Regazzoni	33

1971

Stewart	62
Peterson	33
Cevert	26

1972

Fittipaldi	61
Stewart	45
Hulme	39

1973

Stewart	71
Fittipaldi	55
Peterson	52

1974

Fittipaldi	55
Regazzoni	52
Scheckter	45

1975

Lauda	64.5
Fittipaldi	45
Reutemann	37

1976

Hunt	69
Lauda	68
Scheckter	49

1977

Lauda	72
Scheckter	55
Andretti	47

1978

Andretti	64
Peterson	51
Reutemann	48

1979

Scheckter	51
Villeneuve	47
Jones	40

1980

Jones	67
Piquet	54
Reutemann	42

1981

Piquet	50
Reutemann	49
Jones	46

1982

Rosberg	44
Watson	39
Pironi	39

1983

Piquet	59
Prost	57
Arnoux	49

1984

Lauda	72
Prost	71.5
de Angelis	34

1985

Prost	73
Alboreto	53
Rosberg	40

1986

Prost	72
Mansell	70
Piquet	69

1987

Piquet	73
Mansell	61
Senna	57

1988

Senna	90
Prost	87
Berger	41

1989

Prost	76
Senna	60
Patrese	40

1990

Senna	78
Prost	71
Piquet	43
Berger	43

1991

Senna	96
Mansell	72
Patrese	53

1992

Mansell	108
Patrese	56
Schumacher	53

1993

Prost	99
Senna	73
Hill	69

1994

Schumacher	92
Hill	91
Berger	39

1995

Schumacher	102
Hill	69
Coulthard	49

O

Oatley, Neil: 111

Oliver, Jackie: 61, 78

Opel: 123

Oporto: 31, 35, 41, 58

Österreichring: 49, 55, 65, 81, 83, 84, 85, 87, 90, 91, 101, 105, 109, 110, 117, 129, 138, 142, 144

Oulton Park: 35, 45, 76, 77, 84

P

Pace, Carlos: 61, 83, 94

Panis, Olivier: 152

Parkes, Mike: 37, 61, 63, 69,

Parnell, Reg: 10, 12, 52, 58

Patrese, Riccardo: 93, 131, 140, 144, 145, 150

Pau: 70, 93

Paul Ricard circuit: 49, 67, 79, 94, 125, 128, 129, 142, 144, 147

Pedralbes circuit (Barcelona) 11, 12, 21, 23, 29

Penske, Roger/Team: 101

Pescara: 20, 25, 30

Pescarolo, Henri: 49, 78, 138

Peterson, Ronnie: 65, 78, 79, 80, 81, 85, 87, 89, 93, 94, 100, 101, 103, 146, 147

Peugeot: 123, 149

Phillipe, Maurice: 100

Phoenix: 119, 140, 144, 147

Phoenix Park: 67

Pironi, Didier: 13, 111, 112, 122, 127, 128, 147

Pininfarina: 10, 104

Piquet, Nelson: 89, 110, 111, 114, 115, 116, 117, 118, 119, 121, 122, 128, 129, 130, 139, 142, 144

Porsche: 36, 41, 42, 43, 45, 46, 50, 51, 54, 59, 65, 66, 71, 76, 81, 83, 99, 130, 147, 149

Postlethwaite, Harvey: 94, 95, 121, 147

Prost, Alain: 19, 90, 91, 113, 116, 118, 119, 122, 123, 126, 127, 128, 129, 130, 131, 132, 133, 137, 138, 139, 140, 141, 142, 144, 145, 147, 149, 150

Pryce, Tom: 109

Pukekohe circuit: 59

Purley, David: 80, 81

R

Ralt: 115

Ratzenburger, Roland: 141, 151

Rees, Alan: 63, 69, 71

Regazzoni, Clay: 71, 78, 79, 80, 83, 88, 93, 103, 110, 111

Renault: 103, 105, 107, 112, 116, 127, 128, 129, 132, 135, 145, 147, 151

Reutemann, Carlos: 25, 79, 94, 101, 103, 111, 116, 119, 122

Revson, Peter: 65, 69, 80, 94

Rheims-Geux: 10, 11, 13, 16, 17, 20, 21, 22, 25, 26, 29, 34, 35, 36, 37, 41, 42, 45, 50, 54, 58, 60, 63, 69,

Ribeiro, Alex: 115

Riley: 28, 29

Rindt, Jochen: 37, 43, 49, 64, 65, 68, 69, 70, 71, 77, 78, 83, 84, 147, 149

Riverside Raceway: 36, 41, 58

Rodriguez, Pedro: 43, 48, 49, 64, 78, 79, 83, 100

Rodriguez, Ricardo: 42, 46, 53, 79

Rosberg, Keke: 85, 90, 91, 120, 121, 122, 123, 129, 142

Rosier, Louis: 10, 21

Rouen-les-Essarts: 12, 16, 17, 30, 43, 47, 54, 55, 59, 60, 64, 70

Russell, Jim: 83

S

Salvadori, Roy: 27, 31, 34, 35, 53, 59, 76

Sandown Park: 36

Sanesi, Consalvo: 10, 11

Sauber: 151

Scarfiotti, Ludovico: 37, 60, 61, 63, 69, 70

Schell, Harry: 23, 29, 31, 35, 46

Scheckter, Jody: 80, 81, 88, 94, 102, 103, 104, 105, 110, 127, 147

Schenken, Tim: 61

Schetty, Peter: 61

Schlesser, Jo: 57, 69, 70

Schlesser, Jean-Louis: 139

Schumacher, Michael: 91, 113, 133, 137, 141, 145, 147, 148, 149, 150, 151, 152, 153

Schuppan, Vern: 121

Sebring: 30, 35, 40, 41, 43, 70, 100

Senna, Ayrton: 67, 96, 99, 117, 118, 119, 127, 130, 131, 132, 133, 136, 137, 138, 139, 140, 141, 142, 144, 145, 147, 149, 150, 151, 152

Serra, Chico: 115

Servoz-Gavin, Johnny: 78

Shadows: 80, 96, 101

Shelby, Carroll: 41, 43

Shelby Daytona Cobra: 43, 60

Siffert, Jo: 48, 55, 60, 63, 64, 77, 78, 79

Silverstone: 10, 11, 12, 16, 21, 22, 23, 26, 29, 30, 31, 34, 35, 45, 46, 49, 54, 58, 67, 76, 77, 83, 94, 101, 104, 105, 109, 111, 118, 119, 124, 125, 139, 144, 146, 147, 151, 152, 153

Simon, André: 41

Simtek: 141, 151

Snetterton: 33, 35, 70, 76, 83, 124, 137

Solitude: 36, 45, 60

Southgate, Tony: 101

Spa-Francorchamps: 16, 20, 21, 22, 24, 25, 29, 31, 35, 41, 42, 45, 47, 48, 53, 54, 55, 56, 58, 59, 60, 63, 66, 70, 75, 77, 80, 113, 118, 119, 124, 128, 129, 133, 142, 144, 145, 149, 153

Speedwell Engineering: 45

Spence, Mike: 57, 77, 141

sponsorship: 96

Sports Car Club of America: 40

Stacey, Alan: 35, 53

Stanley, Louis: 87

Stewart, Jackie: 25, 37, 44, 48, 49, 51, 56, 57, 64, 65, 66, 68, 70, 71, 74, 75, 76, 77, 78, 79, 80, 81, 85, 100, 104, 130, 142, 145, 147, 149

Stiller, Harry: 109

Stommelen, Rolf: 61, 78, 109

Surtees, John: 35, 37, 46, 47, 53, 54, 55, 58, 59, 60, 61, 63, 64, 69, 76, 100, 109

Picture Credits

Goddard Picture Library: 8, 11, 12, 13, 14, 15, 16, 18, 19, 20, 21, 22, 23, 24, 26 (t), 28, 29, 30, 31.
Phipps Photographic: 26 (b), 27 (both), 32, 34, 35, 36, 37, 38, 40, 41, 42 (both), 43, 44, 46, 47, 48, 49, 50 (both), 51, 52, 53, 54, 55, 56, 58, 59, 61, 62, 63, 64, 65, 66 (both), 67 (both), 68, 69, 70, 71, 72, 74, 75, 76, 77, 78, 79, 80, 81, 82, 84, 85, 86, 88, 89, 90, 91, 92, 93, 94, 95, 96, 97 (t), 98, 100, 101, 102, 104, 105, 106, 108, 110, 111, 112 (both), 113 (t), 114, 116, 117, 118, 119, 120, 122, 123, 124, 126, 128, 129, 130, 131, 132, 133, 136, 138, 139, 140, 141, 143, 144, 145, 146 (both).
Sutton Motorsport Images: 6, 97 (b), 113 (b), 125 (both), 134, 147 (both), 148, 150, 151, 153.
t = top, b = bottom